Hellenism and Reconciliation in Ireland from Yeats to Field Day

Hellenism and Reconciliation in Ireland from Yeats to Field Day

NATHAN WALLACE

CORK UNIVERSITY PRESS

First published in 2015 by
Cork University Press
Youngline Industrial Estate
Pouladuff Road, Togher
Cork, Ireland

British Library Cataloguing in Publication Data
A CIP catalogue record for this book is available from the British Library.

ISBN 978-1-78205-068-1

Typeset by Tower Books, Ballincollig, County Cork
Printed in Malta by Gutenberg Press

www.corkuniversitypress.com

For Sara,
just in time

Contents

Acknowledgements

This book has been a long time coming, and in writing it I have benefited greatly from the conversation, encouragement and inspiration of many people. I would first like to thank my two dissertation directors at the University of Notre Dame, Chris Vanden Bossche and Seamus Deane. I also owe a debt of gratitude to my committee members Jim Smyth, Luke Gibbons, Kathy Alexis Psomiades and Jay Walton (may he rest in peace). While at Notre Dame I benefited greatly from knowing and working with the scholars at the Donald and Marilyn Keough Institute for Irish Studies. This distinguished group has included Kevin Whelan, Mary Burgess, Susan Harris, Margaret O'Callaghan, Brian Ó Conchubair, Éamonn Ó Ciardha, Mary Burke, Brendan Ó Buachalla, Maud Ellmann, Breandán Mac Suibhne, Peter MacQuillan, John Waters and Michael Griffin. I thank Christopher Fox for the vision, ingenuity and generosity with which he has overseen the entire project. While at Notre Dame I was very fortunate that my graduate-student cohort included Skip Thompson, Sean O'Brien, Willie Murphy, Julie, Kipp, Erich Hertz, Jim Hansen, Renee Trilling, Anne Enenbach, Heather Edwards, Julie Henigan, Scott Smith, Julie Bruneau, Harry McCandless, John Witek, Gavin Foster and Surajit Bose. For their scholarly example and their encouragement, I thank Elizabeth Butler Cullingford and David Lloyd. I also thank Sonia Gernes and John Matthias for running such wonderful creative-writing courses at Notre Dame, and for overseeing my MFA in poetry. Among my professors and mentors at Trinity University (San Antonio), I thank Frank Kersnowski for teaching me Irish poetry, Joan Burton for teaching me Athenian drama, Larry Kimmel for teaching me Nietzsche, Richard Newhauser for teaching me Chaucer, and Douglas Guthier for spiritual guidance.

In the writing and researching of this book I have benefited from colleagues at Union College and at the Ohio State University (OSU). Our time in Schenectady, NY was particularly brightened by the friendship and conversation of Ed Pavlic, Chanette Romero, Christopher Pizzino and Judith Lewin. In the OSU English Department, Stuart Lishan, Clare Simmons, Ben McCorkle and Debra Moddelmog deserve the most gratitude. I also thank Catherine Braun, Morris Beja, Jill Galvan, Leslie Tannenbaum, Amanpal Garcha, Luke Wilson, Valerie Lee, Richard Dutton and Sebastian Knowles. Among my colleagues in OSU Marion, I thank Greg Rose, Bishun Pandey, Christopher and Amy Friesen, Tim McNiven, David Steigerwald and Tracy Tylka.

I thank the librarians and archivists of the National Library of Ireland, the Irish Film Archive in Dublin and the Abbey Theatre. I thank Bill Shipsey, Mary Lawlor and Stephen Rea for their generosity in giving me interviews. I thank Nobby Clark for allowing me to use his photographs of the original Field Day production of *The Cure at Troy*. I thank Cormac Deane (Ó Duibhne) for his advice on materials in the Field Day Archive. I also thank Maria O'Donovan and Michael Collins at Cork University Press for their patience and hard work, and I extend special thanks to Dominic Carroll for expertly copy-editing the book.

I thank my parents, Chris Schoellman and Preston Wallace, and my siblings, Lyndon Smith, Maya Parry, Marcia Schoellman, Leah Wallace and Gina Wallace (may she rest in peace). I thank my grandmother, Rebecca Bowen Wallace, and my daughter Simone. Sara Crosby – my wife, best friend and fellow traveller – has marched beside me on every step of this campaign. More was deleted than was saved. The best remains, and better was added. I dedicate it all to her.

Introduction

Over the past twenty years, the concept of reconciliation has garnered a tremendous amount of scholarly and political attention with regard to various conflicts around the world, from South Africa to South America, to the Middle East and to Northern Ireland.[1] Along with the strongly allied ideas of democracy and human rights, reconciliation has become one of the most widely used and frequently invoked aspirational concepts in the world. Reconciliation is hardly a new idea, however, and neither is it new to Ireland. The language of reconciliation, in fact, has been a major feature of Irish writing since the eighteenth century, and a favoured term for Irish peacemakers from Edmund Burke to John Hume.

Historically, the language of reconciliation has meant many things to many people, and this ambiguity has not always been productive. During the Troubles in Northern Ireland, for instance, outside observers regularly urged unionists and nationalists to reconcile with one another according to the principles of liberal democracy. Unfortunately, the many proponents of democratic reconciliation have often failed to trust each other's formulations of it. Richard Bourke has argued in *Peace in Ireland* that unionists and nationalists both lay claim to 'rival democratic aspirations', and that this inhibited the development of any 'concordant sense of equality' between the communities.[2] In its most reductive form, the following question hung in the air over such discussions: would the Troubles be resolved into a Protestant unionist democracy or into a Catholic nationalist democracy? Who would get to vote on such a decision? Furthermore, what protections, if any, would be available to the minority in either case? Either one of these possible reconciliations seemed coercive, and so talking about democratic reconciliation at all could fan the flames of conflict.

The language of reconciliation became increasingly prominent in discussions about Northern Ireland during the 1980s.[3] In her well-known 'no political murder' speech of 5 March 1981, for instance, the British Prime Minister Margaret Thatcher advised Catholics and Protestants to reconcile with one another so that they could go after the IRA together. 'We all have a common interest in peace and reconciliation', she told her audience at Stormont;

> we all have a common interest in creating a society where the gunman has no place and where he'll no longer be able to kill and main [sic] innocent people . . . [however] There is no such thing as political murder, political bombing or political violence. There is only criminal murder, criminal bombing and criminal violence. We will not compromise on this. There will be no political status.[4]

This has been Thatcher's most-oft-quoted speech with reference to the Troubles, not only because it expresses a remarkably uncompromising policy, but also because it is so memorably put. Less well remembered, however, is the degree to which Thatcher adopts the language of reconciliation as a framework for her own expression of intransigence.[5] Thatcher returned to this rhetorical mode at the time of the Anglo-Irish (or 'Hillsborough') Agreement in 1985. Defending the agreement in a debate in the House of Commons on 26 November, she declared that 'reconciliations between these two [nationalist and unionist] communities' was the chief 'goal of this agreement', although it more immediately signalled the common 'commitment of the United Kingdom and the Irish Republic to work for reconciliation'.[6] From her government's perspective, this common commitment would primarily mean a greater level of cooperation between North and South on border security.

Like Thatcher, the Northern Irish constitutional nationalist leader John Hume also used the language of reconciliation. In contrast with Thatcher, however, Hume associated that language with the idea of all-party negotiations and cross-border institutions rather than simply with two-state legal and military cooperation against republicanism. The language of reconciliation used in the Hillsborough Agreement encompassed both of these concerns, along with the notion of human rights. In 1983 Hume engineered the New Ireland Forum in Dublin Castle; this forum included all of the Irish nationalist parties except for Sinn Féin, and it also led the way to Hillsborough. Hume gave a speech at that forum, 'Reconciliation of the irreconcilable', in which he alluded to 'a minority . . . who furiously abhor the work of reconciliation', announcing that '[our] clarion message to the men and women of violence is: "Reconciliation Yes, Destruction No, Democracy Yes, Your Fascism Never."'[7] Hume's ultimate vision of reconciliation in Northern Ireland would have to involve both Sinn Féin and the unionist leadership, and this strongly contrasted with Thatcher's strategy to marginalise Republicanism.

Also in that decade, Conor Cruise O'Brien criticised the language of reconciliation as it was used in relation to the Anglo-Irish Agreement. 'Readers may ask', O'Brien wrote in the *New York Review of Books* in 1986,

> what solution to the problem I envisage? None. I think the language of 'problem' and 'solution' is inappropriate to the case. What we have here is a *conflict* . . . No tinkering will reconcile these irreconcilables and the effort to reconcile them only serves to inflame the conflict, by arousing conflicting hopes and fears. On the other hand, if the Governments in London and Dublin learn, from unhappy experience of this Agreement, that it is better to stop tinkering with ambitious 'solutions', and return to the quiet co-operation in security matters, then the level of the violence involved in the conflict of irreconcilable wills could in time be reduced.[8]

According to O'Brien, the very idea that Irish Protestants and Catholics were capable of reconciliation in the first place lay at the root of the conflict. He agreed with the 'Ulster Says No' campaign of Revd Ian Paisley that the Anglo-Irish Agreement amounted to a British betrayal of Northern unionism, and with its demand that the Irish Republic cooperate with the British against the IRA without asking for any kind of input on the North's internal affairs.

The language of reconciliation has also been a major concern in Irish literature, and has been subject to scrutiny by literary critics. In his 'General introduction' to *The Field Day Anthology of Irish Writing*, Seamus Deane cautions the reader to distrust the innocuous language of reconciliation, which merely pretends to be salutary, pleasing or balanced. Deane identifies 'the aesthetic ideology, which claims autonomy for the work of art' as nothing less than

> a political force which pretends not to be so . . . [its] ideological appeal is embodied in the claim that a work of art achieves, in Coleridge's famous phrase, 'a reconciliation of opposites'. 'Reconciliation' is a key term in art criticism, in translation theory and in political crisis. In Ireland, the linkages between these fields are so close that there is scarcely a distinction in the vocabularies deployed for each. Art, however, is given priority even in this close-knit family, because it gives the example of how tensions, strains, raw authentic experience and processed emotional values can be brought together in a harmonious and triumphant wholeness. The idea that that which is

> chaotic, disorganized and 'rude' can be converted to civilization was shared by English colonial writers and English literary critics, at least until very recent times.[9]

In Deane's formulation, reconciliation is the colonial and neo-colonial discourse of power par excellence, and he further argues that in modern Ireland the ideological function of reconciliation, encapsulated and reproduced through the aesthetics of Coleridgean organicism, lamentably overdetermines a great deal of modern Irish poetry and drama. The argument of this book will bear out the first half of Deane's argument, but it will also argue that some modern Irish poets of reconciliation actually do transcend nineteenth-century colonial ideology.

In 2004 the British journalist Philip Dodd interviewed the Sinn Féin president, Gerry Adams, on the BBC radio programme *Night Waves*.[10] The occasion was the publication of *Hope and History*, Adams' book about his role in the peace process in Northern Ireland. The title of this book came – as many people interested in the peace process would have recognised – from a poem by Seamus Heaney. To be exact, it came from a chorus at the climax of his play *The Cure at Troy: A Version of Sophocles'* Philoctetes (1990). These lines have become the most oft-quoted in Heaney's *oeuvre*:

> History says, Don't hope
> On this side of the grave.
> But then, once in a lifetime
> The longed for tidal wave
> Of justice can rise up,
> And hope and history rhyme.[11]

A creative interpolation on Heaney's part, these lines are in many ways the point of the play that acts as their frame; their importance was often noted in the many interviews Heaney gave in 1990–91 to promote and explain the play. They offered a visionary ethical challenge to the traditionally pessimistic stereotypes of Irish history, and they also reflected the international euphoria that followed the fall of the Berlin Wall in Europe and the crumbling of Apartheid in South Africa. The 'Hope and History' chorus is the most famous example of what Richard Rankin Russell has called Heaney's 'reconciliatory poetics'.

The optimistic, visionary momentum in these lines seemed to inaugurate Ireland's optimistic spirit of the 1990s. In fact, the play was in performance at the Abbey Theatre in November 1990 when Mary Robinson won the election for president of the Irish Republic. The following month,

Robinson quoted it in her inaugural address: 'May I have the fortune', she told her audience in Dublin Castle on 9 December, 'to preside over an Ireland at a time of exciting transformation when we enter a new Europe where old wounds can be healed, a time when, in the words of Seamus Heaney, "hope and history rhyme".'[12] Robinson is also the first political figure to associate Heaney's poem with the language of reconciliation – an idea that has been key to its significance in that sphere.

Following upon Robinson's importation of the chorus into Irish public discourse, a long line of political figures would quote them throughout the peace process of the 1990s. In a letter to Tony Taccone, Heaney mentions his pleasure that the lines 'got lodged in Mary Robinson's consciousness', and that he

> was gratified when later on as President of Ireland, she quoted those lines – in response to the distresses of famine in Africa for example, as well as in other contexts. And I was delighted and surprised when, at the opening of the post-cease-fire Forum for Peace and Reconciliation in Dublin last autumn the lines were quoted again, directly, by Dick Spring, the Irish Minister for Foreign Affairs, and . . . [then] by Gerry Adams, the leader of Sinn Féin.[13]

Heaney's comment that he was pleased to have been quoted by Adams is noteworthy; the IRA ceasefire had only been called the previous year and the Belfast Agreement lay three years in the future. The bonuses continued to accrue after 1995: in 1996 President Bill Clinton published an election-year book, *Between Hope and History.*[14] Shortly after the signing of the 1998 Belfast Agreement, moreover, Clinton quoted the lines as the conclusion of a radio address, further personalising the quotation with a story of how he met Heaney in Ireland and received from him a copy of the poem 'that today hangs on the wall of my office in the upstairs of the White House'.[15] That same week, two days after the signing of the Belfast Agreement, British Prime Minister Tony Blair spoke before the Irish Parliament in Dublin, *Tithe an Oireachtais*, and before speaking was addressed by the *Ceann Comhairle* (Speaker), who included the famous Heaney quotation. 'The overwhelming democratic endorsement of the Agreement', he told Blair,

> demonstrates the clear desire of the people of this island for change to a better and brighter future. Seamus Heaney wrote:
>
> Once in a lifetime, the longed for tidal wave
> of justice can rise up and hope and history
> rhyme.
>
> Prime Minister, by your contribution to peace on this island, hope

> and history do indeed rhyme as the dark days are hopefully forever in the past and a new dawn of peace and reconciliation beckons forth . . .[16]

In that moment of political euphoria, it was almost common sense to say that Blair was a good peacemaker because he had adopted Heaney's ethos of reconciliation in the political sphere. As a historical reconciler, he actually 'got' what Heaney was talking about.

Half a decade later, however, when Adams named his book after Heaney's poem, 'hope and history' was a recognisable meme that had lost some of its rhetorical punch – and in some cases, credibility. After a peace process spoiler group, the Real IRA, carried out a devastating bombing in the Northern Irish town of Omagh, U2's Bono wrote a song, 'Peace on Earth', which bitterly declared that 'hope and history don't rhyme'. In the more discouraging period after 2001, even the former Irish president Mary Robinson took to quoting alternate sections of the chorus in her speeches. In March 2008, for instance, Robinson opened a panel at the PEN (Poets, Essayists and Novelists) World Voices Festival with the words 'It is a bleak time for human rights', a statement she followed with the stanza that comes directly after the one about 'hope and history' in that famous chorus:

> So hope for a great sea-change
> on the far side of revenge.
> Believe that a further shore
> is reachable from here.
> Believe in miracles
> and cures and healing wells.[17]

'Maybe there was too much hope and history', the historian Kevin Whelan reflected, in 2009, when considering how the chorus had been used in the late nineties.[18] Whelan played a major role in framing the bicentenary commemorations of the 1798 United Irish Rising in terms of the peace process, and has more recently suggested that the 'unreal or unrealistic' rhetoric of that year was sometimes 'too easy'. In retrospect, it could even be 'insulting', he continues, in its suggestion that 'people who have lost loved ones' – and to whom 'every day the loss is apparent' – could put the past behind them abruptly.[19] No doubt cognisant of how the poem could be used or misused, Heaney himself has subsequently voiced regret about having included the chorus in *Cure* at all; if anything, however, its afterlife should draw greater critical attention to the poem rather than less.

Reviewing Dodd's 2004 radio interview with Adams on *Night Waves*, the *Independent*'s commentator Robert Hanks noted that it raised questions about the relationship between poetry and politics. 'Can a politician ever be truly cultured?' he asked, continuing that

> If being 'cultured' means anything at all, it is not just knowing a lot of stuff about poetry, music, whatever, but responding to it with intelligent discrimination; and discrimination is something that politicians, by and large, aren't very happy with . . . Asked what Heaney meant to him . . . [Adams would only reply:] 'I'm a big fan.'[20]

This exchange raises the question of just how literary it is possible for political discourse to be, and also just how politically significant a poem can be. That is, one could have asked the question of any number of other politicians who invoked the chorus, and probably have received similarly vague answers. How many of these political figures had actually read Heaney's play, much less seen it in performance? How many knew it was a version of Sophocles' *Philoctetes*, or considered how it fit into Heaney's larger *oeuvre*? In terms of political messaging, it would not have made any difference one way or the other; the point of the quotation is that the lines are inspirational, and that Heaney was an extremely sympathetic poet who was also soon to be a Nobel laureate.

Dodd's question and Adams' answer shed more light on the culturally specific relationship between poetry and politics in Anglo-Irish history than on either the interviewer or the interviewee on that occasion. That is, Dodd did not pose this question to the realm of politics as such, but, rather, to the leader of Sinn Féin in particular.[21] If this was a trick question, what it presumably exposed was that Adams had never truly adopted the ethos of reconciliation that was meant to inform the entire Northern Ireland peace process. The suggestion was that he had no idea of what reconciliation was really about – and it assumed that a critical journalist could expose this fact by demonstrating that Adams really did not know as much about the poetry of Seamus Heaney as he said he did. The cultural logic underlying this discussion of poetry and politics deserves analysis. First, it tells us something about Heaney's status as an Irish literary celebrity. Both as the pre-eminent Northern Irish poet and as a well-respected moderate nationalist, Heaney is widely accepted as an ethical, as well as literary, authority. His ethos of reconciliation commands so much respect in the political sphere, in fact, that it actually becomes possible for an English journalist to put Adams on the spot by asking him to comment on Heaney's poetry with discernment. I would also question this moment, however, and use it to open up some questions about the rhetoric of reconciliation in modern Ireland. How did it ever come about that a proper engagement with Heaney's poetry, whatever that might entail, could be seen as a legitimate test of any political leader's (and especially a republican leader's) genuine commitment to peace and reconciliation in Northern Ireland?

One compelling answer to this question, informed by Deane's comments on reconciliation in the 'General introduction' to *The Field Day Anthology*, would be that a Romantic discourse of organicism has permeated Irish political discourse – so much so, that one might dismiss Irish nationalism in aesthetic terms. In the previous section, we saw how Deane asks us to consider the similar uses of reconciliation among 'English colonial writers and English literary critics'.[22] According to the logic of reconciliation Deane critiques, it would seem Adams cannot be seen as a good reader of Heaney's poetry because he, being the President of Sinn Féin, is too 'chaotic, disorganized and "rude"' to follow Heaney's footsteps towards the 'harmonious and triumphant' Arnoldian 'reconciliation of opposites' in Northern Ireland.[23] Also according to that logic, moreover, it would seem that Heaney actually was 'converted to civilization' in the course of his study of Wordsworth. If this is an ideological assumption underlying Dodd's question, it also raises questions about Heaney's role in the reproduction of Coleridgean ideology of the aesthetic. In order to explore these questions further, I will now introduce the concept of the 'icon of reconciliation'.

By the term 'icon of reconciliation', I mean a literary figure (in this case, Heaney) who comes to be frequently invoked (by Robinson, Adams, Clinton et al.) as an ethical guide to the politics of peace and reconciliation. 'Ethical guide' might sound like a strong term for the origin of what has sometimes degenerated into a catchphrase, but in this book I will be arguing that Heaney's formulation of 'hope and history' has a much more complex history and meaning than that. More specifically, I will argue that the icon of reconciliation has an ethical significance as well as a rhetorical function. To illuminate this dual function, therefore, I will turn to Aristotle, whose rhetorical and ethical philosophies were closely linked by his versatile notion of ethos. In Aristotelian rhetorical terms, then, one might say that the icon of reconciliation combines the ethical proof on one hand, with an appeal to authority on the other.

First, let us consider the icon of reconciliation as an ethical proof. In his *Art of Rhetoric*, Aristotle proposes a tripartite model of persuasion in which we find 'three forms of proof' (*pisteôn tria eidê*).[24] 'The first', he writes, 'depends upon the moral *character* [or *êthos*] of the speaker, the second upon putting the hearer into a certain frame of mind, the third upon the speech itself, in so far as it proves or seems to prove.'[25] In the first of these, the ethical proof, the speaker would present a persona that would win the audience's *eunoia*, or goodwill.[26] During the 1980s, Heaney established tremendous goodwill in his audience through his prose, poetry, interviews and work for Amnesty International. By the end of the decade he was recognised as a major contender for the Nobel Prize in Literature. When *Cure* premiered in 1990, therefore, he was not simply trusted as a poet of peace but, indeed, began to be invoked as an authority on the topic over the next decade.

This leads us to consider the idea of the icon of reconciliation in terms of the appeal to authority. Aristotle described this kind of appeal as a 'previous judgment in regard to the same or a similar or contrary matter' (*ek kriseos peri tou autou e homoiou e enantiou*).[27] These authoritative judgements derived from earlier decisions by the wise (*sophoi*), the good (*agathoi*), the audience themselves, or 'those whose judgment they accept, or those whose judgment it is impossible to contradict . . . for instance, the gods, a father, or instructors'.[28] By 1990 Heaney had established for himself a pre-eminent reputation as a fair-minded, trustworthy poet of the Troubles, and was therefore seen as both wise and good in something like the Aristotelian sense. If Heaney was accepted as a good and wise authority on the Troubles, however, it was partly because he so scrupulously refused either to endorse or wholly condemn republicanism. Therefore, no one could credibly invoke Heaney's 'previous judgment' as a case either for Irish partition or unification.

In the sense that his trustworthiness was widely recognised, and even that he was taken as a kind of authority on the spirit of reconciliation, Heaney is the exemplary contemporary Irish icon of reconciliation. At the same time that he was an icon, however, he was also what I would call an *iconographer* of reconciliation – in the sense that he was invoking another authority, namely Sophocles, to back up his argument. The politicians who quoted the 'Hope and History' chorus throughout the peace process usually cited Heaney without mentioning the play from which it was taken – and neither would it have seemed particularly important to them that it was a modern version of an ancient Greek play. The choice of translating Sophocles was of course highly significant to Heaney, however, and he was aware that it connected him to a century-long traditional of Sophoclean meditations on peace in Ireland that started with Matthew Arnold and ran through the writings of W.B. Yeats, Conor Cruise O'Brien and Tom Paulin (the other primary subjects of this book).

Long before reconciliation became a key term in Irish politics, Sophocles had been associated in various ways with the concept. If the ancient Greeks themselves had had a word for 'reconciled', they would almost certainly have used it to describe him. Indeed, Aristophanes comes close to doing so when, in *The Frogs*, Dionysus calls the recently deceased tragedian *eukolos* ('well-contented' or 'good-natured') both in life and in death.[29] The comic poet Phrynichus also remembered the tragedian as 'a happy man … who wrote many beautiful tragedies'.[30] Even Plato remembers Sophocles as being content with old age, because it had freed him from the tyranny of sexual desire.[31] Perhaps most memorably, however, one classical biographer records that Sophocles actually died of happiness upon learning that his penultimate play, *Oedipus at Colonus*, won first place in the Athenian tragic festival of 406–05 BCE. If this story is true, it means that Sophocles' own death was as serene and happy as that of Oedipus himself.

In addition to these biographical anecdotes, Sophocles' aesthetics have also been associated with reconciliation. In his *Poetics*, for instance, Aristotle famously says that tragedy causes its audience to experience a *catharsis* through 'the arousal of pity and fear'.[32] This enigmatic phrase has been interpreted in various ways, but there can be no doubt that Aristotle saw this in a positive light. Like any other form of purgation, the tragic catharsis suggests cleansing and the maintenance of balance and health. This description of Sophoclean catharsis seems fitting in light of the fact that Sophocles was a priest of Asclepius, a Greek god of healing. When the cult of Asclepius came to Athens, Sophocles reportedly made his own home into a temporary sanctuary; he also wrote a lyric poem to the god, and for this was posthumously made into a kind of hero the Greeks called *deksiôn*. Building on this ancient reputation, moreover, a number of modern scholars have written on Sophocles and reconciliation, even going so far as to compare him later in life with the later Shakespeare.[33] The parallels between *Philoctetes* and *The Tempest* – each of which was its respective playwright's final play – are indeed striking, and Heaney signals his awareness of this when he echoed the language of *The Tempest* in *Cure*.

In Heaney's use of Sophocles, we can see how the iconography of reconciliation combines the Aristotelian ethical appeal with the appeal to authority. That is, like Yeats, who often likened himself to great poets and dramatists of the past (for instance, Dante, who exemplified 'unity of being'), Heaney presented himself as the transmitter of Sophoclean poetic wisdom. Moreover, in order to recommend a Sophoclean ethos of reconciliation with any authority, Heaney would have to demonstrate he had himself genuinely absorbed that ethos through his own art. This was clearly a major concern in *Cure* and in *Seeing Things* (1991), and also in his 2001 poem 'Out of the Bag', in which the poet recounts a therapeutic visit to the temple of Asclepius at Epidaurus. The most frequently quoted phrase of this last poem is 'the cure / By poetry that cannot be coerced', because it so beautifully describes his aesthetics of reconciliation. The incident Heaney relates in that poem, moreover, emphasises his identification with Sophocles as a fellow-poet of visions and miracle cures.

Another aspect of Heaney's Sophoclean persona came through his emphasis on ethics – a major concern of Athenian drama as a civic art – alongside his visionary poetics. If Heaney avoided lending his cultural authority to any side other than a middle-of-the-road liberal-nationalist one, he was going against the kinds of expectation that had historically been directed at major Irish poets during times of conflict. This is an ancient expectation, and while this is a less obvious feature of ancient Greek poetry, Aristotle does point out instances where poets had been invoked to bolster sides in disputes.

In another part of *Rhetoric*, for instance, Aristotle identified poets as witnesses (martyrs) in judicial cases, such as when

> the Athenians, in the matter of Salamis, appealed to Homer as a witness, and recently the inhabitants of Tenedos to Periander of Corinth against the Sigeans. Cleophon also made use of the elegiacs of Solon against Critias, to prove that his family had long been notorious for licentiousness, otherwise Solon would never have written: Bid me the fair-haired Critias listen to his father.[34]

Aristotle's example of how poetic tradition was used in the ancient Greek world to support historical claims between city states for territory, or even to provide character witnesses in disputes between families, has strong echoes in the history of Irish poetry and politics. In pre-Christian and early medieval Ireland, for instance, a highly learned class of poets called *filidh* played important roles as historians, geographers and lawyers. From the twelfth to the seventeenth century, moreover, an elevated caste of bards kept schools where students learned such topics as history, genealogy and law, as well as poetry.

Both as a contemporary *dinnseanchas* poet and translator of the Middle Irish *Buile Suibhne*, Heaney is widely recognised as an inheritor of the medieval Irish poetic tradition, and this has given him a kind of authority to speak on the public stage. Attempting to do this without endorsing either the Northern unionist establishment or the republican resistance to it, Heaney cast himself as a modern version of the mad King Sweeney: someone disoriented by the pull between worlds. This is not an approach that one most readily associates with the old Irish poets, whose cultural and political functions for more than a thousand years were more often concerned with the conservation of traditional knowledge, and even the maintenance of political and cultural identity, than with exhortations towards their native audiences to cultivate a trustworthy reputation for non-partisanship.

Heaney's way of addressing Irish politics is nonetheless rhetorical, but his rhetoric is more Aristotelian in the sense that it links up with ethics, poetics and psychology. Let us consider Book II of *Rhetoric*, which contains the first study of psychology in Western literature. Here is where Aristotle enumerates the emotional states the rhetor must understand (and exploit) in order to be persuasive, such as pity (*eleos*) and fear (*phobos*).[35] He also discusses the paired emotions of envy (*phthonos*) on one hand, and emulation (*zelos*) on the other.[36] One way to convince people is to manipulate their capacity for envy, which is small-minded because it not only wants something good but also wants others not to have it or anything like it. *Zelos*, on the other hand, is where one emulates the good, in the way of 'the young and high-minded', who believe that everyone deserving good can share it without a sense of scarcity.[37] This is a non-territorial good that enriches the community. Aristotelian *zelos* is very close to what Heaney attempted to evoke in his audience through the 'Hope and History' chorus. The poet's situated ethos was also necessary to that appeal to the emotions, and in a way Aristotle speaks to this when he says 'those are emulated whom many want to be like . . . or . . . whom many admire.'[38] In other words, the effect of the 'Hope and History' chorus depends upon Heaney's being an icon of reconciliation, an authoritative poet-witness for peace.

Heaney did not mean to be taken as a witness for a particular settlement or policy in the way that, say, the ancient Athenians invoked Homer. In his decision to adapt Sophocles in *The Cure at Troy*, Heaney signalled that he was moving beyond the bardic territorialism of the Homeric tradition, and emulating the newer concerns with ethics, psychology and citizenship that were essential both to Aristotle's philosophy and the drama of Sophocles.[39] This Hellenism does not mean a renunciation of the Irish tradition, however, because in the 'Hope and History' chorus Heaney combines poetry with prophecy. While these are both forms of authority in *Rhetoric*, Aristotle distinguishes between them as reliable witnesses for the past and future respectively. In medieval Ireland, however, the *filidh* also delivered prophecies as well as poems. In the 'Hope and History' chorus, therefore, Heaney brings the old Irish association between poetry and prophecy together with the ancient Athenian notion of drama as a civic art.[40]

To readers who remain suspicious of reconciliation as a rhetorical trope cloaking colonial ideology, my use of Aristotle to explain the icon of reconciliation may raise further red flags. While the Greek philosopher has, of course, never stopped being foundational to Western thought, he has often been read as a foil to critical theory. In *Totality and Infinity*, for instance, Emmanuel Levinas likens 'the god of Aristotle' to Hegel's coercive concept of infinity that excludes 'all multiplicity', and which 'can only encompass all relations'.[41] Levinas thus associates Aristotle's *Metaphysics* with the kind of idealist and ultimately totalitarian impulses with which Western philosophy has been associated since the Second World War. Levinas called these impulses in Aristotle's thought 'the imperialism of the same', and likens it to 'the sovereignty of the state'.[42] Furthermore, whether or not one considers it a stretch for an Adorno or a Levinas to relate Aristotle's totalising philosophy to totalitarianism, it should be kept in mind that he was the tutor of Alexander the Great: the first European who ever made any real progress towards a stated project of world conquest. The treatise *Alexander, or On Colonies,* probably makes him the first philosophical sponsor of Western imperialism.[43] He may also have been its first intellectual beneficiary; according to tradition, Alexander sent zoological and botanical samples back to Aristotle from the lands he conquered.

Over the past twenty years, however, a number of theorists in diverse fields have sought to bring Aristotle into more fruitful dialogue with modern thought. In his essay 'The ethical culmination of Aristotle's *Metaphysics*', for instance, Christopher Long takes Levinas' challenge to Aristotle as an 'invitation to re-read the history of Western philosophy as something other than a history of totalizing ontologies, searching all the while for the trace of that ethical impulse that is eclipsed by the traditional preoccupation with systematic totality'.[44] The most popular and compelling way to do this, so far, has been to revisit Aristotelian 'ethos', a move which in turn has been key to what we know as the 'ethical turn' in literary study. One critique of the ethical turn has been that if we look to ethics as an autonomous category, separated out from aesthetics, politics, economics or rhetoric, we end up with a worldview riven by a series of specious autonomies. In Aristotle, however, we find no such spurious discontinuities. While he does admittedly universalise a culturally specific definition of characterological virtue, he also refuses to partition ethics off from any other part of his wide-ranging philosophy, and this offers some grounds for retrieving it.[45] It is through his refusal to philosophise *separately*, through *distinct* categories, therefore, that Aristotle helps us to liberate ethics from quarantine, and restores it to its rightful place in discussions of poetics, rhetoric and politics.

Whereas some modern theorists have taken encouragement from the idea that Aristotelian ethos offers connections between seemingly distinct areas of Aristotle's thought, this mobility of the term has also long troubled readers concerned with the disconnect between ethics and rhetoric to begin with. When Aristotle in *Rhetoric* first explained what has subsequently come to be known as the communication triangle, he gave the passions a priority to which Plato – whose ban on poetry in *The Republic* arose from his conviction that the passions that poetry excited would corrupt the state – would surely have rejected. Rather than protesting against the fact that ethical proofs and appeals to the emotions are more persuasive than logical argument, however, Aristotle detailed at length how the speaker's character can be faked and the audience's emotions ascertained and manipulated. In this sense, Aristotle's rhetorical theory seems to fly in the face of his ethical philosophy. Many readers of Aristotle have long argued they are incompatible because his *Nicomachean Ethics* were about the cultivation of actual virtue and this was hard to square with *Rhetoric*'s artful projection of trustworthiness.[46] Others have maintained, however, that Aristotle's sense of ethos is philosophically consistent.[47] Eugene Garver, for instance, argues that in *Rhetoric* Aristotle reconciles art (*technê*) and virtuous behaviour (*praxis*) in a way that remains relevant to discussions about civic art (such as theatre) to the present day.[48] According to Garver's reading of Aristotle, rhetoric and theatre are both civic arts to be defended in the same terms he uses at the end of *Politics*, to justify 'ethical music' and 'catharsis'.[49]

Aristotle's comments on Sophocles, his favourite dramatist, offer some clues towards solving the problem of reconciling the seeming contradiction between his rhetoric and his ethics. This is because Aristotle sometimes referenced Sophocles' dramas to illustrate the delicate balance between rhetorical ethos and ethical character. In *Rhetoric*, for instance, he draws attention to the scene in *Antigone* where the protagonist explains that she has performed funeral rites over her brother Polyneices because she valued her brother over any other relative. According to Aristotle, she is acting ethically by being honest, while at the same time making the best case for herself rhetorically.[50] Making a similar connection in the *Nicomachean Ethics*, moreover, Aristotle identifies *Philoctetes* as an ethical drama because Neoptolemus uses rhetoric in an unethical way and then tries to make up for it by living up to his true ethical character.[51]

Modern Irish literature is deeply informed by the ancient Athenian notion that the dramatic arts perform a vital civic function. This is in fact a major premise upon which the Abbey Theatre and the Field Day Theatre Company have justified their existences, and this assumption has been shared by the admirers and detractors of both organisations. The idea was hardly new to the National Theatre Society in the 1890s, however. Even looking back as far as *Reflections on the Revolution in France*, for instance, we can see that Burke considered drama in Aristotelian terms when he argued that his reaction to the revolution was

> *natural* . . . because we are so made as to be affected at such spectacles . . . because in those natural feelings we learn great lessons . . . We are alarmed into reflection; our minds (as it has long since been observed) are purified by terror and pity; our weak, unthinking pride is humbled under the dispensations of a mysterious wisdom.[52]

For Burke, tragedy is a civic art because it draws out the passions reminding us of the political morality naturally imprinted on human nature. One of Burke's most influential nineteenth-century British readers, moreover, Matthew Arnold, also invoked a similarly Aristotelian notion of civic art as part of his programme of cultural Hellenism. This book will trace the Arnoldian legacy in modern Ireland by examining some key dramatists' and critics' invocations of Hellenism in relation to the problems and promises of political and cultural reconciliation. I have focused my attention on the Field Day Theatre Company, which during the 1980s, continually kept in mind the example of W.B. Yeats as a historical forerunner, and Conor Cruise O'Brien as a hegemonic cultural and intellectual presence to be overturned.

In chapter one, 'W.B. Yeats' Free State Hellenism', I argue that Yeats, rather than being a poet of reconciliation during the 1920s, was trying to balance between an anti-foundationalist poetics of the emblem on one hand, and Arnoldian cultural Hellenism on the other. First, I draw upon arguments in Paul de Man's and David Lloyd's essays on Yeats, that the poetics of the emblem represent radical alternatives to traditional Romantic aesthetics (de Man) and the founding ideology of the Free State (Lloyd).[53] I also draw on the argument from Lloyd's and Paul Thomas' book *Culture and the State*, that the exemplary man of Arnoldian culture is a figure of statist ideology, and argue that Yeats accepted just such a role when he became a senator in the Irish Free State.[54] These antithetical impulses therefore come to a crisis in *The Tower* (1928), most particularly in 'Among School Children' and 'Colonus's Praise'.

In chapter two, 'Conor Cruise O'Brien's sacred dramas', I argue that these Yeatsian antitheses are also present in O'Brien's thinking from as early as the 1950s, but that he ultimately commits himself to a statist ideology as an opponent of the IRA, starting in the 1970s. In the late 1960s, O'Brien developed an idea of 'sacred drama' as a model for the United Nations to pursue world peace during the Cold War. A remarkable double standard appears in O'Brien's theory when he suggests that Ireland is a country that produces sacred dramas for the world but cannot benefit from them at home. I track this double standard through O'Brien's writings about Yeats, Heaney, Sophocles and the United Nations.

In chapter three, 'Tom Paulin at the gates of Thebes (and Derry and Hillsborough)', I argue that Paulin's essay 'The making of a loyalist' laid down a foundational idea for the Field Day Theatre Company by reclaiming Antigone from O'Brien's Sophoclean analogy for the Troubles in *States of Ireland*.[55] In this response to O'Brien, furthermore, Paulin delinked Hellenism from the state, thereby undoing the Arnoldian connection that had bedevilled Yeats and O'Brien alike.

In the fourth chapter, 'Seamus Heaney's poetics of human rights', I draw on Theodor Adorno's utopian notion of a world where one might be 'different without fear' to describe the poetics of human rights Seamus Heaney developed in the 1980s.[56] I will use this to address David Lloyd's argument, from the well-known essay 'Pap for the dispossessed', that Heaney's poetry of the 1970s and early eighties reproduced the identarian logic of nineteenth-century Romantic Irish nationalism.[57] I conclude the chapter by reading *The Cure at Troy* as an allegory for Heaney's poetics of human rights.

The fifth chapter of this book, 'Field Day's daylight gods', counters the charge implied by some of Seamus Deane's more pessimistic comments about Field Day, that *The Cure at Troy* reproduced an ideology of the aesthetic, and by extension a coercive notion of reconciliation in Ireland. Placing this problem in the context of Heaney's long-term conversation with Deane about poetics and politics, I present *Cure* as a paradigmatic example of Field Day's civic art. I also show, through a reading of Deane's review of *Cure*, 'Oranges and Lemnos', that he endorsed Heaney's play as an ethical drama of reconciliation, despite any reservations about Heaney's aesthetic paradigm.

This book's conclusion, 'Anthologising reconciliation', considers the discourse of reconciliation in *The Field Day Anthology of Irish Writing* (5 vols). It will argue that the anthology's first instalment (vols 1–3) is largely informed by the rhetoric of reconciliation that the Northern liberal nationalist leader John Hume used around the time of the Anglo-Irish Agreement in 1985. The final two volumes, however, demonstrate a feminist critique of the peace process' discourse of reconciliation in the 1990s.[58]

These writers, from Yeats to O'Brien to Paulin and Heaney, invoke Sophocles as a kind of figurehead for a civic drama of reconciliation, and all negotiate with the legacy of Arnoldian cultural Hellenism while doing so. They often conceive of rhetoric, politics, ethics and poetics in different ways, but in their thinking about Sophoclean drama in relation to Ireland they do maintain a very Aristotelian insistence (shared by Burke and Arnold) that they all go together. I will argue that Deane's ideological critique of aesthetic reconciliation is most justified in the cases of Yeats and O'Brien, who were the most intellectually indebted to Arnold. When it comes to such Field Day plays as *The Riot Act* and *The Cure at Troy*, however, I will make the case that the poetics of reconciliation can and does transcend the colonial discourse from which it initially emerged in Ireland. Moreover, I will argue that it offers something akin to what Aristotle called an ethical music to a world in conflict.

Chapter One

W.B. Yeats' Free State Hellenism

In a remarkable 1960 essay on W.B. Yeats, Paul de Man described a formative antithesis between a poetics of the natural image and a poetics of the emblem running through the poet's entire career.[1] In his reading, the natural image is a traditional Romantic idea referring to something actually seen and believed to hold meaning in and of itself. The emblem, on the other hand, derives its meaning from poetry itself (whether traditional or personal) rather than from the divine. Both the image and the emblem, moreover, are mutually exclusive paths to reconciliation. As de Man asserts, 'the former leads to a (problematic) vision of unity that transcends the opposition between object and subject, while the latter finds unity preserved in meaning as a carrier of a divine.'[2] According to de Man, then, Yeats began as a traditionally Romantic poet committed to the poetics of the natural image, but came to experiment with this radical emblematic approach in *The Wind Among the Reeds* (1899) and in the essays contained in *Ideas of Good and Evil* (1903).

The conflict between emblem and image continued to haunt Yeats' poetics through the rest of his career, however, and this led de Man to his main argument with Frank Kermode's *The Romantic Image* (1957), which posited Yeats' '"Among School Children", with its seductively dazzling imagery of unity', as the paradigmatic poem of the 'reconciling image' because its 'image of the dancer is said to be the supreme instance of reconciliation . . . [of] the ideal attributes of both body and imagination'.[3] De Man thereby contests Kermode's reading of the 'reconciled' Yeats, arguing, instead, that the critic has overlooked the 'controlled violence of [Yeats'] late work'.[4] Indeed, taking Kermode's 'reconciling image' of dancer and dance head on, de Man reads the final line of 'Among School Children' as an anxious literal question about whether to follow the path of the image or the emblem, rather than as a rhetorical question affirming the conservative poetics of the Romantic image. In the poetry of the 1930s, he concludes, Yeats would finally commit to the emblem and this would lead to his increasingly violent and apocalyptic imagery – ultimately resolving itself into nihilistic collapse in 'The Circus Animals' Desertion'. 'Image and emblem' therefore concludes with de Man telling us that Yeats was anything but a poet of reconciliation.

Like de Man, in his 1989 essay 'The poetics of politics: Yeats and the founding of the state', David Lloyd also promotes an anti-reconciliationist reading of Yeats. Rather than targeting Kermode's version, however, he points the finger at the Irish Republic itself, which, to his mind, had long since channelled the poet's radical poetics into the de-politicised and de-historicised containment zone of cultural education. Before the Easter Rising of 1916, Lloyd's argument states, the cultural nationalist Yeats claimed a poetic status as organic representative of the Irish nation. After 1916, however, the martyrs of the Easter Rising displaced Yeats from this privileged representative position, and the experience of being cast out from the narrative of national reconciliation revealed to him that organicism was a political and aesthetic ideology that could and should be de-stabilised on the level of his poetics.[5] From this point on, therefore, Yeats would write increasingly 'anti-foundationalist' poems, exemplified by such works from *The Winding Stair* (1933) as 'Dialogue of Self and Soul', 'Coole Park and Ballylee, 1931' and 'Byzantium'. What de Man had seen as Yeats' commitment to the emblem over the natural image on the level of sheer poetic experimentation becomes, in Lloyd's reading, an estranged ex-national poet's critique of the new state's ideology of political and aesthetic reconciliation.

Another key to the politics of Yeats' poetics is to be found in de Man's observation, at the beginning of 'Image and emblem', that Yeats had no sense of *Bildung* in the sense of Matthew Arnold's cultural education, because he instead modelled his study on the example of William Blake. While this is true about Yeats' own method of self-education, I would maintain that the poet actually had a very clear sense of *Bildung* on the national level because he believed the Irish sorely lacked an education in Arnoldian cultural Hellenism.[6] Lloyd's comment that Yeats' radical poetic critique of the state was muted by the Irish culture industry, while largely true, nonetheless overlooks the degree to which Yeats actually courted the discourse of cultural education as the necessary precondition for his participation in the state from 1922 to 1928. Even while taking on board Lloyd's brilliant ideological analysis of the Yeatsian emblem, we must still consider that Yeats consciously sought to reproduce, in the interests of the state, many of the ideological functions Lloyd and Paul Thomas ascribed to Arnoldian culture in their 1989 book *Culture and the State*.

Therefore, in this chapter I will take as a point of departure Lloyd's ideological analysis of the emblem, but I will also retain a dialectical element from de Man's approach. That is, whereas Lloyd periodised the distinction between Yeatsian symbol and emblem, de Man's original argument described a back-and-forth struggle between image and emblem running more or less throughout the course of the poet's career. I will also revisit the terms of fundamental opposition we find in de Man's and Lloyd's respective accounts. Where de Man opposed *image* to emblem, and Lloyd opposed *symbol* to emblem, I will be opposing *culture* to emblem. Yeats tries to reconcile these two mutually incompatible influences in his project to shape Irish national character, but this tension reaches a crisis with the foundation of the Irish Free State and yields spectacular results in *The Tower* (1928). In order to explain this formative conflict in Yeats' high modernist phase, however, it will be necessary to show how the poet, in the earliest stage of his career, developed the poetics of the emblem as a critique of Arnold's ideology of culture, even as he was adapting the latter for a cultural nationalist project.

In his series of lectures 'On the study of Celtic literature', Arnold drew most famously upon the French Celticists Ernest Renan and Henri Martin, who invoked racial theory to argue that the Celts were unfit 'to form powerful states'.[7] Arnold took their pseudo-scientific 'findings' to a larger historical narrative of racial expansionism, which seemed to make the British Empire in Ireland inevitable. 'The fusion of all the inhabitants of these islands into one homogenous, English-speaking whole', he wrote triumphantly:

> the breaking down of barriers between us, the swallowing up of separate provincial nationalities, is a consummation to which the natural course of things irresistibly tends; it is a necessity of . . . modern civilization . . . a real, legitimate force . . . [whose] accomplishment is a mere affair of time.[8]

According to this argument, British authority in Ireland was inevitable because 'true science . . . recognizes a law of ultimate fusion, of conciliation', and like 'her elder sister, poetry', science also recognised 'the substantial unity of man'.[9] Arnold also relied on German Romantic aesthetics to support his theory of inevitable Irish reconciliation. Those very theorists' preoccupations with reconciliation derived largely from their Hellenism, which assumed that we fallen moderns had lost the sense of unity once enjoyed by the ancient Greeks, but could retrieve at least some of that lost unity through cultural education or *Bildung*. Ideas such as these lay, for instance, at the heart of Friedrich von Schiller's *Letters on the Aesthetic Education of Man* (1794–95) and *On Naive and Sentimental Poetry* (1795–96), two treatises that influenced Arnold's writings of the 1860s. In the latter work, Schiller associated naive poetry with the classical Greeks and sentimental poetry with the moderns. In 'On the study of Celtic literature', therefore, Arnold took this distinction and mapped it onto the Anglo-Irish relationship. According to this argument, the English are not Hellenised but they could regain some of that Hellenic naivety through culture. The Irish, by contrast, are sentimental because of their race; and this predisposes them to modernity in the worst sense, and cuts them off by nature itself from the spiritual and material fruits of cultural education. 'The true art', Arnold says, 'the *architectonicé* which shapes great works, such as the Agamemnon or the Divine Comedy, comes only after a steady, deep-searching survey, a firm conception of the facts of human life, which the Celt has no patience for.'[10] As Celts, Arnold implies, the Irish come from a dilettantish racial family and should therefore cease trying to make good art, and instead concentrate their diffuse faculties on the challenging task of reconciling themselves to the imperium of a people who actually are capable of creating great art.

Arnold found another model by which to correlate literary achievement with political talent in Friedrich von Schlegel's *On the Study of Greek Poetry* (1797), which contains the idea that Sophocles had mastered the aesthetic principles of 'subordination', 'integration' and 'unification'.[11] All of these characteristics also belonged to an idealised picture of Periclean Athens, and in Arnold's imagination they could be just as applicable to a culturally renovated Britain if only his ideas could gain traction there. According to Schlegel, Sophocles had taken 'the mature and full-grown organization' from previous Greek artists such as Aeschylus and Homer and 'carried [it] out to a completeness . . . [in which] everything evolves *necessarily* out of a unity and even the smallest part belongs unconditionally to the *great law of the whole*'.[12] Schlegel's Sophocles also shows 'moderation' in renouncing 'even the most beautiful outgrowth and . . . even the most alluring temptation to do damage to the equilibrium of the whole'.[13] In contrast with this achievement, Arnold held that the Celt 'runs off into technic . . . employs the utmost elaboration, and attains astonishing skill', but cannot get past 'the first dash of quick, strong perception', or move beyond his 'want of sanity and steadfastness'.[14] One would, therefore, never be able to say about the Irish what Schlegel said about Sophocles: that 'his law-governedness is free, his accuracy graceful, and his richest abundance organizes itself of its own accord to a perfect yet pleasing harmony.'[15] Unable to reconcile themselves in proper Sophoclean fashion, the Irish need to be reconciled from without.

Yeats was very attentive to Arnoldian Celticism, and in his 1897 essay 'The Celtic element of literature' he responded to Arnold's aesthetic and pseudo-scientific arguments about Anglo-Irish reconciliation with his own theory of reconciliation through symbols. He was particularly attentive to the contrast Arnold had drawn between English organicism and *architectonice* on one hand, and the Celtic natural magic and Titanism on the other.[16] In his personal copy of *The Study of Celtic Literature*, Yeats folded down a page including the description of *architectonice*, and underlined passages relating to natural magic and Titanism.[17] He accepts Arnold's attribution of natural magic to the Celt, but elevates it rather than devalues it. 'I do not think he [Arnold] understood', Yeats wrote, 'that our "natural magic" is but the ancient religion of the world, the ancient worship of Nature and that troubled ecstasy before her, that certainty of all beautiful places being haunted, which it brought into men's minds.'[18] Where Arnold had associated natural magic with Keats and the Celt but starkly contrasted this with Sophocles, Yeats associated it with Keats and the Celt and thereby affiliated them with the Greek tragedian.

In response to the anti-Irish dimension of Arnoldian Hellenism, therefore, Yeats argued that Sophocles had linked into something primal and ancient that had survived in Ireland, while only vestiges of it were visible in the imperial art of Rome or modern Britain. Looking back on his Sophoclean translations of the 1920s, Yeats would later write in *On the Boiler* that 'when I prepared *Oedipus at Colonus* for the Abbey stage I saw that the wood of the Furies in the opening scene was any Irish haunted wood.'[19] In contrast to this Sophoclean wood, he continued, no 'nymph-haunted or Fury-haunted wood described in Roman poetry' could inspire awe and fear in the 'passing beggar or fiddler or benighted countryman' who still existed in Irish folk culture.[20] For Yeats, Sophocles' choruses proved that he was in tune, like the Irish, with the *anima mundi*.[21] In this regard, he and the Irish poets were also more imaginative than the Roman poets, or John Keats or Shakespeare – all of whom only saw nature in a 'friendly and pleasant . . . way of people who have forgotten the ancient religion'.[22] Therefore, whereas Arnold assigned 'natural magic' in a minor key to a particular race (the Celt), Yeats associated it with the more sublime 'great Memory' of the entire human race. Yeats draws on a theory of folklore to define and explain 'natural magic', while Arnold had drawn on a racial-science theory to explain it. Arnold's racial science had divided national literatures such as Irish from the English, French or Greek, so that only a cosmopolitan culture of Hellenism could bridge the gaps. Yeats, however, filled those gaps with his theory of symbols as a link back to the Great Memory. For him, the Irish were more attuned to the ancient sensibility of natural magic than the rest of the modern world, and therefore were more like the ideal audiences of Shakespeare and Sophocles at their most 'folkloric' than any other people. Yeats answered Arnold's unionist synthesis of Celticist and Hellenist arguments with an Irish cultural-nationalist synthesis of his own.

Even as he was composing this symbolist response to Arnold, however, Yeats was promoting the Irish Literary Theatre (and, later, the Abbey Theatre) in terms of Arnoldian cultural Hellenism. Yeats' use of cultural Hellenism can particularly be seen in his comparisons of the Abbey Theatre with great dramatic periods in world history, namely fifth-century Athens and Elizabethan London. In 'The function of criticism', Arnold had written that those epochs enjoyed 'a current of ideas' (sadly lacking at the present time) 'in the highest degree animating and nourishing to the creative power'.[23] It was the modern critic's highest calling, therefore, to work towards recreating this environment. 'Even when this [current] does not actually exist', he explained,

> books and reading may enable a man to construct a kind of semblance of it in his own mind, a world of knowledge and intelligence in which he may live and work. This is by no means an equivalent to the artist for the nationally diffused life and thought of the epochs of Sophocles or Shakespeare; but, besides that it may be a means of preparation for such epochs.[24]

Indeed, Yeats had devoted himself to just such 'preparation' for an Irish literary revival all through his career. We can see this in his first essay on 'The Irish Literary Theatre', which appeared in Dublin's *Daily Express* on 14 January 1899. In it he compared the incipient Irish dramatic project to Athenian drama, which had also built a national character. To this end he cited Victor Hugo's idea that 'in the theatre the mob became a people', and added that

> though this could be perfectly true only of ancient times when the theatre was a part of the ceremonial of religion, I have some hope that, if we have enough success to go on from year to year, we may

> help to bring a little ideal thought into the common thought of our times. The writers, on whom we principally depend, have laboured to be citizens, not merely of that passing and modern Ireland of prosaic cynicism and prosaic rivalries which it may be their duty to condemn, but of that eternal and ancient Ireland which has lived from old times in tender and heroic tales and in the unwearied love of many thousand men and women who have been poor in all other things.[25]

A number of enduring themes of Yeatsian Hellenism are already present in this first announcement. First is the Aristotelian notion of drama as a civic art, which Yeats realises will never be reproduced perfectly because the theatre is no longer an actual religious ritual. There is also the more Arnoldian desire (ultimately frustrated) to transcend the 'cynicism and prosaic rivalries' of modern life by way of a common cultural education. Yeats, of course, also linked this cultural Hellenist argument to a Romantic idealist version of Irish folk culture, however, and thereby arrived at conclusions wholly at odds with Arnold's own cultural Hellenist arguments about Ireland in the 1860s. We also see here the attempt, which was constant throughout his entire life in theatre, to balance symbolist doctrine with his Hellenist project to form the national character. Yeats would create a theatre that would form the people, but would do so by returning the Irish to their oldest folk wisdom, leading always towards 'the gates of peace'. The new Irish drama combined a Hellenist ethos of national *Bildung* with a revival of ancient folk wisdom, and would, thereby, become a civic art of reconciliation.[26]

In his writings about Irish drama, therefore, Yeats tried to balance a nationalised version of Arnoldian Hellenism with his intellectual and spiritual commitment to symbolist doctrine. We can also see him trying to do these things in the essay 'Theatre', which first appeared in 1899 but which he revised for inclusion in *Ideas of Good and Evil.* He began by suggesting that Greek dramatic principles were lost in the modern English 'plays of commerce', which 'have substituted [nervous tremors] for the purification that comes with pity and terror to the imagination and intellect'.[27] If 'the poetic drama is at an end' for modern English audiences, however, it might only just be beginning in Ireland because '[T]he audiences of Sophocles and of Shakespeare and of Calderon', he wrote, 'were not unlike the audiences I have heard listening in Irish cabins to songs in Gaelic.'[28] The Irish, though not yet accustomed to drama, would not have any problems visualising 'the horses and the fields and flowers of Colonus as one listened to the elders gathered about

Oedipus, or to see "the pendent bed and procreant cradle" of the "martlet" as one listened to Banquo before the castle of Macbeth'.[29] Unlike the vulgarised modern English audiences who required painted sets to keep their interest in what was happening onstage, the Irish peasantry could, like the Greeks and Elizabethans, visualise scenes from mere poetic description. The Irish peasants and the ancient Greeks shared what Schiller would have called a naive poetic sensibility, and Yeats brought together this German Romantic attempt to recapture that Greek naivety with Blake's idea that 'all art is a labour to bring again the Golden Age, and all culture is certainly a labour to bring again the simplicity of the first ages, with knowledge of good and evil added to it.'[30] In short, Yeats envisioned Irish drama from the very beginning as a project to balance Blakean symbolism with Arnoldian cultural Hellenism.

Sophocles was always Yeats' model Greek dramatist, just as he had been Arnold's. Even as early as his 1893 lecture, 'Nationality and literature', Yeats had (like Arnold) grouped Sophocles with Shakespeare as the supreme dramatists who had shaped Greek and English national character, respectively. According to the stadial model of literary and national development Yeats outlined in his lecture, therefore, 'the period of narrative poetry, the epic or ballad period' was followed by 'the dramatic period', in which 'Agamemnon and Clytemnestra and Oedipus dominate the stage', and this is followed by 'the period of lyric poetry'.[31] In some of his writings in that decade, Yeats suggested that Ireland was in the first period, because Sir Samuel Ferguson and Lady Gregory had a sort of Homeric quality. By 1899, however, when he was promoting the Irish Literary Theatre, he tried to place Dublin in a position analogous to Sophoclean Athens. Just as Sophocles had placed the larger-than-life figure of Oedipus in the Theatre of Dionysus, so would Yeats eventually place Cuchulain in the Abbey.

The greatest challenge to Yeats' appropriation of Arnoldian cultural Hellenism, however, was Irish nationalist philistinism, a force with which he clashed most famously during the controversy over J.M. Synge's *Playboy of the Western World* at the Abbey Theatre in 1907. He did not feel like he won this battle, and so while Synge was dying in 1909, Yeats kept a journal recording his response to the seemingly insurmountable obstacles to cultural development in Ireland. The Abbey's explicitly Hellenist project had fizzled out because the audience had rejected it, and Yeats subsequently struggled with a loss of purpose. 'Could we create a vision of the race as noble as that of Sophocles and of Aeschylus', he wrote, 'it would be attacked upon some trivial ground by minds that prefer Young Ireland rhetoric.'[32] Yeats would later publish selections from this journal under the titles of *Estrangement* (1926) and *The Death of Synge* (1928).[33]

As arranged for publication, however, *Estrangement* also tells the story of how Yeats emerged from this low point armed with a revised strategy for shaping Irish national character by cultural means. In the earlier entries, Yeats notes that Dublin has no culture, and that he himself has no advice for young Irish intellectuals other than that they should spend their early adulthoods seeking it in other countries.[34] As the journal progresses, however, he begins to rally by adopting further ideas from Arnold. One such idea, taken from *Culture and Anarchy* (1869), is that philistinism had rigidified morality to the point of anarchy, and, therefore, Ireland required authoritative cultural institutions (such as the Abbey) to promote traditional moral ideas around which the nation might cohere.[35] Yeats' ideas of culture and authority in these journals were also overtly hegemonic. 'No art can conquer the people alone', he writes in section forty-eight of *Estrangement*, because 'the people are conquered by an ideal of life upheld by authority. As this ideal is rediscovered, the arts, music and poetry, painting and literature, will draw closer together.'[36] This almost seems like a critique of Arnold, but it is actually a description of what Yeats wanted to emulate.

As for the dissemination of these moral ideas, moreover, Yeats returned to the idea of architectonics that Arnold used in *On the Study of Celtic Literature*. Yeats agreed with Arnold that the Irish required a cultural structure. 'You cannot keep the idea of a nation alive', he wrote, 'where there are no national institutions to reverence . . . [or] a model of it in the mind of the people.'[37] Unlike Arnold, however, Yeats believed such a model actually could be achieved in Ireland. Further diverging from Arnold, moreover, Yeats conceptualised that model as a collection of images. For instance, the Young Ireland poets had 'created a mass of obvious images that filled the minds of the young . . . [with] ethical ideas . . . of necessity very simple'.[38] He and Lady Gregory had attempted to improve on this earlier and simpler mass by giving the nation 'a complex mass of images, something like an architect's model'.[39] Nationalist philistines had attacked this model but failed to provide an alternative to it, and so the job would still fall to 'a school of journalists with simple moral ideas' who could give 'sensible images to the affections' and 'a moral diagram' that would in time produce 'a historical and literary nationalism as powerful as the old and nobler'.[40] Yeats' proposal for a 'moral diagram' sounds simple at first, but when we realise that he intends the material for this architectural structure to come from modern Irish writers such as himself and Synge, the process becomes far more complicated.

Yeats does not delve very deeply into this problem in *Estrangements*, but he does explore it further in a journal entry sometime in May 1910, taken down after arguing about Synge while touring Normandy with Maud and Iseult Gonne.[41] He noted that:

> A nation can only be created in the deepest thoughts of its deepest minds – the literature that makes it (and this making takes a long time) – who have first made themselves fundamental and profound and then realized themselves in art. In this way they rouse into national action the governing minds of their [time] . . . [and] create national character.[42]

Yeats is using Synge as an example, but he naturally means himself as well when he talks about these 'deepest minds'. The idea that the artist's personality could have such an impact on national character is also Arnoldian and recalls the critic's famous comment that Wordsworth's poetry, at its best, was 'inevitable as nature herself'.[43] According to Lloyd and Thomas, the cultivated subject of Schillerian aesthetics becomes the representative subject of the 'ethical State' against whose example all citizens will measure themselves ethically.[44] This means the representative subject appears not simply as an ideal type of the citizen but also as the representative type of universal human nature. In the 1860s, largely inspired by his inspections of schools and universities in Germany, Arnold adopted this concept as part of his cultural Hellenist ideal, and also ascribed this representative status to Wordsworth. While Yeats generally disliked Wordsworth, he was, nevertheless, impressed with the example of a poet whose fundamental influence on the modern English consciousness came from the sheer realisation of his own personality through art.

We have seen that Yeats was particularly critical of the colonial ideology of Arnold's cultural writings from the 1860s, but despite his attempts to subvert Arnold for nationalist purposes, he nevertheless absorbed the idea of this representative subject from Arnold and made it a key figure in his writings. As he wrote of Synge, for instance, 'Only that which does not teach, which does not cry out, which does not persuade, which does not condescend, which does not explain, is irresistible. It is made by men who expressed themselves to the full, and it works through the best minds.'[45] The cultural nation-forming personality recalls Lloyd and Thomas' neo-Gramscian critique of the 'bourgeois intellectual' whose '*organic* nature . . . is structural even before it is explicitly or self-consciously "political" in any sense', the index of whose rhetorical effectiveness lies in the credibility of his or her ethical claim to 'disinterest'.[46]

As Arnold had done with Wordsworth for the English in the previous century, therefore, Yeats proposed Synge (and later, himself) as the representative man, identification with whom would provide the Irish not simply with their aesthetic education but also their political assumptions and their relationship to nature. Above all, this representative man would attain dominion over the rhetoric of reconciliation, a dominion that would ultimately be granted, under the heading of culture, to the state ('the governing minds of the time'). It is with a firm grasp of these functions in mind, therefore, that Yeats at the end of *Estrangement* can say that his 'school of journalists with simple moral ideas', sifting the minds of culture heroes such as Synge for fitting images, will 'bid the people love and not hate'.[47] This was the frame through which Yeats wanted Synge to be understood in the long term of Irish cultural history, but, more immediately, it was also the way he would frame his future endeavours as an Irish cultural nationalist.

Even after the rally of Arnoldian cultural mission to spread culture recorded in *Estrangement*, of course, Yeats suffered further defeat at the hands of the philistines who sank the Hugh Lane Municipal Gallery proposal of 1913. In a significant departure from Abbey Hellenism, therefore, he investigated (at Ezra Pound's advice) the Japanese Noh tradition as an aristocratic counterweight to the Athenian model of civic drama. His next play, then, *At the Hawk's Well*, was staged not publicly but privately, in the drawing room of Lady Cunard in London, on 2 April 1916. As the playwright wrote to John Quinn:

> I hope to create a new form of drama which may delight the best minds of my time, and all the more because it can pay its expenses without the others. If when the play is perfectly performed (musicians are the devil) Balfour and Sargent and Ricketts and Sturge Moore and John and the Prime Minister and a few pretty ladies will come to see it, I shall have a success that would have pleased Sophocles. No press, no photographs in the papers, no crowd. I shall be happier than Sophocles. I shall be as lucky as a Japanese dramatic poet at the Court of the Shogun.[48]

Considering the Englishness and unionism of this audience, and the fact that he is identifying himself in some idealised way as their royal servant, it would be fair to say that Yeats had veered some distance from his accustomed project of Irish national *Bildung*. Moreover, Sophocles is a strange presence in this letter. According to some ancient accounts, Sophocles was so happy with the success of *Oedipus at Colonus* that he actually died of joy, presumably in sight of the assembled Athenian audience. Yeats would see his own successes with *Oedipus the King* and *Oedipus at Colonus* a decade later at the Abbey, but these productions would be nothing like the private 'new drama' idea he explored in *At the Hawk's Well*. The Easter Rising took place three weeks after the performance at Lady Cunard's, however, and this directed Yeats' attentions again towards Ireland, where he would ultimately resume a Sophoclean role that Arnold and Schiller would have recognised. When he re-dedicated himself to Hellenism at the Abbey, Yeats would once again become very concerned with both the press and the crowd.

When Yeats re-dedicated himself to the idea of Irish national *Bildung* at the end of the decade, however, he could only do so from a perspective more informed by occult philosophy than had been the case in 1910. Beginning in 1920, therefore, Yeats experimented with a new synthesis of Arnold and Blake, which he called 'unity of culture'. In her 15 December entry into the couple's sixth 'Dream and Sleep Notebook', George Yeats recorded her husband's having been told by a spirit that the 'rapid change in Europe' resulted from 'the mixture of bloods. And with this went a mixture of cultures. Where there was much mixture there was always some part of every man unsatisfied & in every nation unsatisfied classes.'[49] This 'mixture of bloods' idea offered a pessimistic racial explanation for the bloodshed in Europe and Russia. A more active and constructive response was needed for violence much closer at hand, however, and so the spirits offered one under the heading of culture. 'When people have unity of culture', the entry continued, 'the transference of thought & image goes through the whole people. In the past pure races have been made by blood, but bloods are now so mixed that in the future they will have to be made by culture.'[50] This offered a pathway by which the poet might coordinate cultural work with occult study; he could retrieve these images necessary for unity of culture from the world of symbols, and then give them to Ireland via his poems. This was not substantially different from what he had implied about the architecture of images in his journals of 1909 and 1910.

Yeats explored the 'unity of culture' idea further while composing *Four Years*, and on 14 March 1921 wrote to George Russell, hoping that together they might publicise the idea that he believed would 'affect the future of Ireland' in the long run, even if it might not provide immediate 'help in our Irish Crisis'.[51] Yeats wrote again two weeks later, explaining to Russell how important the idea had become to him, and how he thought they could, working together, impact the country in ways that would seem to transcend mere culture. 'The conception of unity and culture has become a cardinal principle in all exposition of the future of my system', he wrote, but he expressed serious concern that the public might dismiss it by its association with an occult poet.[52] In other words, his Blakean reputation might disrupt his Arnoldian cultural mission.

When the Free State government appointed Yeats to a six-year term as senator (1922–28), this transformed the poet's cultural status in relation to the state, practically institutionalising the representative subject position about which Lloyd and Thomas have written. Indeed, the appointment solved many problems Yeats had complained of to Russell. Yeats might not have been a politician, but he had become something more effective for his career-long project of Irish national *Bildung*: a senator appointed not just to represent the Protestant minority but also to oversee matters of culture and education in the Irish Free State. Ultimately, Yeats embraced Arnold almost to the total exclusion of Blake from 1922 to 1928 for three reasons. The first is that it allowed him to describe an Irish identity in a way that tried to bypass race and religion, and might, therefore, also include Protestants in the South. The second was that it allowed him to talk about national education, which could be aimed against sectarianism and anti-intellectualism, and put in the service of ending partition. Finally, it allowed Yeats a role in the founding of 'cultural' institutions of the new state. In short, culture became a key term for Yeats in 1922, because it represented the best way for him to participate in the new nation.

An illustration of Yeats' promotion of cultural reconciliation in the mid-1920s can be seen in a speech he made in Seanad Éireann on the subject of diplomatic relations with Northern Ireland.[53] Yeats told the Seanad on 17 October 1924, when the issue of diplomacy with Northern Ireland came to the floor, that he had

> no hope of seeing Ireland united in my time, or of seeing Ulster won in my time; but I believe it will be won in the end, and not because we fight it, but because we govern this country well. We do that, if I may be permitted as an artist and a writer to say so, by creating a system of culture which will represent the whole of this country and which will draw the imagination of the young towards it.[54]

By his correlation of cultural development with state expansion, Yeats ventured deep into Arnoldian territory. It may be easy to miss the

Arnoldian dimension of this argument, considering that the Irish nationalist Yeats is talking about an aspirational unification of Northern Ireland with the Irish Free State, where the liberal unionist Arnold had been concerned with protecting an existing union between Ireland and Great Britain. Nevertheless, their rhetorical strategies had a great deal in common. Most importantly, by advocating a gradualist approach bolstered by a programme of cultural self-development, Yeats recalls Arnold's own recommendations, in 'On the study of Celtic literature', to combine a 'Burkean' conciliatory Irish policy with a project for national *Bildung*.[55] In that work, Arnold wrote that the English would overcome 'the hard unintelligence, which is just now . . . [England's] bane' in governing Ireland,

> by culture, by a growth in the variety, fullness, and sweetness of our spiritual life; and this end can only be reached by studying things that are outside of ourselves, and by studying them disinterestedly. Let us reunite ourselves with our better mind and with the world through science; and let it be one of our angelic revenges on the Philistines, who among their other sins are the guilty authors of Fenianism, to found at Oxford a chair of Celtic, and to send, through the gentle ministration of science, a message of peace to Ireland.[56]

Yeats and Arnold also both called for a cultural Hellenist transformation of a philistine society so that that society might become politically, as well as culturally, attractive.

During this period, the Arnoldian argument for culture and consent influenced Yeats' occult studies as well.[57] In what appears to be the final entry in the 'Sleep and Dream Notebooks', for instance, Yeats recorded a conversation with the spirits about how Ireland ('at [phase] eight, or eight-nine') was 'affected by the European phase twenty three'.[58] The spirit had replied that Britain was acting in accordance with an imperialist phase, and had only been trying 'to guide their [Ireland's] abundance', even preferring to do so 'with their consent'.[59] Now that the Free State had gained its independence, however, the spirit told Yeats that Ireland 'should not have ideas of glory, of pride, or any idea that suggests dominion over others . . . [because] The cultivation of military power by Ireland as a substitute for the vote . . . conceive[s] the nation as power not abundance'.[60] That is, the Free State should try to attach Northern Ireland not by military means, but, rather, by political and cultural ones. The spirit therefore concludes that 'The nation at 9 . . . must seek a national unity of culture', which in this context correlates very specifically with liberal democracy.[61]

When Yeats finally replicates the Arnoldian argument for cultural Hellenism as a vehicle for state expansion, he aligns the foundational logic of the Free State, which had been founded by the Anglo-Irish Treaty, with the Schillerian idea of aesthetic education as preparation for citizenship.[62] Let us consider how this worked in Arnold's Irish writings, before explaining how it worked in Yeats. As Lloyd and Thomas argue in *Culture and the State*, Arnold assists the British state to achieve its hegemonic status as what Gramsci called the 'ethical state' around 1870, with the passage of the Elementary Education Act. However, the spectacle of Irish recalcitrance was also crucial to Arnold's successful figuration of the cultural Hellenist as ethical exemplar for the new English subject. At first glance, Ireland might only seem to be a threat to British state hegemony, because the English subject could hardly be seen as properly representative of the human race if it could not integrate the recalcitrant Irish into its system. On the contrary, Arnold considered the task of reconciling the recalcitrant Irish as the most practical yardstick for judging whether the English subject had actually attained representative status. Arnold insisted, moreover, that English hegemony in Ireland was inevitable, and that it could only happen by cultural means. As soon as this historical process was accepted as inevitable by the English, the promise of future success secured the ethical power of the British state even in its presently imperfect form. State authority therefore depended upon the idea that the cultural Hellenist was the ethical model for the British subject.

When Yeats adapted this ethical-exemplar formation to the project of Irish cultural and political reconciliation, however, he was adjusting the Arnoldian model to postcolonial conditions. This provided major challenges. Not only was the island partitioned, but it had only recently emerged from a civil war and so could not even claim a monopoly on violence within its own borders. Yeats had been appointed to the Senate not just to oversee matters of culture and education, but also to bolster Protestant representation in the Free State. By all accounts, including his own, Yeats had much greater success in the former capacity than in the latter. Deprived of Arnold's providential self-assurance, therefore, Yeats did not pretend to be aligned with a state anywhere near as hegemonic as the one Arnold had tried to save from 'anarchy' in the 1860s.

For example, in February 1926 Yeats restated his customary analogy between the Abbey Theatre and the Festival of Dionysus in the course of defending Sean O'Casey's latest work, *The Plough and the Stars*. Performances of this play led to nationalist riots and a subsequent police presence in the theatre itself, and so, just as he had done in 1907 during the *Playboy* riots, Yeats took to the stage on 11 February and attempted to educate the crowd about civic art. On 23 February, moreover, he continued the lesson by delivering 'A defence of the Abbey Theatre' at the Dublin Literary Society. Arguing against the nationalist position that 'an intellectual movement' was supposed to 'express a whole people' as it already was, Yeats insisted that 'if those few people' in a small, unrepresentative national movement has 'amongst them a Sophocles or a Shakespeare', they should 'give their character to the people', rather than the other way around.[63] In other words, instead of trying to reflect a flattering image of the Irish nation, the Abbey should still be trying to – as Declan Kiberd has put it – 'invent' Ireland, just as Sophocles had formed the Athenians and Shakespeare had formed the English. Moreover, he seems to have believed it was working. Two days earlier, Yeats wrote to H.J.C. Grierson that 'the theatre has now a great following' despite the riots, and that he had been 'writing the material version of a chorus for a version of *Oedipus* intended for the stage', with 'the Blake illustration to Gray open on a little table' nearby.[64]

Yeats was also at this time deeply engaged in the senate with debates over two education bills, namely the School Attendance Bill (about which he gave speeches on 24 March and 28 April) and the Central Fund Bill (about which he spoke on 30 March). He had delivered 'The child and the state' as a lecture to the Irish Literary Society the previous November, and his essay 'The need for audacity of thought' appeared in *The Dial* in February. During this time period, moreover, Yeats also toured primary schools around the Free State. The most famous of these visits was to St Otteran's School in Waterford, about which he wrote 'Among School Children' in May.[65]

Biographers and editors have generally accepted the thesis of Donald Torchiana's 1965 essay '"Among School Children" and the education of the Irish spirit', that the poem harmonises Yeats' symbolic system with a progressive philosophy of education largely imbued from George Yeats' summaries of Giovanni Gentile (who was reading Maria Montessori). Roy Foster and Ann Saddlemyer also both reproduce George Yeats' considerably less elevated account of the event, but even so, Foster's interpretation of the poem reproduces Torchiana's hegemonic thesis that 'Among School Children' reflects a positive assessment of education in the Free State, and a high point in Yeats' poetics of reconciliation, despite the pessimistic note he jotted down around 26 March:

> Topic for poem – School Children & the thought that life will waste them perhaps that no possible life can fulfil their own dreams or

> even their teacher's [sic] hope. Bring in the old thought that life prepares for what never happens.[66]

This private, bleak assessment of education *as such* was of course very much at odds with the educational policies he publicly advocated as a senator. The same can be said about the major poem he was also drafting in March: 'Sailing to Byzantium'. These contexts should lead us to reconsider the assessment of 'Among School Children' as a poem of reconciliation.

One great strength of Torchiana's reading is that it brings together so many tropes from Yeats' thinking at this time into the Burkean metaphor of the state as a tree. Conversely, a weakness of that same reading is that it underplays the antithetical character of Yeats' thought. Making it seem like he had a solid front was essential to Yeats' success as a senator intent on impacting upon educational and cultural institutions.[67] However, we should consider the fact that he was touring Irish primary schools and coming up with arguments for why education requires greater funding than the Dáil wished to extend, but also composing lines about how 'This is no country for old men' because 'Caught in that music all neglect / Monuments of unageing intellect'.[68] When we also remember, moreover, that Yeats was fantasising about getting to Byzantium where he would no longer be 'fastened to a dying animal', then we must conclude that he was of two minds about the project of cultural education.[69] The fact that Yeats even seems to want to make it hold together calls the entire constellation into question. His first note for 'Among School Children' also indicates the depth of this contradiction. We should also consider that this is the only poem Yeats writes about himself carrying out senatorial business. Whatever antitheses Yeats was able to explore about that office in this poem, however, could only be registered on the level of poetry, and this is where de Man's reading of the poetics of image and emblem, and Lloyd's application of this idea to the Free State, demands most serious consideration.

In other words, 'Among School Children' is where the tension between the anti-foundationist poetics of the emblem and the statist-ideology culture reaches its crisis. As noted above, Yeats wrote 'Sailing to Byzantium' right before drafting 'Among School Children'. When he addresses 'the Presences' in the latter poem, therefore, it is as if the 'sages standing in God's holy fire' whom he addressed in the earlier poem had simply wandered into the middle of a Senate debate.[70] But what are they doing there? Did Yeats think the 'self-born mockers of man's enterprise' would support his position that the Catholic hierarchy in Ireland should be legally obliged to allow local committees to oversee sanitation in religious schools?[71] How did 'the singing masters of my soul' feel about free lunches – another proposal the poet ardently supported?[72] Of course, instead of asking for their advice, Yeats presents them with a theory of education that has inspired Elizabeth Cullingford to call 'Among School Children' Yeats' 'most utopian poem'.[73] Why the Presences need to have this pedagogy explained to them, however, is far from clear. One might have assumed they already knew about the Yeatsian educational Utopia, or even that they had been the ones to tell him about it. The fact that they seem to have done neither points to the real question at the heart of this poem, namely is Yeats' educational philosophy a version of Arnoldian cultural Hellenism or Blakean emblematic revelation?

The poem reflects the friction between the two impulses: it portrays the representative man's symbolist doubts about the project of national *Bildung*. In the first stanza of the poem, Yeats draws attention to his own status as a cultural icon, when he states:

> . . . the children's eyes
> In momentary wonder stare upon
> A sixty-year-old smiling public man.[74]

Here we see Yeats being just as much the object of the children's attention as the school itself is the object of his. According to Lloyd and Thomas, the organisation of space in the modern classroom focused the work of subject formation on the teacher, upon whom all eyes fell.[75] More specifically, they describe the transformation of the British schoolroom into a panoptic, semi-theatrical space that directed student development towards the interrelated goals of aesthetic education and citizenship in a representative democracy. This was a Plato's Cave in which the topics of study were secondary to the primary task of teaching students to accept the teacher – and the entire political and social system he or she represented – as the natural type of human existence. As the authors put it, the children 'may not represent themselves, they must learn to be represented': first by these exemplary teachers, and, later, by an exemplary legislative system.[76]

As a Nobel Prize laureate and a senator, Yeats would presumably be an even more 'exemplary representative of ethical formation' for the students of St Otteran's School than would the children's normal teachers, and this was one reason for the visit. The architecture of 'the long schoolroom' through which Yeats walks and asks his questions in the first stanza, however, is not at all shaped like the gallery of which Lloyd and Thomas write, and this would frustrate the institutional process of interpellation.[77] The fact that the Montessori classroom very significantly does not replicate the seating arrangement of the Abbey Theatre, moreover, allows Yeats to appear in a very different way than he had when defending O'Casey from the stage the previous month. If we are to picture him visiting a Montessori class in action, we will see that the students are not all in one place, they are not all doing the same thing, and when they stopped to stare at him their gazes probably would be directed from multiple directions. Torchiana's essay contains an iconic account of Yeats as an exemplary figure of Arnoldian culture whose presence inspired the students to elevate themselves through aesthetic education, but a more deflationary account of the visit appears in Roy Foster's biography, when he quotes one of the students who may have inspired the reverie recorded in stanzas two through four: 'He was seeing a school-age Maud Gonne, and I was seeing a strange man who briefly interrupted my day.'[78] Yeats' self-presentation in the poem reproduces more of Foster's witness' irony about the visit than Torchiana's more deferential eyewitness recalled; for instance, the opening stanza begins in the first person but ends in the third person with the students' perspective on him.[79]

Let us now return to the conclusion of the poem. De Man has of course written that it is most certainly not about reconciliation, but that it vacillates between an anti-organicist poetics of the emblem on one hand, and a more mainstream Romantic poetics of the 'natural image' on the other. Moreover, while Lloyd's de Man-inspired analysis of Yeats' poetics and politics of this period does not include a reading of 'Among School Children', were one to extend his argument in that direction, it would probably lead to the conclusion that this poem also, like 'Coole Park and Ballylee 1931', subverts the state's foundational ideology of reconciliation through the poetics of the emblem. I would support this conclusion myself, but not without maintaining the dialectical aspect of de Man's argument that the poem vacillates not just between image and emblem but also between culture and emblem. As noted earlier, I see Yeats as far more of an Arnoldian than Lloyd did in 'The poetics of politics'. When I say that this poem uses the emblem against the state, I mean to say that in this poem he is at war not so much with the state as with the persona he has assumed as a senator. As he wrote in his 1917 essay *Per Amica Silentia Lunae*: 'We make out of the quarrels with others, rhetoric, but of the quarrel with ourselves, poetry.'[80] According to this definition, when it comes to the education debate, Yeats the senator can only be a rhetorician. That is, he could only promote the goals of national *Bildung*, and so had to remain silent about his long-standing Blakean critique of Arnoldian culture. He could more freely register this 'quarrel with himself', however, on the level of his poetics.[81] In the reading which follows, therefore, I will say that the poetics of the emblem at the end of 'Among School Children' denaturalises the organicist ideology of Arnoldian culture he has promoted as a senator, specifically by undercutting the idea that a representative man of aesthetic education (such as himself) models citizenship in a representative democracy as the natural form of human life.

I will now read the final stanza of 'Among School Children' in relation to Lloyd and Thomas' idea that the Arnoldian representative man's most important pedagogical lesson for children was in how to be represented. The twisting and turning of Yeats' metaphoric language in that stanza reflects an anti-foundationalist poetics of the emblem, and points towards the arbitrariness of those very systems of representation that the ideology of culture would otherwise naturalise. At the beginning of the eighth stanza, Yeats does not elaborate – for us, or for the Presences – upon what it means for the utopian educational 'labour' to be a 'blossoming' or a 'dancing', but, instead, poses some characteristically enigmatic rhetorical questions to the imperfectly explanatory metaphors themselves. Each metaphor, moreover, suggests a competing impulse in his writing: the blossoming tree suggests organicism, while the dancer suggests the symbolic cosmos of *A Vision*, in which 'Only one symbol exists, though the reflecting mirrors make many appear and all different'.[82] Each metaphor, the tree and the dancer, in its separate philosophical context denotes reconciliation; the philosophical paradigms to which they belong, however, are incompatible.

Let us begin with the first rhetorical question and its addressee. If educational labour is a blossoming, this implies a natural process, such as can be found in Aristotle, who conceives education as necessary to the (male) human being's natural development towards citizenship. The potentiality of citizenship is inherent in the child, just as the potentiality of the oak tree is contained in the acorn. When Yeats asks if the 'great rooted blossomer' is 'the leaf, the blossom or the bole', therefore, it almost sounds like he is talking about the Aristotelian oak – except for the fact that he does not mention the acorn. The fully grown tree has, in fact, already achieved its *telos*, and so now the question is which part should stand in, metonymically, for the whole. In other words, this is not a question for the biologists or metaphysicians, but, rather, one for the poets and rhetoricians. Yeats, the Nobel laureate, is perfectly capable of making a poetic decision like that for himself, but rather than moving forward on his own, he brings the question to the tree itself. This deference makes sense only when we recall that during his senatorial days Yeats frequently repeated the Burkean idea that the state is like a tree. His rhetorical question about the leaf, blossom or bole is, therefore, addressed to the body politic, with two major implications. The first of these is a lesson in liberal pluralism: you are a complex organism whose interdependent parts (that is, Catholics and Protestants) require equal respect and protection in order for the whole to enjoy an integrated natural existence. At the same time, Yeats' question draws attention to the logic of representative democracy itself, which operates on the principle of metonymy whereby a legislator stands in for a constituency, and a state stands in for a nation. It calls to mind that the system of representation is no more preordained than are the choices of elected representatives. The addressee of Yeats' rhetorical question, therefore, reflects the organicism of his statist rhetoric of the 1920s, but the question he poses to it also suggests that the very system of representation it would represent is artificial.

In posing the poem's final rhetorical question, Yeats simultaneously objectifies the addressee and affiliates himself with it.

> O body swayed to music, O brightening glance,
> How can we know the dancer from the dance?[83]

This time, Yeats has actually taken it upon himself to choose the metonym. He chooses two, in fact, and uses each of them to address the dancer with a question about him or herself in the third person. The first choice of metonym, moreover, troubles our common understanding of the term as 'taking a part for the whole', because in most cases (except for when we are talking about people) we tend to equate the body very literally with the whole. These rhetorical oddities suggest objectification in a way that the previous two lines do not, but at the same time Yeats considerably shortens the distance between speaker, addressee and even reader by adopting the first-person plural pronoun 'we' to describe this common effort to tell where dancer ends and dance begins.

The final rhetorical question therefore draws attention away from other reasonable (non-rhetorical) questions, such as: Why is Yeats saying 'we' to a metaphor? Is the metaphor really supposed to know something that the poet does not? Or does Yeats actually share in the metaphor's knowledge, because that knowledge is so self-evident it only needs to be said by way of a rhetorical question? None of these questions are easy to answer, but the fact that they arise at all suggests two possibilities about his stance as a representative man of culture. It may be that Yeats is pointing to his occult philosophy as a way of supplementing his image as the disinterested cultural representative, but I would argue that, on the contrary, Yeats is actually voicing his otherwise unspeakable belief that cultural education is actually a pointless enterprise.

To assess the likelihood of the former reading, we might again consider the poem's relation to 'Sailing to Byzantium'. If 'Among School Children' shows Yeats performing (with reservations) the role of 'smiling public man', the earlier poem shows him far more willingly exemplifying another kind of symbolic function. In the final stanza of that poem, he actually becomes an emblem, and thus directs the audience's attention to occult philosophy rather than cultural Hellenism. In one draft, in fact, Yeats writes that as an artificial golden bird he would 'sing / Of present past & future & to come / For the instruction of Byzantium'.[84] Yeats knew that as a senator of the Free State he had made himself the ethical exemplar of cultural education as a model for citizenship. His educational function had, therefore, become structural. In 'Sailing to Byzantium', however, he imagines a social and political structure in which his exemplary function would reflect his more radical philosophy – embodied in the poetics of the emblem – rather than simply his public commitment to national *Bildung*. Here we should also consider that the Greek sculptor Phidias is a major character in the draft versions of the earlier poem. The character is so prominent, in fact, that Yeats played with the idea of adding 'or Phidias' to the title.[85] Phidias is also a figure who connects classical Athens with medieval Byzantium since he had been responsible for the giant chryselephantine *Athena Parthenos* that stood in the Parthenon for a millennium before the Romans relocated it to Constantinople. Here again, therefore, we see Yeats' attempt to balance a kind of cultural Hellenism with the poetics of the emblem. The effort to achieve this reconciliation continues in 'Colonus' Praise', which Yeats places directly after 'Among School Children' in *The Tower*.

This first chorus from *Oedipus at Colonus* included in *The Tower* lends itself extremely well to Yeats' poetics of the emblem because it features several objects with divine associations that shaped the character not just of Colonus, Sophocles' native deme, but also the Athenian polis to which the deme belonged. Yeats' translation describes the first of these emblems, 'the grey leaved olive tree', as 'The self-sown, self-begotten shape that gives / Athenian intellect its mastery'.[86] Yeats took the poetic liberty of slightly bending the original to echo the 'self-born' Presences of 'Among School Children', and the 'monuments of unageing intellect' in 'Sailing to Byzantium'.[87] There are two further emblems in the poem: an 'oar' and a 'bit', both of which had been gifts from Poseidon, foretelling the feared Athenian cavalry on one hand, and its even more famous naval power on the other.

Yeats adds new material to the Sophoclean original, however, in such a way that gives these emblems an explicitly educational purpose. Yeats writes:

> Because this country has a pious mind,
> And so remembers that when all mankind
> But trod the road, or splashed about the shore,
> Poseidon gave it bit and oar,
> Every Colonus lad or lass discourses
> Of that oar and of that bit;
> Summer and winter, day and night,
> Of horses and horses of the sea, white horses.[88]

The 'triumph' of the emblem's reconciliation with civic education is undercut by two contextual factors, however. The first of these is the fact that this chorus in its original Greek version was recited by Sophocles himself, before a court of family law in Athens, as a way of demonstrating his sanity against his sons' charges of incompetence. However, while the poem vindicated the dramatist in the eyes of the law, it probably did not re-establish him as an ethical exemplar in the hearts of his children. Later, in *The Tower*, Yeats included an altogether more pessimistic chorus from *Oedipus at Colonus*, about how much better it would be never to have been born. This gives Sophocles a far bleaker 'last word' in *The Tower*, which brings him closer to the educational ethos reflected in 'Sailing to Byzantium' than that which is usually attributed to 'Among School Children'. In fact, the 'lesson' that we would all be better off dead is as out of place in the primary-school classroom as would be 'Leda and the Swan' – another Hellenist poem from *The Tower* related to 'schoolchildren', which touched, in its own horrific if subversive way, on the theme of learning when it posed yet another enigmatic rhetorical question: 'Did she put on his knowledge with his power / Before the indifferent beak could let her drop?'[89]

During his senatorial days, Yeats adopted a Sophoclean public persona, but by the 1930s he had lost faith in Arnoldian cultural Hellenism altogether and came to identify with Oedipus instead. We can see this in a two-part open letter he placed in the 'Packet to Ezra Pound' section of his Introduction to the 1937 edition of *A Vision*. He begins the letter by advising his addressee never to 'be elected to the Senate of your country. I think myself, after six years, well out of that of mine.'[90] One reason was his distaste for the political class, and the other was that he found his status as a representative man of culture too limiting. 'Whenever I stood up to speak', he continued, 'unless I spoke of something that concerned the arts, or upon something that depended not upon precise knowledge but upon public opinion . . . I was ashamed until shame turned at last, even if I spoke but a few words . . . into physical pain.'[91] Outside accounts of his speeches also corroborate the discomfort he felt speaking up in this context; the ideology of Arnoldian culture allowed Yeats in the door of the political sphere, but it also kept him quiet (at least relatively).

Even after moving out of senatorial politics, however, Yeats was still thinking about *Oedipus at Colonus*, which he uses in the letter to 'proclaim a new divinity'.[92] By staging his two Sophoclean translations in the 1920s, Yeats concentrated primarily on the character of Oedipus himself: how he discovers his pollution, suffers for it, and is mysteriously redeemed at the end of his life. Let us consider the plot of the second play. It opens with Oedipus and Antigone, having been exiled from Thebes, taking shelter in the sacred grove of the Furies at Colonus. They come under the protection of Theseus, the king who founded Athens and many of its institutions. Theseus fends off Oedipus' sons Eteocles and Polynices, each of whom wish to use their father against the other in a civil war. In an effort to force Oedipus' compliance, Eteocles abducts Antigone, but Theseus rescues her and brings her back to her father. He then oversees Oedipus' mysterious death, which secures good fortune for Athens. Yeats describes this mysterious death scene:

> Oedipus lay upon the earth at the middle point between four sacred objects, was there washed as the dead are washed, and thereupon passed with Theseus to the wood's heart until amidst the sound of thunder earth opened, 'riven by love', and he sank down soul and body into the earth.[93]

Although they show up in the Sophoclean original, the arrangement of Oedipus' body between 'four sacred objects' suggests, in this context, Yeats' fascination with Blakean symbolism.

Yeats delves deeper into the poetics of the emblem, however, when he says that the gods and heroes of this new religion will only have the meanings invented by himself:

> I will have him [Oedipus] balance Christ who, crucified standing up, went into the abstract sky soul and body, and I see him altogether separated from Plato's Athens, from all that talk of the Good and the One, from all that cabinet of perfection, an image from Homer's age.[94]

The expression 'I will have' makes clear that Yeats is taking it upon himself to invent Oedipus' meaningful connections to Christ, Homer and Plato. Even here, however, whether he is making himself a Sophocles at the Abbey Theatre or speaking as an Oedipus from *On the Boiler*, Yeats maintains the goal of shaping national character. Oedipus' 'rage against his sons', Yeats wrote,

> was noble, not from some general idea, some sense of public law upheld, but because it seemed to contain all life . . . He knew nothing but his mind, and yet because he spoke that mind fate possessed it and kingdoms changed according to his blessing and his cursing. Delphi, that rock at earth's navel, spoke through him, and though men shuddered and drove him away they spoke of ancient poetry, praising the boughs overhead, the grass under foot, Colonus and its horses.[95]

The main character is therefore a paradox. Whereas he had been exiled from Thebes because he polluted the state with his crimes, it was nevertheless foretold that he would be a blessing to whatever place he would die in. This mysteriously purifying corruption appealed to Yeats, who came to see in Oedipus an image of a chthonic, self-centred genius who ignored logic, law and the state but, nevertheless, shaped the characters of nations.

And yet, even when he turned into an emblematic, anti-foundationalist Oedipus, the Treatyite settlement remained the *non plus ultra* past which Yeats would not march. That is, even though the emblematic impulse of Yeats' Hellenism ultimately distanced him from the organicist aesthetics of Arnoldian Hellenism, Yeats nevertheless figures *Oedipus at Colonus* as an allegory for the artistic genius and the Free State. The idea that Oedipus' happy demise requires the protection of a philosophical founder-tyrant, moreover, recalls Yeats' admiration for the Cumann na nGaedheal government's strongman Kevin O'Higgins, with whom he dined on the evening of *The Plough and the Stars*' premiere.

The political implications of the Sophoclean analogy become more obvious, however, when we consider the fact that Yeats never completed the Theban cycle begun by *Oedipus the King* and *Oedipus at Colonus* by translating *Antigone*. This had been Sophocles' most profound dramatic meditation on politics, but were one to look for contemporary resonances, it would be impossible to escape a critique of the Free State. The drama opens in Thebes on the morning after the final battle of the civil war that was brewing in *Oedipus at Colonus*. Both Polynices and Eteocles have been killed during the siege of Thebes, and so Creon, who is both their uncle and king of Thebes, decrees that Eteocles will have a hero's burial, but that Polynices' corpse must be left to rot in the street without ceremony. Risking execution, Antigone defies this law by performing a burial ritual over her disgraced brother. Her subsequent arrest leads to an ethical debate over the conflict between unwritten laws and the authority of the state. Antigone goes willingly to her death, but the chorus and the prophet Tiresias both side with Antigone. Even Creon's son Haemon kills himself in protest at his father's inflexibility. Creon's wife, moreover, also commits suicide from grief at her son's death. While Yeats may have admired the idealised image of authority suggested by the analogy between O'Higgins and Theseus, an analogical reading of O'Higgins as Creon would have, conversely, painted a more damning picture of the tyrannical victor in Thebes' fratricidal civil war, and one who was, furthermore, all too ready to execute the death penalty on breakers of his arbitrary law.

If he were to look to *Antigone* as a modern Irish allegory, Yeats would have had to consider the claims of republican women against the Treatyite settlement. This would have meant allowing a Constance Markiewicz or a Maud Gonne to talk back within his poetry. Indeed, these were unlikely Yeatsian heroines in the 1920s and thirties. Instead of translating *Antigone* in its entirety or considering any parallels between it and contemporary Irish politics, therefore, he figures the character passively, comparing her to Shakespeare's Cordelia – another daughter who 'seemed less attendant upon an old railing rambler than upon genius itself'.[96] Even in the brief translation from *Antigone*, that Yeats used to conclude *The Winding Stair and Other Poems* in 1933, the chorus defines her in relation to her father. 'Pray I will and sing I must', the chorus laments as the protagonist descends into her living tomb for no apparent reason, 'And yet I weep – Oedipus' child / Descends into the loveless dust'.[97] In this regard, Yeats was on the side of Arnold, who considered Antigone irrelevant to modern life.[98]

This judgement tells us volumes about the ideological limitations of cultural Hellenism in the political sphere, and Yeats' tacit concurrence is similarly revealing. That is, Yeats' and Arnold's versions of Hellenism were ethical in the Aristotelian sense that they sought to form the character of a nation through civic art, but they were not at all concerned with raising ethical questions for audiences to consider as citizens of a democratic society. Neither presented thorny issues in an open-ended way designed to promote debate and self-reflection among audience members after the show. This was not Field Day. Parting ways with Arnold and Aristotle alike, moreover, Yeats entertained a heroic narrative of the artist culminating in the marginal, luminous and supremely unreconciled figure of Oedipus: a blessed–cursed man whose vatic presence and raging voice were powerful enough to shape the fates of nations. Yeats' notion of national *Bildung* relied upon the idea of exemplary characters who vacillated between antithetical impulses within their own heroic personalities, and derived from these struggles images and emblems that could be arranged into structures that would provide unity of culture. This formula for political and aesthetic reconciliation was inherently coercive, however, and lent itself to political authoritarianism.

The Field Day Theatre Company would revisit this Yeatsian problem of reconciliation and culture again throughout the 1980s; when Heaney was giving interviews all around Ireland to promote the forthcoming Field Day production of *The Cure at Troy* in 1990, he was careful to stipulate that his version of Sophocles was Yeatsian in the sense that it was a symbolic drama. He knew that Field Day was taking up questions about reconciliation and the border that Yeats had left unanswered. Indeed, all throughout the 1980s the Field Day board of directors signalled its respect for Yeats' and Gregory's achievement – and a wariness about their shortcomings. Its main argument was not so much with the Abbey, however, as it was with the subject of our next chapter: Conor Cruise O'Brien.

Chapter Two

Conor Cruise O'Brien's Sacred Dramas

From the 1960s until around 1985, Conor Cruise O'Brien was the most famous Irish intellectual in the world; in the 1970s and eighties he was also the most ardent and influential opponent of Irish republicanism in the South. By 1968, when the Troubles began, O'Brien was already an author, literary critic, historian and academic with an international career. As a member of the Irish delegation to the United Nations, O'Brien had played a major role by leading the UN mission to Katanga during the Congo Crisis of 1960. He had also been vice-chancellor at the University of Ghana. He was an outspoken critic of American foreign policy, and when he taught at New York University (NYU) in the late 1960s, O'Brien took part in student protests against the Vietnam War. He alienated many of his liberal admirers, however, when he sided with the loyalists at the beginning of the Troubles in Northern Ireland. For that, he had been called perverse and irresponsible: a Southern nationalist turned tendentious unionist ideologue.[1]

O'Brien entered Dáil Éireann as a member of the Labour Party in 1969, and when Labour formed a coalition government with Fine Gael he became minister for posts and telegraphs (1973–77). Given his earlier criticism of his Fianna Fáil predecessor's use of section 31 of the 1960 Broadcasting Act to censor the IRA, it had been widely expected that O'Brien would adopt a more liberal approach when he took responsibility for censorship policy himself. On the contrary, he applied the ban with a severity that even his sympathetic biographer Donald Akenson has called 'increasingly ruthless' and 'increasingly frantic'.[2] In 1974 he proposed an amendment bill to clarify and strengthen section 31, and this became the Broadcasting (Amendment) Act, 1976.[3] Also that year, O'Brien wrote section 3 of an amendment bill to the criminal code that would have extended his authority to censor print media. After he shared his draft of the section with *Washington Post* reporter Bernard

Nossiter, and suggested he would use it to imprison newspaper editors (such as Tim Pat Coogan of the *Irish Press*) for publishing letters from IRA supporters, public outcry prompted the authors of the bill to drop section 3 from the proposed legislation.[4] The public was further outraged in February 1977 when *The Irish Times* revealed that a 'Heavy Gang' in the Garda Síochána had been employing illegal coercion to obtain confessions from people suspected of IRA membership.[5] Despite these shocks to the public's confidence in the government, section 31 would continue to be renewed every year by successive Cabinet ministers for well over a decade after O'Brien left politics. It was finally allowed to lapse in January 1994, several months before the IRA ceasefire.[6] O'Brien would spend the rest of that decade inveighing against the Northern Irish peace process, alienating himself more and more from even those Irish readers who admired him up until that point.[7]

The president of Ireland from 1997 to 2011, Mary McAleese, has recalled the 'culture shock' she experienced when she and her family moved from the North of Ireland to the Republic in those years, only to discover O'Brien, 'an extraordinarily arrogant man . . . in the process of revising everything I had known . . . about Irish history – and who set in motion a way of looking at Northern Ireland that we are only now beginning to grow up and grow out of'.[8] One of the reasons O'Brien's criticisms were taken so seriously on the international stage was that he came from a Catholic nationalist background. However, he often rejected the idea that he had abandoned his tribe. In his 1972 book *States of Ireland*, for instance, he argued that:

> In fact the reverse accusation would contain more truth. It is to the Irish Catholic community that I belong. This is my 'little platoon', to love which, according to Edmund Burke (whose family were in that same platoon), 'is the first, the germ, as it were, of publick affections'. I am motivated by affection for that platoon, identification with it, and fear that it may destroy itself, including me, through infatuation with its own mythology.[9]

This was a backhanded identification, to be sure. A brilliant stylist and polemicist, O'Brien channelled this jumble of competing impulses into a persona that came to be known popularly in Ireland as 'the Cruiser'. By the time he published *States of Ireland*, some observers had come to see him as the most effective of all unionist ideologues. In response to that book, in fact, John Hume argued that O'Brien made the unionist arguments more effectively than did the unionists themselves.[10] When the Fine Gael–Labour coalition government lost the 1977 general election,

O'Brien was nevertheless elected to Seanad Éireann, where he remained until 1979, after which he became editor-in-chief of *The Observer*. In 1985 he invited further controversy by joining Revd Ian Paisley's 'Ulster Says No' campaign against the Anglo-Irish Agreement. The rise of the Field Day Theatre Company's profile, moreover, diminished O'Brien's mastery of the conversation about the Troubles, in cultural and historical terms. By the end of 1996, he had alienated the last of his liberal nationalist followers by joining the right-wing fringe UK Unionist Party, led by Robert McCartney.[11] Fintan O'Toole expressed disgust in May 1998, for instance, when O'Brien aligned himself explicitly with Ian Paisley in opposition to the Good Friday Agreement.[12] And finally, O'Brien alienated even the far-right unionists he had embraced when he published an excerpt from his memoirs in the *Sunday Independent* advising Ulster unionists to join a united Ireland voluntarily.[13]

O'Brien's career was defined by paradox, and has therefore attracted searching critical analysis. For instance, in the 1980 review essay 'The making of a loyalist', Tom Paulin attributes O'Brien's 'static and unfruitful contradictions' to the author–politician's 'continuing uncertainty about his identity', which 'is a figment of public opinion and since there are many opinions there must be many identities'.[14] In contrast to Paulin's reading of O'Brien's inconsistency, however, Mark McNally has more recently argued that the apparent incongruities between O'Brien's international liberalism and Irish conservatism are actually consistent with a career-long antipathy to nationalisms of all stripes.[15] In this chapter I will attribute these contradictions in O'Brien's intellectual and political formation to a variety of Irish Hellenism he himself called the 'sacred drama', a synthesis of Arnoldian culture and Yeatsian tragic vision that he developed during the 1960s while teaching literature and politics in Ghana and New York, and meditating on his bygone career at the United Nations.

Between 1965 and 1969, as Albert Schweitzer Chair at New York University, O'Brien identified himself strongly with the Arnoldian critical tradition.[16] Like Arnold, O'Brien was particularly interested in Greek drama, writing in 1969 that, far from being 'politically irrelevant', the drama was 'part of the political process'.[17] He accordingly called for scholars in the humanities to promote the improvement of literary tastes because it would lead to the creation of a culture with a more serious political ethos. 'The task of the humanist', he wrote, 'will be to keep alive . . . the possibility of such growth [of pure mind] . . . in order that politics may be imagined and conducted in a manner transcending the crude fetishisms which now govern the world.'[18] Although O'Brien did not use the word directly, he reproduced the notion of Hellenism Arnold had expounded in *Culture and Anarchy*, particularly in his references to Sophocles, Aeschylus and Thucydides, all of whom Arnold also referenced as touchstones in the 1860s. Furthermore, O'Brien extended the Arnoldian metaphor to describe contemporary American politics in that same essay when he diagnosed racism in America as a 'crudely fetishistic politics' promoted by mass popular culture – what he called American popular culture's 'cunningly debased forms of drama'.[19] O'Brien drew a stark distinction between the culture of a politically progressive society drawn to 'Aeschylus and Sophocles' and a politically regressive one drawn to 'cowboys and Indians' or to 'Superman and Batman'.[20] His interest in the growth of the mind was also very similar to Arnold's 'liberalism of the future', which believed in human perfectibility but also resisted the visionary, millenarian quality of the radical left. O'Brien did not arrive at this Arnoldian Hellenist position by any simple route, nor was his position as straightforwardly Arnoldian as it is described here. In fact, this was only one part of a larger concept he called the 'sacred drama', which he had been developing for thirty years.

At the beginning of his career in the Republic of Ireland's Department of External Affairs, O'Brien was an anti-partitionist ideologue working under the first coalition government's foreign minister, Seán MacBride, son of Maud Gonne and the 1916 martyr John MacBride. However, by 1951, O'Brien was in agreement with the new minister, Frank Aiken, in his opinion that the Republic needed to move beyond its fixation on partition in order to enter the modern era. Dispensing with MacBride's policy emphasis on ending partition, Aiken set out to redefine Irish foreign policy so that it would improve Ireland's international profile and help modernise Irish society itself. O'Brien came to identify himself with these goals, and when Ireland entered the United Nations in 1955, he became the head of the UN section in Dublin. By 1960, he had joined Aiken at the Irish delegation in New York; together they crafted the Republic's foreign-policy image as a non-aligned, human rights-oriented moral authority on the international stage.[21]

In reforming Irish foreign policy, Aiken and O'Brien took inspiration from the Swedish model of international diplomacy. 'For some of us, particularly the younger members of the Department', O'Brien recounted in his UN memoir *To Katanga and Back*, 'the ideal of what constituted good international behavior was exemplified at this time by Sweden . . .

[which] was, as we saw it, independent, disinterested and honorable.'[22] The Swedish example was particularly prominent during Ireland's early years in the UN because the Swedish diplomat Dag Hammarskjöld had been Secretary General since 1953. 'Hammarskjold more than anyone', O'Brien wrote in *Katanga*, 'had given the United Nations a focus of moral authority which could attract an international loyalty, and use it in the cause of peace and justice.'[23] According to O'Brien, the Irish delegation identified with Hammarskjöld as an icon of international moral authority, and therefore joined diplomatic forces with 'the small (and mainly Scandinavian) group of delegations . . . whose sole concern it was to safeguard that moral authority . . . against the interested pressure' from either side of the East–West split.[24] He has described the cult of personality surrounding Hammarskjöld, who was also a mystical poet, as a useful diplomatic tool. This description of the Hammarskjöld mystique, moreover, showed more than a little similarity to his description of the sometimes politically useful cult of personality surrounding Charles Stewart Parnell, who had been the topic of his doctoral dissertation 'Parnell and his Party'.

In addition to supporting the Swedish model, the Irish delegation also cultivated Ireland's international profile as a postcolonial country. Ireland's anti-imperial credentials were high in postcolonial Africa, and particularly in the Congo where the 1916 martyr Sir Roger Casement had exposed Belgian colonial atrocities in 1903–04. This was significant to Ireland's profile at the UN because the number of UN member states was expanding rapidly, as it admitted countries from Africa, Asia, the Middle East and Latin America. By 1960 fully one quarter of the total seats in the UN belonged to these postcolonial 'Third World' countries. This meant that the US and the USSR would have to compete for their votes in the General Assembly. Between its familial connection with Irish America, its postcolonial status, and its cultivation of the Swedish model of conscientious European non-alignment in the Cold War, the Irish were well situated to communicate between the First and Third Worlds. O'Brien applauded the idea that the Americans and Russians would have to compete for the hearts and minds of the Third World, because this would promote international norms of moral behaviour. Through its special ability to communicate between these 'worlds', the Irish might then play a disproportionate role in the articulation of those moral norms. When Hammarskjöld hand-picked O'Brien to be his special representative during the Congo Crisis, therefore, it reflected the success of Aiken's vision for Ireland's place among the nations of the world. It was the UN's first peacekeeping mission, and at home the government's role in it was criticised by the political opposition.

At the end of June 1960, the Belgian Congo's colonial status officially ended, but its independence was merely nominal because its military would continue under European command, as would the country's mining operations. The Congolese soldiers mutinied against this arrangement and began attacking Europeans. The Belgian government then sent European mercenaries to the mineral-rich province of Katanga, which separated from the Congo as its own independent nation under the presidency of Moïse Tshombe. In early July the Congo requested UN assistance to help stabilise the country, and the Security Council hastily worked out an ambiguous military resolution allowing Hammarskjöld to send twenty thousand troops from twenty-five countries (including Ireland) to the Congo. It was unclear, however, what those troops were meant to do when they got there. This lack of clarity would lead to considerable controversy for years to come.

Frustrated with the slow pace of UN assistance, the Congolese Prime Minister, Patrice Lumumba, petitioned the Soviet Union directly for military support. In response to this, the CIA backed a coup (led by the future President of Zaire, Joseph-Désiré Mobutu). UN troops took responsibility for Lumumba's safety, but he was captured anyway and taken to Katanga where he was put before a firing squad of Belgian mercenaries. When the UN's leadership in Africa was implicated in Lumumba's death, there were worldwide protests against Belgium, and the Soviet Union denounced Hammarskjöld as an imperialist stooge.[25] In the upheaval following Lumumba's killing, O'Brien was invited onto the Secretariat for implementing the resolution in Katanga.

By early summer 1961, Hammarskjöld had sent him to the Congo as the Secretary General's special representative in charge of the peacekeeping forces. O'Brien was charged with ending the Katangan secession, and to do this he would have to confront the mercenary army that was supporting Tshombe's government. O'Brien oversaw two operations against it. The first of these, 'Operation Rumpunch' (launched 28 August 1961) was militarily successful but politically ineffective because O'Brien was ordered to release the arrested mercenaries. The second, 'Operation Morthor' (launched 12 September 1961), began well militarily but ended in political disaster when Tshombe pretended to surrender but actually escaped to Rhodesia. O'Brien's career at the UN would probably have ended following this fiasco, but the real tragedy was yet to come.[26] From the safety of Rhodesia, Tshombe declared war on the UN, and the Secretary General came to the Congo to take over the matter personally. After meeting with O'Brien, Hammarskjöld boarded a plane to Ndola, Northern Rhodesia intending to conduct face-to-face meetings with the Katangan leadership; the meeting never happened, however, because the aircraft crashed eight miles from its destination.[27]

Hammarskjöld's death in Africa became instantly mythic. He won a posthumous Nobel Peace Prize, and remains a kind of secular patron saint for the United Nations. For O'Brien, the tragedy was particularly deep because he felt responsible for it. In *To Katanga and Back*, he admitted being haunted by a 'question – inevitable, unanswerable, uncomfortable: whether, if Mr Hammarskjold had made another choice [that is, of special representative], he might now be alive?'[28] According to Akenson, O'Brien spent the 1960s trying to figure out 'what had happened in the Congo, what the character of the United Nations really was, and what mystery lay at the heart of the life and death of the tragically mystic' Swede, whom O'Brien had even looked to as a 'second father'.[29] Akenson also reported that O'Brien had never stopped brooding about Hammarskjöld's death, and that he could never 'accept its tragic illogic'.[30] He was already a controversial figure in the British and French press, but now O'Brien was humiliated and marginalised in the UN itself. In the wake of the disaster, UN officials argued that O'Brien had overreached his mission. The UN's new Secretary General, the Burmese diplomat U Thant, requested his resignation.[31]

Akenson has described the Congo Crisis as the 'watershed' experience of O'Brien's life, and suggested that what he learned in Africa in 1961 strongly informed his subsequent approach – in and out of government – to the Troubles in Northern Ireland. O'Brien's Irish 'antiterrorism campaign' of the 1970s reflected the 'crucial reality', Akenson writes, that O'Brien learned in the Congo: 'that the veneer of civilization is very thin and that social anarchy . . . was only a millimeter away'.[32] From that point on, O'Brien devoted his intellectual, creative and political energies 'to keep[ing] at bay the beast within human society'.[33] Akenson argues that O'Brien learned in the Congo that violence is always threatening to break through the thin veneer of human civilisation. Furthermore, O'Brien would later dedicate his political and writing career to the quelling of such violence in Northern Ireland. However, he did not think that sheer rationalism was the answer; rather, his experience in Africa led him to the conclusion that peacemakers must learn to engage with the irrational as well as the rational aspects of human society. O'Brien outlines this need in *The Suspecting Glance*, and it also appears verbatim in his 1968 book *United Nations: Sacred Drama*. In the passage, he agrees with 'the socialist aspiration . . . towards the placing of the resources of humanity under the control of intelligence responsible to humanity', but says also that this intelligence needs to start thinking about literature and culture, too. Not only would this new science call 'us to be suspicious about ourselves', but would also demand 'more emphasis on zoology', on 'the sensitive development of social psychology and anthropology', and on 'the careful exploration of the interplay of myth, metaphor and ritual forms both in our language and in our institutions and across the two'.[34] He brought this ethos to the programme in literature and society he had started at NYU, and when he returned to Ireland he brought this ethos more directly into the political sphere, as well.

Rather than giving in to pessimism about the UN's capacity to save humanity from nuclear Armageddon during the Cold War after his experiences in Katanga, O'Brien took a reformist attitude and reinvented himself as a prominent critic of the power politics of the Security Council. O'Brien was looking to various modern paradigms with which to reconcile his Enlightenment principles with his post-Katangan conclusion that life had an essentially tragic character. In *United Nations: Sacred Drama*, O'Brien drew heavily on ideas of 'play' in the work of Johan Huizinga, the Dutch cultural historian, to describe how the United Nations had worked at its best, and should strive to work in the future.[35] O'Brien writes:

> Since the United Nations makes its impression on the imagination of mankind through a spectacle presented in an auditorium with confrontations of opposing personages, it may be said to belong to the category of *drama*. Since the personages, individually or collectively, symbolize mighty forces, since the audience is mankind and the theme the destiny of man, the drama may rightly be called sacred.[36]

He leavens this idealism with a degree of realism, however, extending the theatrical conceit. 'To speak of the sacred drama', he qualifies the analogy, 'is not to suggest that the United Nations dwells perpetually on some pure and solemn height: far from it';[37] rather, O'Brien continues,

> This drama swings from tragedy to farce and back again, neither bathos nor buffoonery is alien to it: all the unities, in every sense, are broken . . . the dramatic principles are more like Shakespeare's than Racine's. But we must imagine scenes from Shakespeare performed

> in no coherent order by a motley cast, most of whom have forgotten most of their lines and mangled the remains of what they remember . . . [it] is a Shakespeare of the theatre of the absurd, suffused by nightmare in its form as well as in its content. On its common level it is a desperately serious farce, on whose continued run our lives may depend.[38]

Ultimately, despite the limitations imposed upon it as a symbolic entity, and the failings of its actors, O'Brien's sacred drama offers the potential for reconciliation on the divided world stage. At its best, it has the power to recreate the setting of the Areopagus from Aeschylus' *Eumenides*.

O'Brien also formulated this version of Hellenism as an alternative to the Hellenism to be found in the prevailing 'modern realist' view of international relations put forth by the political theorist Hans Morgenthau.[39] The political philosophy of realism takes Thucydides' *Peloponnesian War* as its founding text, and Thucydides' realist perspective is often summed up by this famous passage (translated here by Thomas Hobbes):

> The causes why they [the Athenians and the Peloponnesians] brake the same [the Thirty Years Peace] and their quarrels, I have therefore set down first, because no man should be to seek from what ground so great a war amongst the Grecians should arise. And the truest quarrel, though least in speech, I conceive to be the growth of the Athenian power, which putting the Lacedaemonians into fear necessitated [*anankasai*] the war.[40]

The key term here is *anagkê*, which Liddel and Scott translate as 'force, constraint, necessity', or 'violence'.[41] There are other possible renderings of *anankasai*, but Hobbes' translation of it as 'necessitated' exemplifies the realist philosophy because it presents the competition for political and military hegemony as a law of human nature. The sheer fact of Athens' ascent made Sparta attack it. This was not because the Athenians or Spartans had any particular character, but because the Athenians and the Spartans were human beings. This means that nations have no choice but to compete for hegemony, and in a bipolar conflict – one between superpowers such as Athens and Sparta, or the United States and the Soviet Union – all smaller conflicts (between Corinth and Corcyra, or North and South Vietnam) are moving parts and minor battlefields of that larger one. Under these conditions, concepts of justice are secondary to strategy.

Even in the supposedly 'realist' Thucydides, however, there is a place for peacemaking and arbitration: the shrine of the Oracle at Delphi. Accordingly, O'Brien devotes an entire chapter to the ways in which the

UN plays a role analogous to that of the Delphic Oracle, before whom the would-be hegemons of ancient Greece would lay down arms, seeking arbitration from a commonly recognised, sacred authority. As in ancient Greece, however, so in the Cold War world: the sacred space of arbitration was also subject to the exigencies of power politics. The UN's limited successes could only be achieved on the basis of its credibility as a disinterested moral authority, but the obvious influence of the US State Department frequently endangered that credibility. The same was true in the fourth century BCE: the Athenian Demosthenes criticised the undue influence exerted by Philip of Macedon on the Delphic Amphyctyony, saying that the Oracle 'philippises'. O'Brien believed that the organisation was still credible because even if the UN is largely an instrument of US hegemony, it nevertheless obliges the US to cultivate the goodwill of smaller postcolonial countries (especially in Africa) in order to maintain that hegemony.

In Greece the same was true with Philip. Thanks to his patronage of the Oracle (and his superior military might), the Macedonian commanded a majority of votes in the Delphic Amphictyony, but the other member states still required a degree of persuasion. The oracle favours Philip but it also obliges him to engage in the art of persuasion rather than merely warfare. O'Brien therefore says that political influence is indeed a part of the Oracle's function. 'Pressures to degrade the shrine', he writes, 'are as old as civilisation; they are indeed part of the shrine and of its drama.'[42] It is only in the overweening abuse, however, that the part destroys the whole. The UN was also like a Delphic Oracle because both allowed 'opportunities for continuous contact, and unpublicised adjustments of matters in dispute'.[43] It allowed space for the superpowers to hammer out agreements even behind closed doors. This was not a wholly idealist suggestion because it presupposed that the superpowers, dedicated both to hegemony and also to the avoidance of nuclear war, would compromise on questions of justice. For example, according to O'Brien, the US used the UN to justify its tacit agreement not to intervene against the Soviet invasion of Hungary.[44] By offering a space for compromise during the Cold War, the UN was a possible instrument of what would in the 1970s be called détente, an alternate strategy to that of containment.

O'Brien continued to use the Greek tragedy analogy in his criticism of Trygve Lie, the UN's first Secretary General (1946–52), who apparently

> neglected the aspect of the sacred which alone gives meaning to the drama. The holder of the office, when he is true to its sacred

> function, must be touched by the spirit of the goddess Athena in the last scene of the *Oresteia*; neither abetting the Eumenides nor rebuking them, safeguarding the retreat of Orestes, applying the holy balm of noble words to all parties, and breaking the cycle of blood and vengeance. A Secretary-General acting on this level might have shortened the Korean war, by sanctifying a Communist retreat, through Soviet pressure on North Korea, accompanied by a solemn ritual of praise for Soviet 'mediation'.[45]

In addition to Lie's failure to recreate the role of Aeschylus' Athena in relation to the very real Korean War, O'Brien also considered Lie's failure to protect Leon Trotsky ('the great tragic hero of the century') from Stalinist persecution as a failure to execute the role Theseus had played in Sophocles' *Oedipus at Colonus*. As Norwegian minister for justice, Lie had offered sanctuary to the exiled Soviet leader but then submitted to Stalinist pressure by deporting him (to Mexico). By bringing this very un-Hellenic cowardice to the UN, Lie had abused the shrine's 'charisma' nearly to the point of dissolution.

Despite O'Brien's insistence upon conscientious maintenance of the UN's shrine, he largely disregards the shrine's usefulness in Ireland. Near the beginning of his chapter on the Delphic Oracle analogy, O'Brien mentions how the UN in its oracular function seeks to promote the reconciliation of divided countries such as 'China, the Koreas, the Vietnams and the Germanies'.[46] He is clearly focused on the Cold War when he compiles that list, but when we consider the context of 1968, his failure to include 'the Irelands' in this list of unreconciled countries is certainly noteworthy. O'Brien did not think that the UN's version of sacred drama could work in Ireland. The major reason was that the United Kingdom, being a member of the Security Council, could keep discussion of Northern Ireland off the table.[47] There was also resistance on the side of the Irish Republic. In *States of Ireland*, O'Brien recalled that as a member of the foreign service around 1960, he had once 'drafted proposals for a possible approach to the problem at the United Nations'.[48] He had projected that if Dublin could assure Belfast that it no longer sought to end partition, the UK might allow a conversation (either in the Council of Europe or at the UN) about the rights of Catholics in Northern Ireland. According to O'Brien, however, political infighting within the foreign service itself killed the proposal before it ever went public. Elsewhere in *States of Ireland*, O'Brien described the 1966 collapse of executive-level diplomacy between the Irish Taoiseach, Seán Lemass and the Northern Ireland Prime Minister, Terence O'Neill. The apex of this diplomatic effort came in 1965 when Lemass visited O'Neill at Stormont. Unfortunately, the effort died when nationalists celebrated the fiftieth anniversary of the Easter Rebellion while unionists commemorated the fiftieth anniversary of the Battle of the Somme. In such a year of commemorations, O'Brien noted, 'ghosts were bound to walk, both North and South'.[49] These commemorations reinforced two competing narratives of Irish history which only agreed on one point: that O'Neill and Lemass were betraying their own communities by engaging in diplomacy at all. Both leaders, therefore, ceased their attempts to normalise relations, and O'Brien concluded that sacred drama in Ireland was a hindrance to any substantial movement towards peace on the island.

O'Brien also belonged to the school of Irish historical revisionism, which took as one of its main tenets that myth and history should not be mixed. This served to strengthen his conclusion that sacred drama would not bring peace to Ireland. In the late 1940s and early fifties, O'Brien had written a doctoral dissertation on Charles Stewart Parnell at Trinity College, Dublin under the direction of Professor Theo Moody, who co-founded the revisionist school with Robert Dudley-Edwards. These historians came from either side of the Protestant/Catholic divide in Ireland, but they met while working on their PhDs in history at the University of London. Upon returning to Ireland, they took academic positions at Trinity College, Dublin and University College Dublin, respectively. In 1936 they co-founded the Irish Historical Society, and their cooperatively produced journal, *Irish Historical Studies*, appeared two years later. As historians and public intellectuals they shared three common goals: first, they wanted to establish modern Irish historiography on a more scientific basis; second, they wanted to build an infrastructure for scholarly publication of the new research; and third, they would supply modern Irish audiences with a less biased narrative of their shared past.[50] Moody and Dudley-Edwards hoped a more enlightened general understanding of the Irish past would foster greater understanding between communities, thereby helping to forestall conflict between nationalists and unionists on either side of the Irish border. O'Brien identified himself with this mission, although his later interest in myth (particularly sacred drama) would complicate this identification considerably and lead to serious contradictions.

O'Brien chose for his dissertation topic a key figure of interest for revisionists because the 'Parnell myth' occupies an important place in the historical imagination of physical-force Irish nationalists. The revisionist historian F.S.L. Lyons in 1972 had written that:

> It was his [Parnell's] myth rather than his record, that most influenced posterity. To the generation that grew up in the poisonous atmosphere of the split which persisted nearly ten years after his death, Parnell stood out as a towering figure, far above the politicians whom he had created and who had repaid him – so the argument went – with betrayal . . .[51]

The generation of 1916 would, therefore, draw upon Parnell's heroic myth to justify their engagement in revolutionary violence rather than the political process. O'Brien's *Parnell and his Party*, therefore, conforms to the Irish revisionist paradigm in that it challenges the popular mythos of Parnell as man of destiny by downplaying the tragic individualist image Parnell projected of himself during the split.

Despite this attempt to keep myth separate from history, however, it has also been true that some of the most prominent historians of the Irish revisionist school, including Lyons as well as Roy Foster, have been major Yeats scholars.[52] O'Brien shares in this paradox, and, indeed, Yeats is a significant presence in *Parnell and his Party*. It is very curious to note that O'Brien concludes the book with a quotation from the poem 'Parnell's Funeral', thereby granting the final word of his revisionist history to the poet most responsible for immortalising the very myth his book was apparently attempting to refute. He introduces the lines, moreover, by way of his own kind of Yeatsian rhetorical question. Referencing the Parnell split, he asks:

> Did this collective emotional explosion of 1890 help to set free the imaginative forces which, for a time in the early 1900s, made Dublin – the Parnellite city – an important centre of world literature? One cannot prove it to be so, but one does sense in that literature the Parnellite shock. Those who feel – as does the present writer – that the Parnell of the split deviated from politics into literature, may reflect that, in the second field as in the first, he made his power felt:
>
> And here's a final reason,
> He was of such a kind
> Every man that sings a song
> Keeps Parnell in his mind.[53]

The historian has become poetic, and, thereby, gestures beyond the standard revisionist critique of the Parnell myth to the idea that some aspects of Parnell's history are better explained by poets. O'Brien says he thinks he can feel the shock, suggesting that its reverberations have imbued Irish literature with some kind of knowledge or power, and thereby given it global significance.

In that passage, O'Brien was also drawing on Yeats as a historical source on the relationship between poetry and politics. Yeats famously told his audience at Oslo in his Nobel Prize acceptance speech that:

> The modern literature of Ireland, and indeed all that stir of thought which prepared for the Anglo-Irish war began when Parnell fell from power in 1891. A disillusioned and embittered Ireland turned from Parliamentary politics and the race began, as I think, to be troubled by that event's long gestation.[54]

When he came to write *States of Ireland*, moreover, O'Brien would use this quotation as the epigraph for the first chapter, 'The fall of Parnell'. Giving Yeats' idea such pride of place in *Parnell and his Party* called the 'scientific' basis of his revisionist study into question and seems to have inspired some Yeatsian meditation in the author. That is, by reflecting Yeats' description of the 'stir' and 'gestation' in a rhetorical question about an 'explosion' and a 'shock', O'Brien suggests an analogy between Parnell, literary Dublin and the Easter Rising on one hand, and Zeus, Leda and the Trojan War on the other. According to this scheme, Parnell appears to be a Zeus figure who transforms himself (from politics into literature) in order to shock and make 'his power felt' on a Leda figure (Dublin and/or Irish literature). The 'emotional explosion' of Parnell's fall in Dublin is like the 'shudder in the loins' of Zeus on Leda, and in both cases the explosion prefigures violence to come, whether it be at the walls of Troy or at the General Post Office in Dublin.

If the conclusion to *Parnell and his Party* featured an implicitly 'Ledean' rhetorical question, O'Brien invoked the poem more explicitly in the conclusion to his pivotal 1965 essay 'Passion and cunning: an essay on the politics of W.B. Yeats'.[55] It is instructive to compare the conclusion of this essay with that of *Parnell and his Party* because both contain the suggestion that art has a kind of clairvoyance with regard to political history. The '"telepathic waves of violence and fear" make themselves known', O'Brien writes,

> not in the form of calculated practical deductions, but in the attempt to reveal, through metaphoric insight, what is actually happening. The poet, like the lady, is
>
> so caught up
> So mastered by the brute blood of the air
>
> that he does indeed take on the knowledge of what is happening with the power to make it known. The political man had his cautious understanding with Fascism, the diplomatic relation to a great

> force; the poet conveyed the nature of the force, the dimension of the tragedy.[56]

Many have taken O'Brien's 1966 essay as a condemnation of Yeats' politics, but O'Brien was much more interested in the idea that 'the purity and integrity' of Yeats' wholesale commitment to 'the truth about politics as . . . [he] apprehended it' resulted in the creation of 'metaphors of such power that they thrust aside all calculated intent: bird and lady take possession of the scene'.[57] According to this argument, therefore, when it came to politics, Yeats lost sight of democratic ethics but not of his own poetics.

Even despite his attention to the poet's later anti-democratic ideology, O'Brien recognised and valued the strain of cultural Hellenism in Yeats' promotion of civic art in Ireland. The most incendiary comment O'Brien made about Yeats in the 'Passion and cunning' essay was that he would have cooperated with a fascist state should Germany have prevailed in the Second World War and he had lived to see it. 'In Ireland', he wrote, 'one would have expected to see him [Yeats] at least a cautious participant, or ornament, in a collaborationist regime.'[58] As an ornament, O'Brien surely must have meant that Yeats would have reassumed something like the senatorial role of the 1920s, but one in which he exemplified culture in perhaps more of a Nietzschean rather than an Arnoldian light. Rather than signalling O'Brien's distance from Yeats, however, this claim reflected O'Brien's imaginative sympathy with Yeats as a public figure at the crossroads between literature and politics in dark times.

O'Brien could relate to Yeats' hypothetical situation because, at the time he wrote that essay he was vice chancellor at the University of Ghana. In the early 1960s Ghana was not a totalitarian state, but under the presidency of Kwame Nkrumah it had many features of a dictatorship. O'Brien was critical of Nkrumah's rule, but he collaborated with it in order to build the university and protect its ideals – ideals he affirmed in the last address he gave as vice chancellor: 'Respect for truth; intellectual courage in the pursuit of truth; moral courage in the telling of truth . . . the qualities of a real, of a living university'.[59] Having decided that promoting these ideals in the academic sphere was worth collaborating with a government averse to them in the political sphere, O'Brien persevered in this diplomatic relationship until the end of his three-year contract.[60] Turning back to the vice chancellor's address quoted above, O'Brien concluded that:

> The university has a duty, not only to transmit intact that [universal intellectual] heritage, but to provide intellectual conditions in which

> a modern African genius can make his own fresh and unpredictable contribution to the development of the human mind. We are here to provide, in Yeats's phrase:
>
> *. . . not what they would,*
> *But the right twigs for an eagle's nest.*[61]

O'Brien may have scandalised the Yeatsians by pointing out Yeats' antagonism to democratic culture and politics, but when he ends his speech on academic freedom in Ghana with the closing lines of 'To a Wealthy Man', it is clear that he saw Yeats very much as his companion in a project of anti-colonial, cosmopolitan enlightenment.[62]

It was on the basis of Yeats' imaginative integrity, over and above his ideology, that O'Brien thought of him as an exemplary sacred dramatist for the United Nations. His book on the UN contained a supplementary bibliography on 'the mysterious confines where religion, drama, and politics meet', and this included, alongside Shakespeare, Milton and Greek dramatists, such Irish texts as 'Meditations in time of civil war', 'Cuchulain Comforted', and *Cathleen ni Houlihan*, in addition to Burke's *Reflections on the Revolution in France* and *Letters on a Regicide Peace.*[63] O'Brien also listed W.I.M. Thompson's history of the 1916 Easter Rising, *Imagination of an Insurrection*, along with his own *Parnell and his Party*. This sounds like the reading list for a college seminar on Yeats' poetry and politics, and indeed O'Brien had been giving a lot of lectures on Yeats at NYU at the time he published this book. By privileging Ireland as a source of sacred dramas for the UN, but excluding Irish partition from the list of problems that the UN sacred drama might arbitrate, O'Brien inscribes the double standard that the UN had been forced to accept by the exigencies of power politics into his theory of literature. He posited that Irish political, religious and literary history is saturated with sacred drama, but even if knowledge of this Irish drama might heighten the consciousness of tragic actors at the UN as they try to save the human race from nuclear Armageddon, the mixture of poetry with politics can only ever offer the gravest of threats to the tenuous peace in Ireland itself.

This double standard is powerfully reflected in O'Brien's criticism of Seamus Heaney's poetry of the 1970s. In 'A slow, north-east wind', his well-known review of *North* (1975), O'Brien compared the book to Yeats' *The Tower*. In addition to many other reasons for doing so, Heaney more or less invited O'Brien to explore the comparison. He did this first by calling O'Brien out, in 'Whatever you say, say nothing', for his constant invocations of Burke to support a unionist perspective. He did it secondly, moreover, by naming the book's final section after the 'singing school' of 'Sailing to Byzantium'. In response to these invitations, O'Brien sharply argued that Heaney was a very good poet but a very poor Yeatsian because he failed to transcend the limitations of his background by renouncing Catholic piety and denouncing republican violence. No matter how far he travelled from Derry, Heaney remained too much of a Northern Catholic whose home territory 'is always with him, the ash, somehow, now standing out even more on his forehead'.[64] Until he followed O'Brien's path to cosmopolitanism, moreover, Heaney would never be able to exemplify reconciliation on the level of culture or politics.

By framing Heaney's failure to live up to Yeats' example in terms of ethics rather than aesthetics, O'Brien reaffirmed the Yeats of *The Tower* as an exemplary man of culture. What Heaney missed about Yeats' example, apparently, was his disinterested play of mind with relation to the Troubles of his time which left Yeats 'free to try . . . on . . . different relationships to the tragedy' unfolding around him in the Anglo-Irish War and then the Irish civil war.[65] 'Heaney's relation to a deeper tragedy', by contrast, 'was fixed and pre-ordained; the poet is on intimate terms with doom, and speaks its language wryly and succinctly.'[66] In wording that further suggested O'Brien thought tragic experience was pre-ordained, the critic also suggested that Heaney's poetry reified the Troubles, presenting 'the thing itself, the actual substance of historical agony and dissolution, the tragedy of a people in a place'.[67] O'Brien blamed this dark vision on Heaney himself, declaring that the 'bleak conclusiveness of these poems' are by far the most 'pessimistic analyses of "Northern Ireland"' that he had ever come across.[68]

The double standard between O'Brien's judgement of the 'bleak' Heaney and the more optimistic potentialities of the UN's sacred drama stands out in his criticism of the most controversial of all bog poems. 'Punishment' is often faulted for its too-sympathetic portrayal of the IRA's violence against Catholic women whom they believe to be fraternising with, and/or passing along secrets to, British soldiers. O'Brien objects to the poem on the grounds that it legitimates an illegal system by which the woman is judged 'guilty', and to illustrate the point offers the following quotation:

> My poor scapegoat,
> I almost love you
> but would have cast, I know
> the stones of silence . . .

> I who have stood dumb
> when your betraying sisters,
> cauled in tar,
> wept by the railings,
>
> who would connive
> in civilized outrage
> yet understand the exact
> and tribal, intimate revenge.[69]

O'Brien identifies the word 'exact' as being what 'hurts the most: Seamus Heaney has so greatly earned the right to use this word that to see him use it as he does here opens up a sort of chasm.'[70] His quotation, however, was not so exact because it elided five lines between 'silence' and 'I who have stood dumb', lines in which the poet denaturalises his own spectatorial relationship, calling himself 'the artful voyeur'.[71]

O'Brien's critical objections to that passage have been very widely adopted, but when we consider the review in relation to the sacred-drama idea, it is remarkable that O'Brien has overlooked the very obvious similarity between 'Punishment' and a poem that Hammarskjöld had written around the time that O'Brien had played his own tragic role as Special representative in the Congo. O'Brien had taken the poem seriously enough that he reproduced it, with commentary, in *United Nations: Sacred Drama*.

In this section of the book, O'Brien was describing Hammarskjöld as the ideal Secretary General because his lineage and cult of personality made him a kind of mystical philosopher king. This outward image was also reflected in the poems he kept in his private notebook, found in his New York apartment after his death, and published posthumously under the title of *Markings*. O'Brien quotes from the book:

> 'You are dedicated to this task,' he wrote in his diary in 1955 – 'because of the Divine intention behind what is, in fact, only a sacrificial rite in a still barbarian cult: a feeble creation of man's hands – but you have to give your all to this human dream for the sake of that which alone gives it reality.' About five years later – apparently at the time of the Soviet and other attacks on him over the Congo – he is sure that the victim in the sacrificial rite is himself:
>
> > I have watched the others:
> > Now I am the victim
> > Strapped fast to the altar
> > For sacrifice.

> Dumb, my naked body
> Endures the stoning, dumb
> When slit up and the live
> Heart is plucked out.[72]

It is remarkable that O'Brien failed to compare these two poems, which he quoted and analysed in print only seven years apart from one another. Each poem deals with a similar situation. In both we see a sacrificial victim who is stripped and strapped or handcuffed to a railing or an 'altar', ready to be stoned, and who is only one in a series. Second, we have a similarity of diction: both are primarily monosyballic and disyllabic and prominently feature the adjective 'dumb'. Third, we find the same poetic form in each: slender quatrains of two- and three-beat lines. The only real difference is context, and the distance between the contexts is the distance between parochialism and cosmopolitanism. On the global stage of the UN, poetry about Hammarskjöld's punishment offered a spiritual key to humanity's last, best hope. In Northern Ireland, however, poetry about Catholic women's punishment proved that sacred dramas only lead to terror. The strange double standard here reproduced one argument at the root of Arnoldian Celticism, namely that the Irish are predestined for political failure for reasons that can also be found in their artistic failures.

The contradiction in this formulation was more than just a double standard between his thoughts on Ireland and those about the UN. Even within those internationally focused works, O'Brien reproduces something like the Yeatsian friction between culture and emblem I have described in relation to *The Tower* in chapter one. In *To Katanga and Back*, and in the passage from *United Nations: Sacred Drama* quoted above, O'Brien described Hammarskjöld as a sacred dramatist in the positive, 'best-self' Arnoldian sense. Hammarskjöld's positive cult of personality, something like Parnell's before the split, features a transformative aura of reconciliation like that which Coleridge had attributed to the Sophoclean tragic chorus. In this way, the drama would coax forth the better self through aesthetic and religious experience.

This was not the only way O'Brien thought about Hammarskjöld in relation to the sacred drama, however. There was also a darker aspect that served as a reminder of human evil, and, therefore, also the moral limitations on political and social life. During the international furore after Lumumba's death, the Soviet Union denounced Hammarskjöld as an imperialist stooge, but supporters such as O'Brien stood by him. Over the course of the 1960s, however, O'Brien came to question this position, and in 1968 he published a play, *Murderous Angels*, that revisited the Secretary General's role in Lumumba's death in the mode of Greek tragedy. Hammarskjöld does not come off nearly as well in this work. When O'Brien makes his sacred drama centre on ethical questions rather than aesthetic (or ritual) ones, therefore, his outlook becomes much more pessimistic and he transitions from an Arnoldian vocabulary to a Nietzschean one. In this light, he stresses that even the most sincere faith in reconciliation is at best self-deluding because it merely hid (often from the self) the basic will for power that had inspired the conflict to begin with. Like the Nietzsche of *The Gay Science*, O'Brien came to see himself as a defender of the Enlightenment, albeit one with tragic wisdom. In his conclusion to *The Suspecting Glance*, a series of lectures on Machiavelli, Burke, Nietzsche and Yeats delivered in 1969, O'Brien emphasised this specific link between all of these writers, calling them 'suspicious' thinkers because they 'are profoundly aware of the resource and versatility of violence and deception in man, in society, and in themselves. They all believe most firmly in the existence of what Christians call original sin.'[73] This pessimism is sorely lacking among young members of the left because they tend to ignore 'what man is actually like' (by O'Brien's post-Katangan lights, at least) and, therefore, they make 'wildly optimistic assumptions about transforming man through education, or through revolution'.[74] O'Brien was at this point beginning to advise Northern Irish activists to be more suspicious of themselves, and he used the trappings of Arnoldian cultural Hellenism to do it.

The back and forth over *North* was not the first time O'Brien and Heaney had taken opposing sides in print. As early as October 1968, they had both published articles on the escalating events in Derry and Belfast in the same issue of *The Listener*. Not surprisingly, they offered opposing viewpoints. O'Brien blamed the civil rights protesters for provoking a unionist power structure that could only be expected to respond violently to their demands. Heaney, on the other hand, blamed the unionist political class for dismissing the civil rights protestors as communists and republicans, because they could only transform a liberal and non-violent movement into a radical and violent one by doing so.[75] Heaney grounded the argument of his article, 'Old Derry's walls', with a greater level of historical and cultural detail than O'Brien, who took a more abstract approach to the problem by employing an analogy between Northern Ireland and Sophocles' *Antigone*. This analogical argument suited O'Brien's purposes because it was universal rather than particular; it allowed him to speak about the crisis in an international context including the US, France, China and Czechoslovakia. O'Brien did not use the *Antigone* analogy because he thought Northern Ireland was uniquely tragic, but, rather, because he thought it summed up a global moment of which Northern Ireland was a part.

Likening the Northern civil rights protesters with Antigone and the unionist establishment with Creon, O'Brien warned that Antigone was playing with fire by challenging a delicate balance that kept civil war in Ireland at bay. 'The subordination of Catholic to Protestant in Derry', he wrote, 'is a result of force and the threat of force. The condition of Derry may be thought of as one of frozen violence: any attempt to thaw it out will liberate violence which is at present static.'[76] More than half the blame for the coming Troubles would be on Antigone/Bernadette Devlin's head: her 'free decision, and that alone . . . precipitated the tragedy', while 'Creon's responsibility was the more remote one of having placed this tragic power in the hands of a headstrong child of Oedipus.'[77] Having decided that Antigone's rash action was responsible for Creon's violence, therefore, O'Brien made the more moderate and practical-minded sister, Ismene, a key figure in the analogy.

O'Brien's primary focus in the 1968 article was not on advising Antigone how to act, but, rather, on addressing the larger question of how the smaller conflicts between little Antigones and little Creons all over the world might impact on the larger and more precarious balance between the two great Creons on either side of the Cold War. With this problem in mind, it was therefore important for O'Brien to represent the protesters as idealists rather than communist spies or republican propagandists. 'Creon and Antigone are both part of our nature', O'Brien wrote, 'inaccessible to advice, and incapable of living at peace in the city.'[78] This was just a part of political life – a problem even the Greeks had tangled with in Athens, the original laboratory for democracy and drama. Sophocles, moreover, had been correct in teaching us to respect the conscientious objector. 'Without Antigone', O'Brien therefore concluded the essay,

> we could attain a quieter, more realistic world. The Creons might respect one another's spheres of influence if the instability of idealism were to cease to present, inside their own dominions, a threat to law and order . . . At present every Creon thinks that some other Creon is behind the Antigone that is plaguing him. The communists, thinks Creon, are behind the student activists at Columbia: the CIA, thinks Creon, are behind the Czech intellectuals. We should be safer without the trouble-maker from Thebes. And that

> which would be lost, if she could be eliminated, is quite intangible: no more, perhaps, than a way of imagining and dramatising man's dignity. It is true that this way may express the essence of what man's dignity actually is. In losing it, man might gain peace at the price of his soul.[79]

It is understandable for you to send in the riot police, O'Brien tells Creon, but just realise that you are suppressing internal dissent (which is not really that terrible a thing in and of itself) rather than defending yourself against external enemies.

One of the many reasons O'Brien's *Antigone* article has been taken so seriously is that he wrote it during the very month in which historians have said the Troubles began. At the date of publication, People's Democracy was a fortnight old, and its marchers would not undergo the infamous loyalist attacks at Burntollet Bridge for more than another two months. The Provisional IRA would not split off from the Dublin-based Official IRA until more than a year later, and Bloody Sunday still lay three years away. By drawing his analogy at that moment, O'Brien was initiating a much longer conversation about a much larger crisis than he or many of his readers envisioned. The analogy would reverberate through intellectual discussions of the Troubles in Northern Ireland for decades, although the figures, and the stakes of the argument, would change significantly over time. When O'Brien initially published the critique, for instance, Creon was a stand-in for the unionist power structure in Northern Ireland. The British army intervened in the province in 1969, however, and in 1971 the British government introduced the infamous policy of internment without trial. In March 1972 it dissolved the Northern Ireland Parliament and instituted direct rule of the province.

Given the complexity and magnitude of these developments, the stakes and implications of the original analogy had changed drastically. One might not think so from the fact that he repeats the original article almost verbatim, but his comment on the essay registers a significant shift:

> Reading that essay now, three years afterwards, I find myself no longer in sympathy with the conclusion. Antigone is very fine on the stage, or in retrospect or a long way off, or even in real life for a single, splendid epiphany. But after four long years of Antigone and her under-studies and all those funerals – more than a hundred dead at the time of writing – you begin to feel that Ismene's commonsense and feeling for the living may make the more needful, if less spectacular element in 'human dignity'. In any case the play has

> been moving – like so much else in Northern Ireland – *backwards*, away from the ceremonial act of non-violent disobedience, and into the fratricidal war, which precedes the action of the play.[80]

O'Brien's major qualification here was that Antigone deserved less sympathy now than she had done several years before because she was responsible for so many more deaths. When we consider the shift in analogues, however, the article takes on new meanings. For instance: who was he talking about when he referred to Antigone's 'understudies'? Did O'Brien mean here the remnants of the non-violent civil rights movement, some members of whom would later be shot on Bloody Sunday for marching against the policy of internment without trial? Or would these 'understudies' include the IRA gunmen whom the British army would insist had been among the marchers, and whose supposed presence would be used to justify the massacre? The failure to distinguish between violent and non-violent opponents of British policy was very often, as in this case, responsible for the radicalisation of the former. This was a point Heaney had made in 'Old Derry's walls', and this makes that essay (which has never been reprinted) even more 'Tiresian' than O'Brien's, because in it he strongly recommends that the unionist establishment deal more justly with the civil rights movement so as not to radicalise the situation. Even in his own article, O'Brien identifies the writers of exactly this kind of argument as modern Tiresiases on account of the fact that their opinions were both correct and ignored. In 1972, however, he would no longer show sympathy with Antigone or allow the wisdom of Tiresias' advice; he would denounce them both as IRA sympathisers.

The most important shift in this analogy, however, was in its identification with Creon. Having entered the Dáil, O'Brien replaced the avuncular persona who advised his students at NYU to read more Burke just to know what the other side thought, and to read more Nietzsche so as not to assume the best about themselves, with the more visceral anti-republican polemic for which he is most often remembered today. He went, for instance, from simply giving lectures on Machiavellian ruthlessness to promoting authoritarian policies and, in some cases, overlooking ruthless and illegal behaviour. It was therefore chilling when he wrote in *States of Ireland* that current difficulties in the North would have been avoided if the original Ulster plantation had been more Machiavellian than it actually was.

O'Brien's *Antigone* essay, in both of its incarnations, neatly encapsulated the double standard inherent in his formulation of sacred drama. It was meant to be understood as a sacred drama of reconciliation, but it was not about reconciliation in Ireland, but, rather, one to prove a larger, more global point. It was instructive to know about from a distance, but unwise to dwell upon at home. In this sense, the Irish could generate, and even enact, sacred dramas that would help the process of reconciliation on the world stage, but these dramas could only spell disaster at their point of origin. The Irish might learn something from a Greek sacred drama, but even under optimal conditions this would only be a salutary reminder of their worst selves rather than an inspiring call to achieve their best selves. Once the Troubles were under way, however, O'Brien started to look at the Irish drama in a more specific way and realised from this that the *Antigone* model was not working there in the way he had predicted. The failure of the analogy might have prompted him to rethink the problem, but it did not. Instead, the disparity confirmed for O'Brien his original Arnoldian assumption that the Irish would never live up to any normative model of politics or aesthetics. Reconciliation would therefore remain an impossibility for them until the twin ideologies of culture and the state finally monopolised all violence and defined all possibilities of ethical life on either side of the border. In the next chapter, we will see that these would be the stakes of the Field Day Theatre Company's profound engagement with Sophoclean drama.

Chapter Three

Tom Paulin at the Gates of Thebes (and Derry and Hillsborough)

> Thebes has seven gates
> and the sun shines on each one:
> just take a look
> at the triangle
> and the compasses –
> dead clear they are,
> like an open book.
>
> Tom Paulin, chorus from *The Riot Act* (1985)[1]

> I waited outside the gate-lodge,
> waited like a dog
> in my own province
> till a policeman brought me
> a signed paper.
>
> Tom Paulin, 'An Ulster Unionist Walks the Streets of London' (1987)[2]

Nothing raises questions about political and cultural identity in quite the way a borderland does. Likewise, there is nothing like a Greek tragedy to draw our attention to the proximity between the origins of drama and democracy. In retrospect, therefore, the fact that Conor Cruise O'Brien had once used Sophocles' *Antigone* as an analogy for the Troubles in Northern Ireland, and then also to censor news coverage and public discussions of the crisis, seems profoundly counter-intuitive.[3] Particularly when we consider the prevalence of Hellenism on the Irish stage over the past thirty years, it is hard to understand how substantial discussions of Irish identity and politics could ever have been inhibited (rather than actually promoted) with reference to Sophocles.[4] We owe a large part of the difference between now and then, therefore, to the success of the Field Day Theatre Company. Field Day, in turn, owed to Tom Paulin the group's larger understanding of what re-appropriating Sophocles could mean during the Troubles.

In the 1980s Field Day prompted a major shift in Irish public discussions about Irish culture and politics, moving the conversation beyond O'Brien's polemics against the IRA into more searching ways of thinking about identity, history and conflict. This did not happen without controversy, and, therefore, a large part of this conversation had to do with the attempt to characterise Field Day itself.[5] As Seamus Deane told Dympna Callaghan in a 1993 interview, Field Day had 'been associated with terrorism by [Edna] Longley, Conor Cruise O'Brien, and all the usual suspects who have said that we're the cultural wing of the Provisional IRA'.[6] In the typescript for an unpublished essay on the company, moreover, Deane gave a more extended description of the hostile characterisations that had been aimed at the group, such as:

> . . . an elitist grouping of intellectuals preoccupied with arcane academicisms while Belfast burns, as defenders of or as subverters of the status quo, as a worthy little cultural fizzle, as a sort of nuclear anti-unionist and anti-protestant league. Most people do not know what Field Day is for or about and many have protested that it is either too vague to be interesting or too interesting to preserve its vagueness.[7]

The project started in 1980 when Brian Friel, a Derry Catholic, and the actor/director Stephen Rea, a Belfast Presbyterian, founded the group (which rhymes with 'Friel–Rae') in order to produce Friel's now-classic landmark of modern Irish drama, *Translations*.[8] In a 2006 interview with Cormac Ó Duibhne, Rea commented on what he valued about this first collaboration with Friel. 'In *Translations*', he told Ó Duibhne, the audience

> experienced the act of colonization, you saw these people losing everything. You saw the loss of language actually happening. And that is essentially political . . . all areas of that debate are in there . . . So, what that play does, the great value of drama, and I don't think I've ever seen it as poignantly and as clearly as at the opening of *Translations*, is that it offers ideas in an unthreatening way, it allows the audience to complete the ideas.[9]

Rea's enthusiasm for Friel's even-handed appeal to the audience's own critical faculties suggests that contemporary denunciations of Field Day's supposedly 'radical' ideology were overblown.[10] The premiere was also a major event in the cultural history of Northern Ireland because it brought together a fractured community; its audience contained prominent members from across the political spectrum, and they came together in the Guildhall of Derry, a highly symbolic setting which strongly emphasised the idea of civic art. The drama performed further service to a divided society, moreover, by dramatising Ulster's contested history in a way that questioned the assumptions about national and cultural identity underwriting either side of the conflict. In addition to playing this civic role in Derry itself, part of Field Day's original mission was to bring its theatrical tours to larger and smaller venues all over the island, thereby finding audiences that might not otherwise go to see dramatic performances.[11]

Inspired by the critical and popular success of *Translations*, Friel and Rea decided to turn what was initially conceived as a single project into an ongoing organisation. As they embarked on their first decade of theatrical and publishing projects, Friel and Rea invited a handful of notable cultural figures from the North of Ireland to form a board of directors and to take on a more ambitious programme. In addition to Seamus Heaney and Seamus Deane, both of whom had gone to St Columba's School in Derry with Friel, the augmented board included the poet Tom Paulin and the musician and television producer David Hammond. Later, this group was joined by the playwright Thomas Kilroy, who is from the Republic. As Deane told an interviewer in 1988, 'it quickly became obvious' to him, as a new board member,

> that Stephen and Brian had ideas of expanding beyond the Theatre, into publishing . . . and into creating in Field Day some kind of focus, nucleus, a group that would have a political and cultural . . . set of preoccupations. We knew that the pamphlets had to have as one of their preoccupations language and its use and its abuse and the political force which it had even in apparently innocent situations.[12]

Their two-pronged approach was aimed at raising the level of public conversation about the North of Ireland above what they saw as the stultifying hegemony of O'Brien, who, blaming the Northern crisis entirely upon the Provisional IRA, tendentiously argued for a military rather than a political solution. The pamphlets, like many of the plays, sought to complicate the simplistic notions of Irish character and identity that were seen to contribute to the ongoing conflict in the North.

Paulin's 1980 essay 'The making of a loyalist' initiated what would become a longer conversation among Field Day directors about Sophocles, beginning as a psychological assessment of Conor Cruise

O'Brien's career as a unionist commentator on Northern Ireland.[13] According to Paulin, O'Brien's politics reflected the insecurity of his colonised intellect, and he therefore required approval from the international community. Thus, Paulin accounted for the apparent contradiction between O'Brien's liberal cosmopolitanism and his conservative statism in Ireland. 'The making of a loyalist' was also a crucial essay in Paulin's own intellectual and political trajectory because it marked his conversion from a unionist to a nationalist perspective on Northern Ireland. Paulin explained this in an article for the *Independent on Sunday* to accompany a revival of *The Riot Act* in 2003. 'I first encountered the play as a teenager in Belfast', he wrote,

> in the city's innocent dreamtime in the mid-1960s . . . I went to a late night cinema in the city centre and saw a version in modern Greek, with subtitles . . . Then I read an essay by the great Shakespearian critic, AC Bradley – 'Hegel's Theory of Tragedy'. I began to see that the play had a philosophical as well as a historical and political meaning . . . As a student in England, I followed obsessively what was happening in the North of Ireland . . . [but] supported neither side . . . then in and about 1980, I read a book by O'Brien called *States of Ireland*, which drew centrally on Antigone . . . [and] realised that I did not agree with his interpretation . . . like O'Brien I had clung to the view that the Unionist state of Northern Ireland could be reformed. Without supporting violent attempts to change it, I came to the view that it was an indefensible statelet.[14]

In this account, we can see that, with remarkable symmetry, Paulin's psychological history of O'Brien's becoming an ex-Catholic intellectual unionist from the South has, as its own backstory, Paulin's own improbable 'making' as a Protestant Republican from the North.

Paulin also notes that O'Brien sympathises with Creon rather than Antigone because he is a proponent of the state. 'O'Brien's political analysis is inspired and supported by his interpretation of Sophocles' great tragedy', he writes,

> so it is crucial to recognise how badly he misinterprets the play. According to Hegel, for whom *Antigone* was 'the perfect exemplar' of tragedy, the sacred laws which Antigone revered are 'the instinctive Powers of Feeling, Love and Kinship, not the daylight gods of free and self-conscious, social and political life.' As Hegel shows, in the play 'neither the right of family, nor that of the state is denied; what is denied is the absoluteness of the claim of each.'[15]

Paulin's reading of the play is more critically productive than the relatively simple refutation of O'Brien would suggest, however. It is easy enough to criticise one person's reading of *Antigone* as a one-sided appropriation of a two-sided work, but this gesture alone merely skims the surface of Hegel's thinking about the play. When Paulin brings the Hegelian frame in to refute O'Brien, however, he is going beneath the surface – far enough to propose a new way of thinking about conflict in the North: not as a fight between civilians and barbarians, but as a conflict between legitimate ethical systems. Paulin has drawn upon this distinction in a number of places subsequently, and they have resonated with Deane and Heaney, who have repeated it in essays of their own.[16] In 'Field Day's Greeks (and Russians)', for instance, Deane expanded upon Paulin's reading of O'Brien, applying to a Thatcherite Creon who 'did invoke, in however vicious and suburban a spirit, the idea that the state had to obey ethical imperatives that were senior to all other ethical demands – familial, tribal, religious (sectarian) – by virtue of their universality and impartiality'.[17] In his reading of *Antigone*, however, Paulin actually plays O'Brien and Hegel off one another to recast the play as an ethical drama about identity.

In some ways, Paulin's reading of *Antigone* resonates with Patricia Jagentowicz Mills' Adornian and feminist response to Hegel's reading of the play.[18] First of all, she reminds us that, in Hegel, the Spirit progresses historically towards self-realisation through the sublation, or *Aufhebung*, of the universal and the particular. For Hegel, in the pagan world the universal and the particular cannot actually be reconciled because the former is in the masculine sphere of the polis, and the latter is in the female sphere of the family. Therefore, Creon and Antigone are evenly matched only because of the period in which they meet. In the modern world, by contrast, the Creons always have to win. Particularity is subsumed into the universal, and the progress of Spirit continues on its reconciled and reconciling way to ultimate self-realisation and the end of history. Mills therefore objects to Hegel's *Antigone* as an identarian narrative. 'Adorno's critique of Hegel', she writes, 'allows for the emergence of Antigone as the particular, the representation of difference, beyond the domination of a logic of identity.'[19] That is, Hegel admires how Antigone champions the traditional religious ethos of family (governed by women) in its resistance to the state (governed by men), but nevertheless argues that, even in their conflict, the two figures exist as 'a diverse self; and this contradicts the unity of the self, and constitutes their unrighteous and necessary destruction'.[20] Despite the power of its description of difference, Hegel's historical model does not respect Antigone's ethical claim forever. Like a colonial empire, the state sustains itself by 'consuming and absorbing into itself the separatism of the Penates, or the separation into independent families presided over by womankind, and by keeping them dissolved in the fluid continuity of its own nature'.[21] Mills has taken this moment in Hegel as a new point of departure. She maintains, however, that 'in criticizing Hegel's interpretation of the *Antigone*, we begin to see another story in Western philosophy, one other than that of Hegelian reconciliation: the revolt of the particular against the subsumption under a universal schema.'[22] In light of Mills' analysis, therefore, we can see that O'Brien's *Antigone* is actually more Hegelian than Paulin's is, in that it makes the modern Creon the inevitable winner.

When Paulin takes on the idea of 'daylight gods' and 'instinctive powers' to describe the Northern Irish Antigone, he is actually borrowing terms from a philosophical system whose identarian ends he does not ultimately endorse. He veers off from Hegel in placing Antigone's claim in the present; he makes her a modern rebel rather than an abstract emblem of some long-ago reconciled, *aufgehoben* particularity. In his own treatment of Sophocles' play, therefore, Paulin arrests Hegel's difference-annihilating reconciliation between Antigone's and Creon's ethical orders, and reframes the dynamic between them as a permanent element in the modern social experience that constructs us as split subjects. Paulin has also written that the Hegelian conflict makes up 'the DNA of social and civic life', whether we recognise it or not.[23] In another retrospective essay on *The Riot Act*, moreover, Paulin suggests that the conflict between Antigone and Creon is more obviously pronounced in relation to postcolonial subjectivity than in metropolitan political life. He writes:

> I knew that the conflict in the play is between what sociologists call *Gemeinschaft* – roughly the family – and *Gesellschaft*, which is civic or public life. It is rare to get this conflict within mainstream white British society, but many members of ethnic minorities appreciate that tension between those two worlds.[24]

That is, the opposition between 'daylight gods' and 'instinctive powers' is more obvious to 'ethnic minorities' than it is to 'mainstream white society', although the opposition is nevertheless present throughout modern life. In continuation of the quotation, Paulin gives a personalised source for this insight: 'For more than a quarter of a century I've been a member of an extended Indian family and have gained some appreciation of how opposed the two spheres are.'[25] Paulin adopts O'Brien's emphasis on Ismene, a crucial character whom Hegel never considers, although he does not really approve of her equivocations. When Paulin, actually following O'Brien, brings her into the equation, it has the effect of stalling the identarian narrative of Hegelian reconciliation.

In his *Antigone* allegory, O'Brien had advised Irish nationalists to take Ismene's advice to Antigone, and not resist Creon's law. Paulin reminded O'Brien, however, that Ismene eventually sides with Antigone. With the exception of Creon, who crumbles at the play's end, Ismene is the only major character who questions herself. Despite the emphasis Paulin places on Ismene, he does not heroise what he calls her 'classically liberal position'; rather, he suggests that Sophocles must have been critical of her because in ancient Athens 'there was a *nomos* (an understood law) which made it accepted practice not to remain neutral in a civil war'.[26] By Paulin's perspective, to be a liberal or seemingly apolitical Ismene makes one a de facto Creon. 'Some people are institutionalized', he has written about post-Thatcherite academic culture: 'they aren't Creons, but they are his shadows, his clones.'[27]

Just as the situation, and, therefore, also the applicability of the *Antigone* analogy, had developed significantly between the publication of O'Brien's article in 1968 and 1972, huge changes had, of course, also taken place between 1972 and 1984. In 1976, for instance, the British government revoked republican and loyalist paramilitary prisoners' special-category status. Over the next several years, this led to various kinds of protests – mainly by republicans – from 'blanket protests' and 'dirty protests' to, most horrifyingly, the IRA hunger strikes of 1981.[28] Despite the international pressures brought upon Margaret Thatcher's government to negotiate with the republican leadership inside the prison, the Prime Minister infamously held fast. It would, therefore, be her image as the 'Iron Lady', steadfastly refusing the symbolic demands of republican prisoners at Long Kesh, that became the inevitable modern analogy for Creon. Deane later linked Paulin's 1984 play explicitly to the IRA hunger strikes, which he likened to

> some kind of terrifying public theatre. So yes, *The Riot Act* was an adaptation of the great theatre that was going on . . . in the streets, so to say . . . This is a critical point in Northern Irish history and this play was critical for much that Field Day was talking about because . . . a transformation actually had begun.[29]

When he talks about 'the street', Deane is referring to the various ways in which the mainstream of Irish nationalist opinion, which had for most of the Troubles refrained from endorsing the IRA's violence, showed their solidarity with the prisoners' demands – not just by attending funeral and protest marches, but also by voting for the hunger strikers in parliamentary elections both in Northern Ireland and in the Republic.

The major transformative aspect of the hunger-strike era, therefore, was that it led to Sinn Féin's entry into the political process. This was probably the most desperate moment of the entire Troubles, but Sinn Féin's electoral victories were, nevertheless, important steps for both communities' progress towards the Belfast Agreement of 1998. This was not a time, however, in which people felt the language of reconciliation was particularly realistic. 'When you get a politics outside of democracy', Paulin told one interviewer, 'then it's a tragic politics and you have to choose one position or the other . . . I chose Republicanism. I don't and never did support violence but it did come down to having to choose.'[30]

In a hostile review of *The Riot Act*, Fintan O'Toole identified Paulin's play with the essential dynamic of Field Day, but this was because both reflected the same ethical and intellectual shortcomings. 'By choosing to do a version of *Antigone*', O'Toole asserted,

> Field Day cannot but have been drawn by the political resonances of the play in modern Ireland . . . The area where myths and modern realities meet is the territory Field Day has staked out for itself . . . But just as Field Day has entered the political arena without stating all of the political consequences of its stance, Tom Paulin's version of *Antigone* exploits the resonances of the classical text without clarifying them. It goes half way and ends up in something of a theatrical never-never land. For the sake of the modern resonances much of the theatricality of the original *Antigone* is lost.[31]

The charge that Paulin's play suffered from the company's political bias was echoed frequently in other reviews. For O'Toole, the idea of political ideology and 'theatricality' are closely aligned, but this was an alignment that Rea, the play's director, told Patrick Quilligan that he was trying to avoid.[32] Rea acknowledged the play's contemporary political resonances but would not 'spell out the parallels in recent Irish history' because this might 'prejudice' the audience upon 'the artistic merits of the play'.[33] These unspoken parallels were obviously between Antigone's symbolic self-sacrifice and those of the IRA hunger strikers at Long Kesh; 'there is a sense in *Antigone*', he explained, 'that if you respond to a fixed position by a Government, in this case Creon, your response is in some way evil or subversive . . . [but] Apart from the obvious political relevance for us, it's a great play translated by an Irish poet and we want it to be primarily theatrical.'[34] Perhaps because of these inevitable prejudices in a strongly polarised atmosphere, however, a number of reviewers attacked the performance as being compromised by political bias on the company's part. Peter Thompson of the *Irish Press*, for instance, called the play 'mercilessly didactic'.[35]

The reviewer in one unionist newspaper, the *Northern Constitution*, complained that *The Riot Act* 'wasn't Sophocles liberated into the modern milieu, it was Sophocles chained to the parish pump'.[36] Whatever he or she thought of the Field Day production, the reviewer nevertheless believed Sophocles would have had a good perspective on Northern Ireland because he recognised 'the necessity for tyranny'.[37] Ironically, the reviewer also praised the actor who played Creon for doing 'more than adequately what was asked' by the director – apparently without knowing that both the actor and the director were Stephen Rea.[38] The mistake suggests that perhaps Field Day may not have been as one-sidedly radical as its critics often accused it of being. Field Day's primarily agreed-upon goal, both as a touring theatre company and as a publishing house, was to call its various audiences to recognise and rethink the seemingly given identity formations underlying their own contributions to the breakdown of Irish civil society. As Rea had put it to Quilligan, 'politics is an important ingredient but not the only one. We tour the whole country in an attempt to reach a fresh identity that will contain everyone and in that we are political.'[39] If Irish audiences could find ways to think about identity as being fluid, of subject positions as being split, then they would be in far better positions to think around and past as well as through it.

When critics dismissed Paulin's own politics as being too biased, however, they missed the underlying questions about identity and reconciliation in his work at that time. That is, the concept of 'daylight gods' in Paulin's creative work is not reducible to the idea of a state power he rejects. Rather, they provide Paulin with critical coordinates for articulating his own paradoxical identity formation.[40] This connection is prominent in *Liberty Tree*, a collection he opens with the poem 'Under Creon'.[41] This poem revisits the connections between Ulster Protestantism and Irish republicanism through a reading of *Antigone*. (The next year, Paulin would place 'Under Creon' in the theatre programme for Field Day's *Riot Act* tour.) In the poem, Paulin figures himself as a lone figure wandering in the night 'below a mountain' – namely, Belfast's Cave Hill,[42] an iconic site for Irish republicans because it is where two founding figures of Irish republicanism, Theobald Wolfe Tone (a Dublin Anglican) and Henry Joy McCracken (a Belfast Presbyterian), met in 1795 to swear an oath that they would raise a united Irish rebellion against English rule. In the aftermath of the United Irishmen's disastrous 1798 rising, moreover, McCracken was arrested on Cave Hill. In the poem's middle two stanzas, Paulin describes how:

> At neapish hour, I searched out gaps
> in that imperial shrub; a free voice sang
> dissenting green, and syllables spoke
> holm oaks by a salt shore, their dark tangs
> glistening like Nisus in a night attack.
>
> The daylight gods were never in this place
> And I had pressed beyond my usual dusk
> to find a cadence for the dead: McCracken,
> Hope, the northern starlight, a death mask
> and the levelled grave that Biggar traced;[43]

During the 'neapish hour' in which he walks, the waters of Belfast Lough are balanced precisely between the high and low tides. He is finding a kind of balance and freedom, but he is out there in the dark by himself. The 'free voice' is an elusive, reconciled version of the poet himself, in that it is both green (as in nationalist) and dissenting (as in Dissenting Protestant sects). Retrieving this identity, moreover, will also mean taking apart the monolithic identity formations of the 'imperial shrub', getting away from 'the daylight gods' so that he can 'find a cadence for the dead' Protestant nationalists such as the Ulster Presbyterians Henry Joy McCracken, James Hope and Joseph Biggar.[44] His predecessors, the earlier 'dissenting green' voices, suggest the lost chances of Irish reconciliation throughout history, and they may also suggest possibilities of future reconciliation on the other side of Creon's identarian reign. He is still finding a dissenting green song for himself, and for the Orangemen he knows will not want to hear it.

For Paulin, at least, the largely submerged tradition of Irish Protestant republicanism means following one's conscience in the most uncompromising of ways and reconciling daylight with the night. The speaker looks for, or to, the 'northern starlight', a reference to the United Irishmen's newspaper, the *Northern Star*, the reading of which was a highly political act in the 1790s. This paper was also published by Ulster Presbyterians, and this was one of the things that got William Orr executed. Paulin, therefore, identifies with Antigone as a figure of radical dissent, much like that of his own hero, John Bunyan, the puritan author of *A Pilgrim's Progress*, who chose to sit in an English jail for seventeen years rather than sign an oath not to preach. Coming at the Sophoclean material from that perspective, Paulin's *The Riot Act* is very conscious of Ismene's liberalism, but is not nearly as sympathetic with it as Heaney was.

As the poem ends, the speaker admits that he has not got the song right yet, but does not give up hope. 'Maybe one day I'll get the hang of it', he concludes,

> and find joy, not justice, in a snapped connection,
> that Jacobin oath on the black mountain.[45]

The play on words in 'find joy' – meaning 'to find satisfaction in what you are looking for' on one hand, and retrieving a critically and creatively productive version of Henry *Joy* McCracken on the other – suggests that the singer will have to come up with an aesthetic model to complete his historical and philosophical retrieval of Presbyterian republicanism.

Paulin described a similar search for joy again when he told the story of the set design for the Field Day production of *The Riot Act*. At one point in rehearsals, the set designer resigned, and Paulin was, to some extent, relieved because he found the existing set 'too ethnic Irish'.[46] The rehearsals were in Derry, and Paulin recounts getting up early to think with his feet about a new set. His early-morning trek through the centre of Derry sounds in a number of respects just like the one the speaker takes outside Belfast in 'Under Creon'. 'I woke at five', Paulin writes,

> got out of bed and walked through the silent city. I looked up at the Victorian gothic Guildhall – *no joy there*. Then something led me down a street I didn't know – Great James Street – and I found myself in front of a disused Presbyterian church. It was a perfect, neo-classical meeting house, which represented *more than a daylight god*. When the new designer, Brien Vehey [sic], arrived, I took him to the church, and then later we got hold of a book of Jefferson's architectural drawings and a new Enlightenment set emerged.[47]

When we consider Paulin's conjunction of Sophoclean meditations with the paradoxical history of Protestant republicanism, his 'new Enlightenment set' in Derry also suggests the setting up of a new Irish Enlightenment.[48] What he comes up with is a profoundly reconciling image. He looks at the Guildhall, which is the seat of local government in Derry, and also where every one of the Field Day tours (but one) has begun. Paulin rejects its Victorian aesthetics and pushes back to the eighteenth century: to Thomas Jefferson, and to Presbyterian neo-classical meeting-house architecture. The tantalising difference between this set-design history and the poet's trajectory in 'Under Creon' is the status of the Hegelian 'daylight gods'. That is, in the poem Paulin goes to where the daylight gods have never been; but in the disused Presbyterian church he finds a place where the daylight god (now meaning a specifically Presbyterian God) is not the only god. This set, balancing Sophocles' *nomous chthonos* ('laws of the earth') with his *dikan theôn* ('justice of the gods'), as they appear in the play's famous 'Wonders of Man' chorus, represents an aesthetics in which Paulin can find joy.[49]

Part of Hegel's inspiration for describing the ethical conflict in *Antigone* comes from the distinctions both the protagonist and the chorus make between the dark laws of the earth and the daylight laws of Zeus. Sophocles does not oppose these laws to one another in quite the way that Hegel opposes the 'instinctive powers' to the 'daylight gods' in his *Aesthetics*, but Paulin splits the difference in *The Riot Act*. The clearest example of this comes when Antigone is first brought before Creon, and she defends her decision to bury her brother at the risk of execution:

> It was never Zeus
> made that law.
> Down in the dark earth
> there's no law says,
> 'Break with your own kin,
> go lick the state.'
> We're bound to the dead:
> we must be loyal to them.
> I had to bury him.[50]

Hugh Lloyd-Jones' prose translation reads:

> It was not Zeus who made this proclamation, nor was it Justice who lives with the gods below that established such laws among men, nor did I think your proclamations strong enough to have power to overrule, moral as they were, *the unwritten and unfailing ordinances of the gods* [*agrapta theon . . . nomima*]. For these have life, not simply today and yesterday, but for ever, and no one knows how long ago they were revealed.[51]

What Paulin preserves from the original is Antigone's acknowledgement of two distinct sources of what modern philosophy would call 'natural law'. One comes from out of the sky and one from under the ground, but both contradict Creon's proclamation to 'go lick the state'. This appeal to unwritten law against the modern rationalist state constituted a major element of Burke's *Reflections on the Revolution in France*, but this clipped, spitting translation of Antigone's defiant speech into Ulster English is distinctively Paulin's own.

The more famous passage from Sophocles' *Antigone* dealing with the sky laws and the underground gods, however, is the 'Wonders of Man' chorus. This chorus has a special place in Northern Irish poetry. Stressing the natural law element of the play, Heaney has invoked and translated this chorus as a human rights poem.[52] In his early poem 'Glengormley', moreover, Derek Mahon imitated this chorus to satirise modern life, and noted that the bygone Antigones, 'those unreconciled in their metaphysical pain', had long since been dispatched so that the Creons of the world could erect the dreary suburbs in which we congratulate ourselves for being modern humans.[53] He recognises that heroic people have died resisting the dull modernity in which we sit today, as banal a triumph of Hegelian reconciliation as could be feared or imagined. Paulin's translation in *The Riot Act* reflects Mahon's sentiment, but in a way that fits with the drama because it shows up the chorus' easy acceptance of Creon's claims to reason and the state.

> There are many wonders on this earth
> and man has made most of them;
> though only death has baffled him
> he owns the universe, the stars,
> *sput* satellites and great societies.
>
> Fish pip inside his radar screens
> and foals kick out of a syringe:
> he bounces on the dusty moon
> and chases clouds about the sky
> so they can dip on sterile ground.
>
> By pushing harder every way,
> by risking everything he loves,
> he makes us better, day by day:
> we call this progress and it shows
> we're damned near perfect![54]

Like Mahon, Paulin jokes about the hollow pretensions of reason and the state in the face of real tragedy, but he leaves out the natural-law argument against Creon that comes later in the chorus, and which Lloyd-Jones renders thus in prose:

> Skilful beyond hope is the contrivance of his art, and he advances sometimes to evil, at other times to good. *When he applies the laws of the earth and the justice the gods have sworn to uphold he is high in the*

> *city; outcast from the city is he with whom the ignoble consorts because of his recklessness.* May he who does such things never sit by my hearth or share my thoughts![55]

As with Antigone's previously described speech, Sophocles again has the chorus distinguish between the '*dikan theon*' and the underground '*nomous chthonos*'. Heaney, whose thinking about *Antigone* was heavily influenced by Paulin, nevertheless paid a great deal more attention to this natural-law argument when he translated the chorus under the name of 'Sophoclean' in the *New Yorker* as a kind of 'open letter' to US President George W. Bush, whose administration was preparing the invasion of Iraq in 2003.[56]

Paulin would continue to think about that chorus even after he wrote *The Riot Act*, however. More specifically, he considered the warning aspect when the chorus announces that the man who ignores justice will be exiled from the human community. Sophocles states the warning antithetically. The leader who respects the divine laws will be 'high in the city' – or '*hypsipolis*'; if he ignores them, however, he will be 'outcast from the city' – or '*apolis*'.[57] The Sophoclean balance between *hypsipolis* and *apolis* neatly suggests that the city will 'un-city' its highest citizen. The economy of this antithesis clearly appealed to Paulin, and while he did not go back and retranslate the 'Wonders of Man' chorus when he reprinted it in *Fivemiletown* (1987), he nevertheless integrated its most interesting term into 'The Caravans on Lüneberg Heath', the long poem with which he concluded the book. This poem concentrates on various displacements and humiliations in the religious, political and cultural history of Central Europe – running from the seventeenth-century Defenestration of Prague, to Martin Heidegger's disgrace after the Second World War.[58] One of its Heidegger sections begins with an image of

> the West's last thinker, part woodcutter
> and part charlatan
> is digging trenches on the Rhine
> – lonely uncanny violent
> the artist and the leader
> without expedients
> *apolis*
> without structure and order
> among all that is –[59]

This was a much-deserved humiliation in Paulin's eyes, but he appreciated the pathos of a Creon who has become un-citied. *Fivemiletown* makes analogies between *Antigone* and the Troubles, but it also makes analogies with the history of the Reformation – particularly in his poem 'The Defenestration of Hillsborough', which is about the Anglo-Irish ('Hillsborough') Agreement of 1985. In his poems about this event, Paulin concentrated on one particular unionist MP, namely Harold McCusker.

The Official Unionist Party (OUP) MP from Armagh (later, Upper Bann), McCusker was a moderately friendly voice towards Field Day (who were seen as being too green for many unionists to like). In an episode of the BBC's *Arena* programme on Field Day's 1988 tour of Brian Friel's play *Making History*, McCusker gave an interview saying that he 'could sympathise' in some limited ways with the Field Day presentation of the sixteenth-century Irish rebel leader Hugh O'Neill because O'Neill had been trying

> to hold onto a way of life that he realized was slipping from him. And I can identify with him because in many ways Unionists in Northern Ireland today are trying to hold onto a Unionist way of life which they feel is slowly slipping away from them. On the other hand, the tactics he [O'Neill] uses . . . are more akin to the tactics used by my political opponents.[60]

McCusker died of cancer in 1990, and his seat in Parliament was subsequently won by David Trimble of the OUP, the politician who would share the 1998 Nobel Peace Prize with John Hume. Paulin was particularly interested in, and even moved by, McCusker's opposition to the Anglo-Irish Agreement, and used his speech against it as the conclusion to the section on Northern Protestantism he was currently editing for *The Field Day Anthology*.[61] Collecting this material as an Irish genre, to be studied alongside other varieties of Irish writing, was a political gesture on Paulin's part; it said a great deal about his own identity formation because it included Ulster Protestants in a larger, productively heterodox formation of Irishness. Paulin's gesture was inclusive in the sense that it insisted on a place for Protestants in a larger narrative of Irish identity, but it could also be seen as coercive because the vast majority of Northern Protestants would prefer to distance themselves from any ideas of Irish national identity.

In constructing this narrative of questionable reconciliation, Paulin begins with several selections from William Drennan, one of the founders of the United Irishmen. Paulin's first selection, therefore, was Drennan's letter suggesting the formation of a republican secret society, 'a benevolent conspiracy' aimed at 'Real Independence to Ireland', which would be like a 'caisson in the dark and troubled waters, a stable unseen power'.[62] Paulin pays special attention to Drennan's metaphor of the United Irishmen as the 'caisson'. As he writes in his editorial introduction, Drennan's caisson 'is ambiguous and revealing' because it can mean 'a water-tight chest, used in the foundations of bridges in deep water', but it 'also means an explosive device'.[63] So it suggests both 'stability, secrecy, political and intellectual power, a new international order' on one hand, and yet on the other hand it is also 'the embodiment of active revolutionary energy and enthusiasm'.[64] Paulin identifies this ambiguous 'caisson' with 'a type of protestant imagination' springing 'ultimately from Pauline theology . . . fuse[ing] the personal life with the civic life'.[65] This Pauline fusion, of course, acts as a possible reconciliation between the Hegelian/Sophoclean 'daylight gods' and the corresponding 'instinctive powers' of private life. Drennan's caisson runs through Paulin's section – from Drennan through Henry Cooke and Edward Carson to Ian Paisley and Harold McCusker – and provides the basis of what Paulin will end his introduction by calling a kind of rhetoric, politics, ethics and aesthetics of 'Protestant écriture'.[66]

The aesthetic argument of Paulin's *Field Day Anthology* section on 'Northern Protestant oratory and writing' complements the historical one because both lead to the Anglo-Irish Agreement and address the daunting challenge of getting unionist consent, beyond 'Ulster Says No' protest politics, towards the peace process that would continue in the 1990s. The section ends with Harold McCusker's 'Waiting like a dog: the gates of Hillsborough' speech, which he delivered in the House of Commons one week after the signing of the Anglo-Irish Agreement in November 1985. This speech exemplifies the politics and poetics of caisson, from its powerful opening narration of Pauline witness, to its conclusive, chilling threats of violence against the British state and Irish nationalists alike. After a two-paragraph exordium about how the speaker hopes to convey his 'bitterness . . . with dignity', McCusker gives a three-paragraph narrative of personal witness, made powerfully memorable by his repeated descriptions of himself going to, or standing outside, the gates of Hillsborough Castle on Friday 15 November and 'waiting like a dog' while the British and Irish governments signed the Anglo-Irish Agreement.[67] Eliding the bulk of the paragraphs, I will quote McCusker's powerful repetition:

> I went to Hillsborough on the Friday morning, despite the obstacles put in my way . . . I stood outside Hillsborough, not waving a Union flag – I doubt whether I will ever wave one again – not singing hymns, saying prayers or protesting, *but like a dog* and asked the

> Government to put in my hand the document that sold my birthright . . . I stood in the cold outside the gates of Hillsborough castle and waited for them to come out and give me the agreement second hand . . . I felt desolate because as I stood in the cold outside Hillsborough castle everything that I held most dear turned to ashes in my mouth.[68]

Paulin discussed McCusker's speech in the *Arena* interview. 'I was very moved' by it, he said, because 'there was something classic about . . . the way it articulated . . . a terrible feeling of historical betrayal.' Continuing on this theme, Paulin expressed his fascination with how

> the Loyalist imagination . . . goes out naked into the world and . . . testifies . . . [and] breaks through . . . conventional ways of speaking . . . [although] I suppose if you want a civilised society you've got to say no [to] unparliamentary language . . . But that means [in Northern Ireland] everybody's got to agree on a common language. That hasn't happened yet. So . . . because the . . . loyalists are . . . so much less sophisticated than the nationalist community . . . in the way in which they present themselves in public that they . . . say extraordinary things and write amazing letters to the newspapers . . . in which a whole political . . . subconscious comes out.[69]

For Paulin, the creative engagement with, and even promotion of, radical dissent actually prefigures a kind of path towards Irish reconciliation because the cause of Irish reunification, in fact, depends upon a kind of dissenters' consent. For this ever to happen, the notion of Irish identity would have to be reimagined, and the notion of political reconciliation itself would have to be reimagined. Paulin also wrestles with the knowledge that this idea of reconciliation is also coercive, and he tries to engage with it on the level of poetic language and as a cultural historian.[70]

In *Fivemiletown*, Paulin included a poem inspired by this speech, 'An Ulster Unionist Walks the Streets of London'. In his own clipped fashion, he includes McCusker's refrain: 'I waited outside the gate-lodge, / waited like a dog / in my own province'.[71] In this reference to the 'gate-lodge' of Hillsborough, Paulin plays once again with the *Antigone* analogy. In *The Riot Act*, the first chorus introduces the setting and mentions the seven gates of Thebes that had been successfully defended from a siege only the day before.[72] This would have suggested not just Thebes but also the walled city of Derry – and its own never-forgotten siege in the seventeenth century. By retrieving that chorus and inserting it as an epigraph to *Fivemiletown*, however, the Theban gates now suggest Hillsborough rather than Derry. In this scenario, the Protestants are actually locked outside rather than fighting off a siege from within. The image of a Protestant locked outside the gates somewhere in Ulster is as powerful an image of a man *apolis* as Paulin could have conjured. The poem ends, of course, with McCusker wandering through Kentish Town,

> walk[ing] the streets
> like a half-foreigner
> among the London Irish.
> What does it feel like?
> I wanted to ask them –
> what does it feel like
> to be a child of that nation?[73]

On one level, the unionist speaker in the poem is asking a rhetorical question: Isn't it a sad state of affairs that the London Irish are allowed on some level to be more British than the Ulster unionists themselves? On another level, however, the question could be the beginning of a dialogue about identity.

In this particular poem, and other selections from this powerful volume of poems about identity, Paulin recognises his fellow Protestants' sense of betrayal at the agreement between Thatcher's government and that of the Irish Republic. He recognises that this is coercive, but he also believes there is a reality of the situation that unionists will have to recognise. In 'The Defenestration of Hillsborough', a companion piece to 'An Ulster Unionist Walks the Streets of London', Paulin begins with a unionist speaker, perhaps McCusker, announcing to his friend: 'Here we are on a window ledge / with the idea of a race', and the poem ends with the speaker's realisation that 'we have a choice: / either to jump or get pushed'.[74] There were several defenestrations of Prague; in the poem itself Paulin mentions Tomáš Masaryk, the first president of Czechoslovakia, whose son Jan had probably been pushed, at the behest of the country's new communist leadership, when he fell from a tall window in 1948. Given Paulin's interest in the Reformation, however, it is more likely that he was thinking of one of the earlier defenestrations. The first defenestration took place in 1419 and precipitated the Hussite Wars. The second came in 1618 and helped lead to the Thirty Years War. Paulin is not suggesting that Ulstermen on the figurative ledge at Hillsborough are about to die, but, rather, that they are about to be coerced into a united Ireland. This would suggest, therefore, that he is thinking of the second defenestration – the one in which the Catholics who were pushed out of the window at Prague Castle did not actually die. Catholics later held that the Catholic lords regent were saved by angels, while Protestants joked that they only survived by landing on an enormous mound of horse manure. If Paulin's allegory suggests that Ulster unionists such as McCusker will have to face the reality of a united Ireland, he is not pretending this 'reconciliation' will smell like a rose.

One of the things that made *Antigone* in the 1980s such a powerful lever against the O'Brienite hegemony of the 1970s was that it allowed one to catch the former minister for posts and telegraphs in a major critical blunder about a canonical play whose relevance to modern politics and philosophy appears to be limitless; this, of course, highlighted the inflexibility of his thought about a complex political and cultural environment. Furthermore, given the extraordinary number of modern thinkers who have placed Antigone at the centre of their thinking about such things as gender, politics, ethics or psychology, O'Brien may just as plausibly have allowed his unionist allegory to depend upon the equally untenable notion that there was only one correct way to stage *Hamlet*. By reclaiming *Antigone* from O'Brien, Paulin showed how the Irish writer could, for the first time since Yeats had fastened the Arnoldian connection during the 1920s, disconnect Hellenism from the ideology of the state.[75]

And while Paulin disdained the figure of Ismene, he also opened up ways of thinking about her that resonated deeply with other members of the Field Day board. The themes were already there in *Translations*, even though Friel would not yet have been aware of Paulin's tangle with O'Brien. The Ismene position was immediately recognisable to Heaney at the time of the hunger strikes, however. In 'Title deeds', a 2004 lecture about how he came to write his own version of the play *The Burial at Thebes*, Heaney also quotes Hegel by way of Paulin to discuss the traumatic moment in 1981 when the RUC (Royal Ulster Constabulary) turned over the body of Francis Hughes, an IRA hunger striker, to a crowd of family and republican sympathisers at Toomebridge. Heaney describes the situation as having had a fundamentally Sophoclean character. 'If ever there was a dramatisation', Heaney told his audience at Harvard,

> of the contest between what Hegel called the 'Instinctive Powers of Feeling, Love and Kinship' and 'the daylight gods of free and self-conscious, social, and political life,' it was that evening when the hearse with its police escort arrived on the village street and the cordon that surrounded it was jostled in fury and indignation by the waiting crowd. The surge of rage in the crowd as they faced the

> police that evening was more than ideological. It did of course spring from political disaffection, but it sprang also from a sense that something inviolate had been assailed by the state.[76]

Heaney is going back to the original Field Day Sophoclean moment of identifying Thatcher's government with Creon, but he is not figuratively identifying Francis Hughes with Antigone. Rather, he is identifying Hughes with Polynices, the dead brother for whom Antigone is willing to die in order to perform the burial rites. The outraged crowd are not so much a crowd of Antigones either, but, rather, a group of people who are in Antigone's and Ismene's situation. Their 'instinctive powers of feeling, love, and kinship' are being violated by the state, but it is an open question at that moment as to how each individual might respond.

By identifying Hughes with Polynices, therefore, Heaney stakes out his characteristically middle ground. In Sophocles, neither Antigone nor Ismene try to justify Polynices' cause; they had two brothers die on either side of what was essentially a Theban civil war. Rather than taking a side between Polynices and Eteocles, the sisters long to see burial rites conducted for *both* brothers and not just for the one whose side won. Likewise, Antigone's conflict with Creon is not political in the sense that she cares who sits at the head of state. It is deeply political, however, in the sense that she insists upon a limit to state power as such. Sophocles gives us no sense that Polynices had a just cause; in fact, if we look to the prequel *Oedipus at Colonus*, it becomes clear that neither brother did. If Polynices had won the battle and denied burial to Eteocles, Antigone would have found herself with the same problem. She objects to an impious rigidity in the state, and this was the problem many nationalists inside and outside of the republican movement had with Margaret Thatcher's persona as 'Iron Lady'.

At the time of the hunger strikes, as Heaney describes it, his ethical and rhetorical position was very much that of an Ismene: largely sympathetic to Antigone's complaints against Creon, but not expressing those sympathies publicly for fear of the political consequences. He describes the ethical and rhetorical situation for liberal nationalists as being challenging and compromising. Like many, Heaney 'felt cautious about expressing public support, however noble their sacrifice', for the hunger strikers.[77] As he put it,

> Support for their fast could be read by the IRA and others as support for their violent methods, so many people hesitated. But in their hesitation they were painfully aware that they were giving silent assent to the intransigence and overbearing of Margaret Thatcher,

> who stated with a too brutal simplicity that 'Crime is crime, is crime. It is not political.'[78]

In another essay, 'Frontiers of writing', Heaney describes the experience of learning about Hughes' death while he was himself at the 'quintessentially Oxford experience' of a college dinner.[79] Heaney's family had known the Hughes family for generations, and as a young man he had known the sister and father, although he did not know the man himself. Heaney did not share this information with his hosts, and, indeed, that night he slept in rooms that had once been occupied by one of Thatcher's Tory ministers. This story exemplifies what Heaney called the 'almost unseemly . . . scruple' that liberal nationalists came to show in that polarising atmosphere.[80] Heaney found himself in Ismene's position, wanting to express support for the Hughes family while not wishing to express or even be seen to express solidarity with the IRA's use of violence. This was the moment for *The Riot Act*, but the moment for *The Cure at Troy* was coming. Heaney's poetry in the 1980s, which will be the topic of our next chapter, is about how he felt his way through that impasse by devising a poetics of human rights.

Chapter Four

Seamus Heaney's Poetics of Human Rights

> It is a private, quiet recognition . . . that you are placed in the Republic of Conscience whether you like it or not.
>
> Mary Lawlor, former executive of Amnesty International's Irish Section[1]

> Art is the negative knowledge of the actual world.
>
> Theodor Adorno, 'Reconciliation under duress'[2]

In 'Human rights, poetic redress', an article that first appeared in *The Irish Times* on the sixtieth anniversary of the United Nations Universal Declaration of Human Rights, Seamus Heaney commented on the wording of the declaration's first article, which reads: 'All human beings are born free and equal in dignity and rights. They are endowed with reason and conscience and should act towards one another in a spirit of brotherhood.'[3] He was responding as a poet critic, as a canonical writer, and as a utopian political thinker:

> In the boldness and buoyancy of these words there are echoes of many of the great foundational texts of western civilisation, from Sophocles' 'wonders of man' chorus through Christ's Sermon on the Mount on up to the American Declaration of Independence and the French Declaration of the Rights of Man. So even if this First Article cannot guarantee what it declares, if its writ cannot be made to run in China or Zimbabwe or Guantánamo, it nevertheless gestures so confidently towards what human beings desire that it fortifies a conviction that the desirable can in fact be realised.[4]

It is strange that while much has been written about the political content of Heaney's poetry in relation to the Troubles in Northern Ireland, his advocacy for human rights has been largely overlooked by scholars. This oversight is even stranger when we consider that Heaney's association with Amnesty International began in the early 1980s, during what were perhaps the darkest days of the Troubles. It is as if Heaney's engagement with the language of human rights, despite its obvious significance to his political poetry for decades, has remained literally invisible from a critical point of view.

How can we explain this oversight? Even in *Stepping Stones*, the interviewer Dennis O'Driscoll only asks about Heaney's connection to Amnesty International twice, and each time in passing.[5] In one of these instances, the interviewer remarks upon how strange it seems to him that Heaney's 'From the Republic of Conscience' is such a good poem, despite the fact that it had been written as a commission. Apparently, not even Heaney himself seems to think that the reader of *Stepping Stones* will have any interest in his human rights advocacy. And yet the rich ideas put forward in 'Human rights, poetic redress' are consistent with a great deal of the thinking behind his poetry and criticism since 1985 (at the very latest). These ideas are especially relevant to any historical understanding of his two staged versions of Sophoclean drama. When Heaney says that the declaration's first article sounds like Sophocles to him, how can we continue to read his Sophocles *without* the first article in mind?[6]

In a country with a long-term cultural, political and, indeed, psychological investment in the human rights idea, Heaney was at least as visible as U2's Bono as a cultural advocate for it. From its beginnings with Seán MacBride, Amnesty International has had a long presence in Ireland. During the Troubles, it reported on human rights abuses by the IRA as well as by the British government.[7] It is likely, then, that Heaney had been attracted to this organisation not just because it allows a principled perspective on the violence of both sides in Northern Ireland, but also because it takes a global perspective as well. Heaney's association with Amnesty, therefore, represented a significant dimension of his public persona in Ireland, and it was ultimately responsible for the profoundest transformation in his political reputation, from being the poet whom Ciarán Carson in 1975 called 'the laureate of violence' to becoming the de facto laureate of the Northern Irish peace process.[8]

During the 1980s Heaney formulated a model of human rights poetry that he distinguished from the poetry of witness. He based this formulation on a key insight that the poetic uses of memory and witness must be carefully qualified in order to speak responsibly to the different contexts of human rights violations. Any responsible poetry about Northern Ireland, Heaney seems to have decided, would have to recognise the context of a violent conflict where the only realistic solution might be reached through political negotiation rather than by military victory. In such a situation, the would-be poet of witness must consider to what ends his/her poetic testimonies might be put by those who would abuse the rhetoric of 'against forgetting' to perpetuate the cycle of violence.

In 1975 Heaney published *North*, his first volume to address the Troubles in Northern Ireland in an extended way. The most controversial poems in that collection are known as the 'bog poems', which turn to the exhumed bodies of Iron Age men and women – bodies that had been preserved in the bogs of Denmark – for metaphors about the violence in Northern Ireland. In 'Feeling into words', his oft-quoted 1974 essay about how he came to write the bog poems, Heaney talks about a deep identification with the bog people, particularly with the most famous one described in his poem 'The Tollund Man'.[9] The first section of the poem begins with the declaration that 'Some day I will go to Aarhus / To see his peat-brown head' at the museum there.[10] This leads to a graphic, sexualised description of the Tollund Man's death by ritual sacrifice, and of his preserved remains now. In the second section, Heaney imagines that his severed head may now 'make germinate' a vague resolution to the Troubles. Then, in the third and final section, he describes what his journey to Aarhus will feel like. He will first experience 'Something of his sad freedom / As he rode the tumbrel'; then his identification with the Tollund Man's alienation will complete itself:

> Out there in Jutland
> In the old man-killing parishes
> I will feel lost,
> Unhappy and at home.[11]

Edna Longley questioned 'the precise "emblematic" relevance of these mummified figures to the "man-killing" parishes of Northern Ireland', and argued that Heaney, 'not distinguish[ing] between involuntary and voluntary "martyrdom", . . . subsume[s] the latter into the former'.[12] She agrees with Ciarán Carson's assessment that Heaney is merely naturalising the violence, as if 'there never were and never will be any political consequences of such acts; they have been removed to the realm of sex, death and inevitability'.[13]

In his 1985 essay 'Pap for the dispossessed: Seamus Heaney and the poetics of identity', moreover, David Lloyd seconds both of these objections and reframes them in more explicitly Adornian terms. He rejects what he sees as Heaney's inherently political ideology of art's 'apparent freedom . . . from politics', and accuses the bog poems of forcing a false unity under the guise of that so-called freedom.[14] It is precisely what Adorno would call a coercive reconciliation. Lloyd writes:

> The political function of aesthetics and culture is not only to suggest the possibility of transcending conflict, but to do so by excluding (or integrating) difference, whether historically produced or metaphysically conceived, insofar as it represents a threat to an image of unity whose role is finally hegemonic. The poetics of identity is involved in both the efficacy and the contradictions of aesthetic politics and political aesthetics.[15]

The profound identification with the Tollund Man that Heaney describes himself as experiencing in 'Feeling into words' is, therefore, identarian insofar as he presents it as a symbolic solution to an ultimately and essentially insoluble conflict. Lloyd argues that this imposes a mythological and 'aesthetic resolution' upon 'conflicts constituted in quite specific historical junctures by rendering disparate events as symbolic moments expressive of an underlying continuity of identity'.[16] This impulse is supposedly encapsulated in an oft-quoted passage from the 1974 essay 'Feeling into words' about the Troubles being 'a struggle between the cults and devotees of a [British imperial] god and a[n Irish nationalist] goddess'.[17] The idea that this essay mythologises the Troubles has been frequently overemphasised, although with respect to 'The Tollund Man', the emblem of adversity he encounters seems to be an exhumed version of himself.[18] The differences between Iron Age Denmark and twentieth-century Ulster come to be erased by a false identification so that, ultimately, Aarhus came to sound like 'our house'.

Ironically, Heaney's poetics had already moved beyond the limitations of identarian thinking by the time Lloyd's essay was published. In the year that Amnesty published 'From the Republic of Conscience', *North* was a decade old. Heaney's human rights poetic envisioned a future of non-coerced reconciliation rather than a past of aesthetic, mythological, unrelieved coercion. It was as if he had already seen what Lloyd was objecting to in his poetry and had already devised a poetic model to counter it.

If Heaney's approach to the Troubles in 'The Tollund Man' was flawed by identarian logic, the theory Heaney used to explain the poem in 'Feeling into words' displayed greater promise; it did mark an early stage of Heaney's search for a poetics of reconciliation. In 'Feeling', he seeks comprehension of two diametrically opposed understandings of the violence in the North, a reconciliation that might be symbolised in what Yeats called 'befitting emblems of adversity'.[19] This hopefully allows him 'to encompass the perspectives of a humane reason and at the same time to grant the religious intensity of the violence in its deplorable authenticity and complexity'.[20] Heaney's critics objected that the poems of *North* afford too much voice to that 'religious intensity' without answering it sufficiently by way of 'humane reason'. The severed head of the Tollund Man represents an attempt to find such an emblem, but, having a past but no future, it ill befits the adversity at hand. This was therefore an early, failed attempt on Heaney's part to invoke a Yeatsian poetics of the emblem for reconciliation in Northern Ireland.

He would keep looking for ways to appropriate the poetics of the emblem, and would ultimately find greater success in such works as 'From the Republic of Conscience', *The Cure at Troy* and *Seeing Things*. One of Heaney's several inspirations for *The Cure at Troy* was Edmund Wilson's 1929 essay 'Philoctetes: the wound and the bow'.[21] Indeed, the name of this essay would provide Heaney with the two symbols needed to achieve the dialectical consciousness of the Troubles where 'The Tollund Man' had failed. Before he could put such a drama on the stage, however, Heaney had to develop an idea of poetic composition that could be both independent of, and yet answerable to, the political sphere. Borrowing from Heaney's own vocabulary, I will call it the lyrical conscience.

In his essay 'The Interesting case of Nero, Chekhov's cognac and a knocker', Heaney makes the case that lyric poetry, or even celebratory music, can count as a conscientious response to suffering.[22] This is, at any rate, his own mode; in his essay 'Place and displacement', he also identifies this mode in fellow Northern Irish poets such as Paul Muldoon, Derek Mahon and Michael Longley.[23] In 'Case', Heaney contrasts this indirect approach with that of Wilfred Owen, who exemplifies

> a type of poet who increasingly appears in the annals of twentieth-century literature, and who looms as a kind of shadowy judging figure above every poet who has written subsequently. The shorthand name we have evolved for this figure is the 'poet as witness', and he represents poetry's solidarity with the doomed, the deprived, the victimized, the underprivileged. The witness is any figure in whom the truth-telling urge and the compulsion to identify with the oppressed becomes necessarily integral with the act of writing itself.[24]

Heaney is obviously trying not to sound irreverent, but it is also clear that he wants to get out from under the 'shadowy judging figure' even while responding to real-life tragedies. The essay began with an anecdote about how he and David Hammond called off a recording gig out of respect for the victims of a bombing, but by the end of it he had described why the moral spirit of the Polish poet Zbigniew Herbert would have advised him to make the recording anyway.

Heaney's claim for a kind of lyrical conscience is most explicit in his description of Osip Mandelstam, for whom 'obedience to poetic impulse was obedience to conscience; lyric action constituted radical witness'.[25] This was a very important idea for understanding Heaney's poetry of the early 1980s. As he explains in his essay 'Envies and identifications', this idea of Mandelstam's exuberantly lyrical conscience inspires the final section of 'Station Island', a poetry sequence based on Dante's *Purgatorio*.[26] In that final section, the shade of James Joyce ultimately authorises Heaney to stop feeling like he has to be a poet of witness. When the pilgrim poet insists that he should continue to maintain the anti-colonial ethos he found in *A Portrait of the Artist as a Young Man*, the shade disparages 'That subject people stuff' as being 'Infantile, like your peasant pilgrimage'.[27] He sneers at 'the sackcloth and ashes' and 'doing the decent thing'. Instead, he recommends 'writ[ing] / for the joy of it', and 'Cultivat[ing] a work-lust'.[28]

Heaney is defending the idea that such a cultivated work lust is a psychological necessity, but this has far greater implications than merely a personal sense of relief. In 'Place and displacement', he describes how, for Northern Irish poets coming into their own during the Troubles, the satisfaction of lyrical creation was 'the only reliable release' from the limitations imposed upon the artist by the intensity of group thinking. It also leads to a particular kind of aesthetic experience. He talks about being 'in that liberated moment when the lyric discovers its buoyant completion', or

> when the timeless formal pleasure comes to its fullness and exhaustion, in those moments of self-justification and self-obliteration the poet makes contact with the plane of consciousness where he is at once intensified in his being and detached from his predicaments.[29]

This idea of poetic escape, and even the idea of that individual's poetic escape being ultimately productive for the social world, may sound Romantic, but it was Romantic in a way that Walter Benjamin and Theodor Adorno both found critically promising.[30] Whether Heaney was consciously attempting to develop a poetic model in relation to Adorno's thinking or not, some of that theorist's key ideas will be important to my explication of the poetics of human rights.

In his essay 'On lyric poetry and society', Adorno locates an 'auratic', utopian possibility in poetic language itself. He also talks about a moment of self-obliteration similar to the one Heaney described above:

> The moment of unself-consciousness in which the subject submerges itself in language is . . . a moment not of violence, nor of violence against the subject, but reconciliation: language itself speaks only when it speaks not as something alien to the subject but as the subject's own voice.[31]

Helen Vendler has analysed the aesthetic individuality of Heaney's poems in Adornian terms, but her 'aesthetic method' has been accused of depoliticised mysticism.[32] Whether or not it is fair to say this of Vendler, Heaney takes care to defend himself against the charge of being an 'ivory tower' poet. He defends 'the link between poetic technique and historical situation', and insists that the Northern poets of indirect witness do not 'conceive of their lyric stances as evasions of the actual conditions' because their '"pure" poetry is perfectly justifiable in earshot of the car bomb, and it can imply a politics'.[33] But how, exactly, might it do so?

Again, we might borrow from Adorno's thinking about lyrical poetry to read Heaney's lyrical conscience in relation to the political sphere. Vendler draws on Adorno while stressing the significance of a great poem's absolute individuality, as when he writes that the lyric poem's 'immersion in . . . individual form elevates . . . [it] to the status of something universal by making manifest something not distorted, not grasped, not yet subsumed'.[34] This is a compelling reason to read poems on their own terms, but we can also relate this to the social world through the notion that lyric poetry's resistance to the logic of identity is a hopeful sign for the human race. That is, Adorno also writes that a successful poem's triumphant particularity, offering us the example of something wholly free from coercion, thus 'anticipates, spiritually, a situation in which no false universality . . . continues to fetter what is other than itself, the human'.[35] A world free of such false universality is one way of describing Adorno's utopian vision.[36]

The reconciled poem's utopian vision also offers something very close to what Heaney called the 'radical witness' of Mandelstam's lyrical conscience. That is, Adorno argues that what seems most harmonious and abstracted from the social world nevertheless 'bears witness to its opposite, to suffering in an existence alien to the subject and to love for it as well . . . its unfathomable beauty cannot be separated from something it makes no reference to, the notion of a world that withholds peace'.[37] Because such a work of art remains non-coerced, it throws a coerced world into relief with a 'negative knowledge of the actual world'.[38]

Heaney's association with Amnesty International dates from the early 1980s. This was a period when a number of Irish artists began to support the organisation in various ways, ranging from the 'Art for Amnesty' auction that allowed Amnesty to purchase its first building in Dublin, to U2's role in the 'Conspiracy of Hope' tour in the United States.[39] Heaney contributed a poetry manuscript to the 'Art for Amnesty' auction, but his most significant contribution has been his poem 'From the Republic of Conscience'. The poem describes an allegorical republic whose cultural and political ethos of conscience therapeutically inspires its visitors to bring home with them the humanising principles of human equality and respect for difference.[40] Issued in a single printing of two thousand copies, the poem was published as a pamphlet illustrated by the Irish sculptor John Behan, and distributed to a group of international visitors who had convened in Dublin for Human Rights Day 1985. It has since then become the iconic Amnesty poem.

In separate interviews, former Amnesty executives in Ireland, Mary Lawlor and Bill Shipsey, each agreed that 'From the Republic of Conscience' has defined a kind of inspiring ethos for the organisation. Shipsey, currently the executive of Art for Amnesty, called Heaney 'without a doubt the spiritual voice for Amnesty since 1985 when he wrote the poem', adding that 'the position he holds in the affections, not just in Ireland but with Amnesty globally' comes from his being 'an enabling voice that allows the front-line activists a space and gives voice to what they are doing'.[41] The poem works, he explains, by

> actually bringing life into a vision of how things could be better. And different. Because it is a mythical republic of conscience but it is also the republic that many of us would want . . . that intellectually we would want to have or to have many of the elements of it.[42]

This idea is very much in line with what Lawlor, who had been the Amnesty executive during the 1980s, has said about the poem as 'a beacon and a call to action and a kind of vision of what is possible'.[43] Both of these human rights advocates in Ireland, therefore, identified Heaney as a voice expressing Amnesty's vision of a non-coerced world that is worth working for. 'Certainly for us in the Human Rights world and particularly in Ireland', Lawlor continued, the poem gave

> voice to what we should all be striving for in a clear accessible way . . . [and] it has had a ripple effect since that day . . . This poem was written in 1985 and it's now 2009 and I reckon that for me, I think

> about it often, I read it often, and I get as much out of it now and I get more out of it as time goes on.[44]

One of these ripples has been the Art for Amnesty's 'Ambassador of Conscience' Award, to which we will turn below.

Heaney spoke on a number of occasions about how he came to write 'From the Republic of Conscience'. In an *Irish Times* article for Human Rights Day 2008, for instance, Heaney recounted how he was approached by a member of Amnesty's Sandymount group, and supplied with what he has called 'a dossier containing the case histories of prisoners of conscience who had suffered everything from censorship and harassment to incarceration and torture'.[45] Heaney found these stories too overwhelming to write about directly. 'I could find no way to invent', he wrote, '"a verbal contraption" that would be anywhere near as strong as the record of injustice and pain in those resolutely unpoetic press releases, and after a couple of weeks I wrote back to say I was unable to deliver.'[46] As he put it in a conversation with Dennis O'Driscoll, 'All I could do at first was quail before that evidence', and so 'I had to recover and "by indirection find direction out"' in order to address the situation.[47] This indirect route meant allowing 'an element of play' to enter into his response. That is, he placed 'the actual cruelty of conditions' to one side and used allegory to describe an ideal republic rather than an intolerable one.

Heaney also explained other inspirations for the poem. Its opening stanza, for instance, 'When I landed in the republic of conscience / it was so noiseless when the engines stopped / I could hear a curlew high above the runway' was inspired by a trip to Orkney. 'I'll never forget the silence there on the airstrip', he told O'Driscoll,

> I was on a small propeller plane: when it taxied to a halt and the engines were shut off, we had to sit and wait for the ground crew; and all the while you could feel the plane shaking slightly in the wind. Then the door was opened, the steps were let down with a clunk and, as I walked across the grass to a little arrivals hut, I heard the cry of a curlew.[48]

'Republic' is a travel narrative, and has the element of a tourist brochure.[49] It was also inspired by a creative-writing assignment he set at Harvard: taking off from Richard Wilbur's poem 'Shame', Heaney's students were to write about 'an imaginary country [meant] to represent a particular state of mind or feeling'.[50] While describing this ideal place, however, Heaney more directly addresses a number of key questions that come up in wider debates about human rights among legal thinkers and/or advocates of international justice.

The first of the questions Heaney takes up in 'From the Republic of Conscience' is how human rights might be defined in the first place. During the Cold War, there were two competing approaches to human rights. The US framed human rights in terms of an individual's right to follow his or her own conscience without state interference. This approach stresses individual liberties over community needs. The Soviet Union's idea of human rights, on the other hand, stressed social and economic rights rather than civil and political ones. In the post-Cold War period, human rights activists have sought to synthesise the two models.

In 'Republic', Heaney advocates a very broad definition of human rights, borrowing from both sides of the Cold War conflict over the term. Upon leaving the airport the speaker finds

> No porters. No interpreter. No taxi.
> You carried your own burden and very soon
> your symptoms of creeping privilege disappeared.[51]

Likewise, the speaker leaves the country with a new sense of property and the embodied self:

> I came back from that frugal republic
> With my two arms the same length, the customs woman
> Having insisted my allowance was myself.[52]

Although Heaney's allegory certainly assumes a definition of human rights that includes such communal concerns as economic and social rights, he also stresses the individual conscience. That is, we hear about the country from the perspective of an individual traveller, and when the speaker becomes a 'representative' of the frugal republic, he or she will work 'independently'.[53] The poem embodies this nexus between the individual conscience and the community through the image of the republic's 'sacred symbol', which is

> . . . a stylized boat.
> The sail is an ear, the mast a sloping pen,
> the hull a mouth-shape, the keel an open eye.[54]

Lawlor refers to these stanzas as the heart of the poem. 'It's just the way you go through all of these things', she says:

> You carried your own burden. The whole notion of the ear, the pen, the mouth, and the eye I mean that there are the four things you need to advance Human Rights, we have it all in ourselves and it's just how you use it. And this kind of, slightly, shot at power.[55]

Lawlor's reading is seconded by John Behan's illustration for the 1985 pamphlet, and Peter Sís' illustration for the first Ambassador of Conscience Award, presented to Czech President Václav Havel in 2003.

In the poem, Heaney also recognises that human rights need to be understood with regard to Enlightenment reason's problematic role in the history of European imperialism. In short, the latter has compromised the moral authority of the former. In this light, it has been argued that the human rights idea imposes a post- or neo-imperialist model of justice upon a world in which the subaltern cannot speak. As if to avoid the overbearing suggestion that the rest of the world needs to act like Europe, Heaney places 'The Republic of Conscience' beyond any specific geopolitical sphere: the curlew it mentions in the first stanza has habitats on six continents. Rather than being vague, however, the Republic of Conscience is a utopian hybrid of times and places. In the last two stanzas of the poem's second section, we find a recognisably European constitutional model coupled with a creation myth that sounds aboriginal:

> At their inauguration, public leaders
> must swear to uphold unwritten law and weep
> to atone for their presumption to hold office –
>
> and to affirm their faith that all life sprang
> from salt in tears which the sky-god wept
> after he dreamt his solitude was endless.[56]

The sky-god's lonely dream suggests that the frugal republic's experience of human rights is communal rather than merely individual, and this revisits the question of how religion bestows political legitimacy. The Latin verb *inaugurare* means to install someone in an office, but the root 'augur' also points to an original religious component, one that to this day has merely assumed alternate forms of observance. And while such sanctification of leadership usually makes leaders seem unapproachably divine, the republic's form of inauguration aligns leadership with a deity in a humanising way. Heaney's oath of office 'to uphold unwritten law' also evokes the history of the human rights idea, which springs from the natural-law tradition.

In another re-envisioning of usual practice in a coerced world, Heaney reimagines the experience of border crossing as humanising.

This is a part of the poem that resonated well with Shipsey, who points to the 'terror we feel with immigration officials, [because] we're all very vulnerable when we go to another country'.[57] It should be little surprise, therefore, that the idea for the Ambassador of Conscience award would come from the final three tercets that make up the most resonantly humanising point in the poem. Before leaving 'that frugal republic', Heaney's visitor character has a significant encounter with 'the old man', who

> . . . rose and gazed into my face
> and said that was official recognition
> that I was now a dual citizen.
>
> He therefore desired me when I got home
> to consider myself a representative
> and to speak on their behalf in my own tongue.
>
> Their embassies, he said, were everywhere
> but operated independently
> and no ambassador would ever be relieved.[58]

We can place this poem in the secular Dantean progression in Heaney's poetry of the late seventies and early eighties: whereas *Field Work*'s 'Ugolino' translates the *Inferno* and the 120-part 'Station Island' draws on the *Purgatorio*, the 3-part 'Republic' echoes the *Paradiso* – from which the poet must return to his own country, recounting his visionary travels in the vulgar tongue.

The 'ripple effect' Lawlor attributes to the poem radiates most strongly from the final stanza. In 2005 Domna C. Stanton brought her 2005 Modern Language Association presidential address 'On rooted cosmopolitanism' to a close with the

> challenge of a cosmopolitan republic of letters and languages to which we and our students belong. Seamus Heaney has called it 'the republic of conscience' and invited us poetically to be its representatives, its public ambassadors . . . This *is* an imagined community to embrace. So, cosmopolitans of the world, unite.[59]

After a decade in which artists were not as involved with Amnesty as they had been in the 1980s, in the early 2000s Shipsey founded a group in Dublin, 'Artists for Amnesty', and collaborated with Heaney on the Ambassador of Conscience Award, which is regularly bestowed on 'ambassadors' who have shown 'exceptional individual leadership in the fight to protect and promote universal Human Rights'.[60] Recipients have included Václav Havel (2003), Hilda Morales Trujillo and Mary Robinson (2004), U2 (2005), Nelson Mandela (2006), Peter Gabriel (2008) and Aung San Suu Kyi (2009).[61] The poem's afterlife also reflects the rich ambiguity of its final line. That is, when we read that 'no ambassador will ever be relieved', it suggests the permanence of one's commitment; cosmopolitan identification with a global human rights ideal is legitimate, and the responsibility to work for human rights is ongoing. Mary Lawlor has called the poem 'a private, quiet recognition . . . that you are placed in the Republic of Conscience whether you like it or not'.[62] Heaney's traveller has seen the republic, but carrying that vision he knows what to work for without the expectation that he will be 'relieved' to find it fully enacted in the world to which he returns.[63]

Rather than identifying Heaney as a laureate of negative dialectics, however, it is important to remember some of the major factors that separate him from Adorno. The masterful balancing of complexity and accessibility to be found in Heaney's work, for instance, places him at some considerable distance from Adorno's famously impenetrable style. Adorno's well-known pessimism contrasts with Heaney's poetic uplift. It is true that Adorno's utopian strain is a necessary balance with his catastrophic view of the Enlightenment, but Colin Hearfield insists that even his 'utopian metaphysics of freedom' are 'Neither positive nor piously hopeful'.[64] While not particularly pious, Heaney's human rights vision is both positive and hopeful. The place where Adorno's pessimism and Heaney's optimism call for the two to part ways most powerfully, however, is in their respective attitudes towards the human rights idea.

As a comprehensive critic of the Enlightenment, Adorno was extremely sceptical of what an organisation like the United Nations might be able to accomplish for the world. For him, the destructive Hegelian logic of identity – where the universal overwhelms the particular, the subject engulfs the object, and difference is reduced to sameness – is responsible for many of the twentieth century's most horrific catastrophes. Imperialism, totalitarianism, dictatorship and global capitalism have all represented coercively universalising attempts to impose various false unifications upon a world of difference, with catastrophic consequences for any who would resist. If we were to put the principle of human rights into Adorno's terms, therefore, we might say that the object has a natural right to be different from the subject. The fact that Adorno elaborated much of his thought about negative dialectics in terms of aesthetics, moreover, means that he offers a convenient poetic of human rights. Carolyn Forché draws upon it explicitly in her description of the poetry of witness. Explaining her choice to include indirect poems in her anthology of human rights poetry, she claims that even these represent a 'dialectical opposition to the extremity' caused by the breakdown of human rights. Such a poetry of dialectical opposition will 'take many forms' in its 'resistance to false attempts at unification'.[65]

One major problem with appropriating Adorno for a poetics of human rights, however, is that Adorno was critical of the idea to begin with. Human rights is a natural-law concept that was secularised during the Enlightenment and enshrined in the United States Declaration of Independence and the French Revolution's Declaration of the Rights of Man and of the Citizen. Therefore, because Adorno regarded the Enlightenment as an unmitigated disaster, he could only regard human rights as misguided at best. As early as 1944 he and Max Horkheimer charged that the dialectic of Enlightenment, brooking no resistance to its destructive logic, would only 'treat its own ideas of human rights exactly as it does the older universals'.[66] In *Minima Moralia*, published only three years after the United Nations made its Universal Declaration of Human Rights, Adorno continued to voice this pessimism:

> If the equality of all who have human shape were demanded as an ideal instead of being assumed as a fact, it would not greatly help. Abstract utopia is all too compatible with the most insidious tendencies of society ... [which] considers actual or imagined differences as stigmas indicating that not enough has yet been done; that something has still been left outside its machinery, not quite determined by its totality.[67]

Taking the many factors that would dissociate Heaney from Adorno into consideration, it makes the most sense to say that Heaney's poetic ethos of human rights can be illuminated with reference to some key concepts from Adorno's thinking.

In summary, we can say that somewhere in the early 1980s Heaney crafted a poetic ethos of lyrical conscience that he would bring with him as a cultural advocate for human rights. This poetic ethos would have the following major characteristics. First, it resists the restrictive pieties of identity politics. Second, it takes seriously the idea that poetry, by being poetry, can model wished-for, non-coercive reconciliations in the social world. Third, it allows itself a kind of visionary optimism about where those reconciliations might lead, despite what he knows of actual conditions in a coerced world.

With *The Cure at Troy: A Version of Sophocles'* Philoctetes, Heaney elaborates on the idea of auratic human rights poetry by integrating it into a

Greek chorus – and thus a larger narrative – rather than just presenting it as a free-standing lyric poem. Because this was a Field Day play, moreover, some members of the audience disliked what they saw as the play's political allegory, and some disliked the fact there wasn't a clearer allegory.[68] Although Heaney very significantly specified that this was a symbolic drama rather than an allegory, the play nevertheless does feature an allegory about poetry itself. Before I can explain how this allegory worked, however, a summary of the Sophoclean original is in order.

By the time the play begins, the Greek hero Philoctetes has been stranded on the island of Lemnos for ten years. He had suffered a snake bite while on the way to the Trojan War with the rest of the Greek fleet, and his affliction had rendered him so noxious to his fellows that they decided to abandon him on the deserted island. Near the end of the war, however, an oracle tells the Greeks that Philoctetes actually needs to come to Troy and be healed by Asclepius, after which he will use the divine bow of Hercules to take the city and end the war. The Greeks send Odysseus, accompanied by Neoptolemus, the son of Achilles, to retrieve Philoctetes and his bow on Lemnos. Neoptolemus is an idealistic young man and a newcomer to the war, and in this way he contrasts with Odysseus, the expeditious veteran. Neoptolemus is opposed to the deceit, but Odysseus nevertheless convinces him to go along with the Greek cause. When he meets Philoctetes, therefore, Neoptolemus accordingly tells a false story about himself also having been betrayed by the Greeks. This wins Philoctetes' trust, and Neoptolemus uses it to steal the bow. The young man has second thoughts, however, and makes the ethical decision to return the bow, knowing that this could be a fatal decision. Philoctetes forgives Neoptolemus. Having re-established his ethical character through ethical action, therefore, he makes an honest rhetorical appeal to Philoctetes to rejoin the Greek cause. Despite his compelling argument (which includes the offer to heal Philoctetes' wounds), however, Philoctetes remains recalcitrant and only relents when Hercules returns and orders him to join the Greeks. The play ends with the three heroes departing Lemnos together, for Troy.

In the original play, Philoctetes would not reconcile with the Greeks until Hercules ordered him to do so. In Heaney's version, however, it is the spirit of Poetry rather than that of Hercules who ultimately convinces Philoctetes. The chorus channels Hercules' words to him, but they also channel the voice of Poetry itself; this is the visionary source for the 'hope and history' that wins him over. Poetry does not win him over by making false claims about itself, however. 'Human beings suffer', the chorus begins,

They torture one another,
They get hurt and get hard.
No poem or play or song
Can fully right a wrong
Inflicted or endured.[69]

These lines reflect both the idea that poetry is separate from the world, but also that it can nevertheless be powerfully responsive to it. It is, moreover, crucial that these lines from and about Poetry appear in place of Sophocles' original *deus ex machina*, because this allows the drama to resolve itself within the internal zone of human psychology rather than through the intervention of an external, coercive 'daylight' god like Hercules. Ironically, this modern addition brought the play more into line with Aristotelian unity of action by fixing the problem of Sophocles' *deus ex machina* conclusion. The opening chorus had already forewarned that poetry would appear at the climax of the play as a volcanic eruption, and so this makes the 'Hope and History' chorus a cathartic release. This gives the 'cure' of the title two meanings, moreover. The first cure comes from Asclepius, who will literally fix Philoctetes' foot. The second cure, however, is poetry itself, and this is what really produces the play's final image of luminously restored human dignity.

Heaney further added to the meaning of Sophocles' original drama when he had *Cure*'s opening chorus explain the theory of poetry according to which the conclusion will make sense. The first lines establish that the problem of the play will be intransigent conflict between 'Heroes. Victims. Gods and human beings. / All throwing shapes, every one of them / Convinced he's in the right'.[70] Their rhetoric sinks

People so deep into
Their own self-pity, self-pity buoys them up.
People so staunch and true, they're fixated,
Shining with self-regard like polished stones.

And their whole life spent admiring themselves
For their own long-suffering.
Licking their wounds
And flashing them around like decorations.
I hate it, I always hated it, and I am
A part of it myself.[71]

On one level, this last admission of the chorus implicates Heaney himself in that endless circle of destructive remembrance; 'the chorus', therefore,

> Is more or less a borderline between
> The you and the me and the it of it.
>
> Between
> The gods' and the human beings' sense of things.[72]

The chorus' self-identification as being between 'the you and the me and the it of it', however, also recalls Adorno's idea that negative dialectics reveal a continuum between subjects and objects. This, in turn, becomes a theory of poetry itself because this continuum is also 'the borderline that poetry / Operates on too'.[73] It is in this philosophical capacity, Heaney lets us know, that the hope-and-history rhyme will nudge our characters towards a noncoercive reconciliation. 'Poetry', says the chorus,

> Allowed the god to speak. It was the voice
> Of reality and justice. The voice of Hercules
> That Philoctetes is going to have to hear
> When the stone cracks and the lava flows.[74]

This reference to 'reality and justice' foreshadows the 'hope and history' to come, but it does so from a transcendent perspective that sees things in the past and future tenses at once.[75]

In some ways, Heaney's utopian lyric poetry sounds like the Coleridgean ideology of the aesthetic about which Deane has shown so much suspicion, because it associates poetic reconciliation with the resolution of political crisis. There are significant philosophical differences between Heaney's and Coleridge's approaches, however. To begin with, Coleridge associated reconciliation with literary genius in an authoritative way that Heaney avoided. All through the former's influential criticism of Shakespeare, for example, we read about how an ideally balanced imagination gives the Bard's dramas (and the cultural clerisy qualified to interpret them, of course) an authoritative wisdom about the political and social order. Indeed, as Deane has pointed out, Coleridge's rhetoric of reconciliation always implied an argument from authority, strongly informed by an underlying ideology of order. Significantly differing from this approach, however, Heaney in *Cure* figures poetry as a depersonalised medium of intersubjectivity: a space where we can see the boundary lines between self and other start to fade, where conflict can be recognised from new perspectives, and reconciliation can be reimagined as well.

The fact that *Cure* is itself a work of poetic drama, moreover, renders the theme of intersubjectivity foundational for our understanding of its action. And while in many ways this approach is diametrically opposed to most traditional understandings of Aristotelian ethics or poetics, Heaney's additions ultimately forward the Greek philosopher's notion that poetry is more philosophical than history and more serious than philosophy. In the sense that it dramatises the mutually constitutive interdependence of self and other, therefore, Heaney's play adds to Field Day's ethical contribution to the Aristotelian tradition of civic drama in modern Ireland. In the next chapter, I will further explore *Cure* as a Field Day play, concentrating attention more closely on the poet's long conversation with Deane.

Chapter Five

Field Day's Daylight Gods

> The internal debates within FD [Field Day] taught me something about the differences between nationalism (cultural) and republicanism; about the pleasure that concerted and cooperative effort can bring; about the need for basic agreement on important issues if that is to flourish. It was a cameo experience of what a real society might, in some respects, be like.
>
> Seamus Deane, early 1990s[1]

> [Field Day's] purpose is to define itself. So it has an inner drama of possibility.
>
> Seamus Heaney, 1987[2]

In the previous chapter I placed Seamus Heaney's *Cure at Troy* in the context of his human rights poetry; in this chapter, I will look at it as a Field Day play. This will mean relating it to the poet's long conversation with Seamus Deane. To begin, let us return to Deane's diagnosis of the aesthetic ideology in modern Irish writing, and how he related this to the tensions within the Field Day board of directors in the late 1980s. To do this, let us return to Deane's 'General introduction' to *The Field Day Anthology of Irish Writing*, in which he links the language of reconciliation to 'the aesthetic ideology . . . a political force which pretends not to be so', but which naturalises colonialism's binary logic of civilian versus barbarian.[3] As he states elsewhere in that introduction, 'When colonialism is successful, it reconciles the colonized culture to its own. When it is unsuccessful, it enforces itself by violence – slaughter, confiscation, the demonizing of those who resist it.'[4] Writing in a distinctly postcolonial mode, therefore, Deane is arguing against what Theodor Adorno has called 'reconciliation under duress'. The question of how to value reconciliation was also significant in the internal debates among the Field Day board of directors. However else they might have agreed on how Field

Day's publishing and theatrical projects might address the Troubles, the group nevertheless entertained competing impulses between advocating a reconciling ethos by way of aesthetic experience and critiquing the aesthetic ideology as a colonial discourse of state power.

Because Deane's critique of aesthetic autonomy was so prominent in that discussion, the competing impulses within Field Day came to resemble the ancient Greek conflict between poetry and philosophy. On one hand, we find something like a Platonic suspicion of poetry in the public sphere.[5] On the other, we find an Aristotelian advocacy of civic art. In a 1992 interview with Dympna Callaghan, Deane called this

> Field Day's problem. Any demystifications or anti-aesthetic gestures we make are more than counterbalanced by the aestheticizing and mystificatory gestures we make in the theater, and sometimes perhaps in the *Anthology*. But the major problem was that we got caught in the ricochet between these so-called polarities rather than pushing on and coming out the other side of it.[6]

Although Deane primarily occupies the anti-aesthetic position against the mystifying ideology of the aesthetic for Field Day, he does not absolutely endorse their 'so-called polarities'.

Deane's lectures and writings reflect a profound suspicion of received aesthetic models in Irish history, his genealogical critiques of which have located deep continuities between postcolonial neurosis, state violence and the ideology of the aesthetic. These continuities are made particularly clear in a set of unpublished interview answers contained in the Field Day archive at the National Library of Ireland. Although the interviewer's surname (his first name is Jonathan) and questions are not contained in the folder, it is clear that the interview was conducted in the early 1990s at a time when Deane was thinking about the group's break-up. One of Jonathan's questions must have touched upon Field Day's mission because Deane begins with a list of Field Day's objectives. Deane explains that the group

> heightened awareness of the fact that discourse is a form of power; that inherited colonial discourses are oppressive; that narration of one's own history, especially in times of crisis, is an act of agency and power; that there is all the difference in the world between being an object of narration and a narrating subject; that it is possible to see and inspect the genealogy of sedimented discourses and to emancipate oneself, to some degree, from their assumptions. We did these things in theatre and in pamphlets and in the Anthology.[7]

This explanation reflects Deane's intellectual grounding in critical theory, and particularly in the Nietzschean tradition of genealogical critique. There are elements of Fanon, Foucault, Lacan and Derrida here, as well. Considering the more pessimistic Adornian perspective with which he has more recently been associated since the publication of his novel *Reading in the Dark*, this is a notably optimistic statement in the sense that it suggests that a kind of talking cure, involving both poetry and philosophy, can 'to some degree' lead to a form of intellectual and psychological home rule. In other words, it becomes apparent that Deane saw in Field Day a chance for some kind of genuine reconciliation in Ireland. In this same interview, for instance, he called Field Day, despite the 'internal debates' within the board, 'a cameo experience of what a real society, in some respects, might be like'.[8] This would make Field Day a reconciling institution indeed.

Given that he was writing after the Friel–Rea quarrel had effectively ended the first stage of Field Day's history, however, Deane described the group's success in measured terms.[9] Their genealogical critique of sedimented discourses in Irish history had not gone far enough, and they had achieved an 'uneven success' in

> liberat[ing] the aesthetic from . . . the natural. This is a very powerful linkage in Ireland – a colonial hangover from the condition of political powerlessness and the accompanying 'permission' to be artistic. I think we played a part in weakening this; but some of the FD directors (Heaney, Friel, Kilroy) were/are anxious supporters of the autonomy of the aesthetic. So, no, I don't think that as a group we were able to change sufficiently; that is one of the reasons the group is breaking up.[10]

In this account, Heaney, Friel and Kilroy compromised Field Day's genuine promise of Irish reconciliation by naturalising, through their art, the false reconciliations of British colonial ideology. Deane had previously used a similar formulation to the 'colonial hangover' in an argument about W.B. Yeats and James Joyce, where he stated that their fixations on English writers such as Shakespeare amounted to a 'pathology of literary unionism'.[11] This earlier twentieth-century pathology had become a hangover, but this was still troublesome. Deane's answer to question six, however, sounds more ominous. Here he denies 'that FD's work is offered as compensation for the violence' in Northern Ireland, and says instead that Field Day was

> a symptom of the violent situation; also an attempt at an analysis of it. We would not at all go with those who say the country's violence

> is compensated for by its 'artistic' productions. Indeed, that is a way of re-establishing the split between the aesthetic and the political which is one of the enabling conditions for state violence.[12]

This sounds more like what Deane might say about Conor Cruise O'Brien's 'sacred drama'. The ideas about Irish poetry that give Heaney a colonial hangover would, therefore, be similar to the ones that made O'Brien an ideological enabler for state violence.

The concerns at the heart of Deane's critique of Field Day actually predated the organisation, and were already prominent issues in 'Unhappy and at home', Deane's 1975 interview with Heaney for the *Crane Bag*. In order of appearance, there are three main issues: an Adornian critique of the aesthetic ideology in Irish poetry; the dialectical relationship between Hercules (daylight gods) and Antaeus (instinctive powers); and the evaluation of Conor Cruise O'Brien's commentary on Northern Ireland. There is a variable level of friction underlying the interview; Deane makes a series of suggestions about Heaney's work, and Heaney mainly agrees with them. About halfway through the interview, for instance, Deane presents Heaney with an Adornian frame for reading *North* and *Wintering Out*, one that says that Heaney achieves a kind of aesthetic 'balance' in his work that reflects its origins in an 'imbalance of hatred or sectarian feeling' experienced in real life. This places the Northern Catholic poet's 'political fidelity' in contradiction with his 'aspiration towards an equipoise and balance of form'.[13] (This was the same issue with the Coleridgean notion of aesthetic reconciliation that Deane would later take up in the 'General introduction' to *The Field Day Anthology*.) 'There is a statement by Adorno', he continues,

> that the conciliatory nature of art is in direct relation to the rage which produced it . . . [I think] the language of much of your poetry has a good deal of violent and physical implication, and yet the poems themselves have a certain poise and balance, even sometimes to a self-conscious degree.[14]

Heaney's response to Deane's critique is positive but ambiguous. Although he does not fully endorse the Adornian frame, he nevertheless acknowledges that Deane's attention to this contradiction gets at 'the very root and intimacy of the poet's act' and points to his own 'metaphorical consideration' of the theme in his own poems 'Antaeus' and 'Hercules and Antaeus' from *North*.[15] 'Hercules represents the balanced rational light', Heaney continues, 'while Antaeus represents the pieties of illiterate fidelity', and adds that he retrospectively decided that 'the rational wins out too strong' in the poem, a resolution he considers 'wrong now'.[16] In response, Deane interprets this to mean that, when writing about Northern Ireland in particular, the Herculean 'humanism' or 'rationality' is misguided when it tries 'to detach itself from' its atavistic origins because 'to be worth the name it must confront or take account of Antaeus' bigotry, or . . . lift itself clear of it'.[17] Lifting itself clear, in Deane's formulation, appears to mean a freedom from history achieved by working through it rather than by ignoring or eliding it. Heaney agrees 'absolutely'. Between the publication of *North* and the interview 'Unhappy and at home', therefore, Heaney has gone from thinking that a poet must go with Herculean 'rationalism', even with nostalgia for Antaeus' atavism, to calling for a more balanced and open-ended encounter.

This level of agreement begins to fray in the interview, however, when Deane brings up Conor Cruise O'Brien. That is, having established that in Northern Ireland Hercules needs to pay more constructive attention to Antaeus, Deane asks if this criticism extends, in Heaney's mind, to O'Brien's commentary on Northern Ireland. The question addresses aesthetic and political theory simultaneously because O'Brien so frequently addressed Northern Ireland in his triple capacity as politician, journalist and literary critic. Considering the fact that O'Brien had recently published the scathing review of *North*, moreover, it is surprising to Deane when Heaney actually defends O'Brien. Deane asks Heaney:

> In view of the inevitability of facing the Northern situation or of bearing some imprint of its experience, do you think that there are any grounds for agreeing with Conor Cruise O'Brien's view that the link between art and politics constitutes an unhealthy intersection?
>
> Heaney: Yes, I think he is correct.
> Deane: Even though he meant this as a criticism [of you]?[18]

Heaney would not agree that O'Brien's aesthetic ideology led to a misreading of Northern Irish poetry or that this misreading of the poetry was equivalent to a misreading of the Northern situation as a whole. Nevertheless, Deane reads Heaney's poetry as a proof that O'Brien's interpretive model for Northern poetry is flawed, and, therefore, finds Heaney's defence of O'Brien troublesome. 'In order to be rational [or Herculean]', Deane told Heaney, 'O'Brien tends to renounce [Antaean] atavisms', while 'poetry . . . to survive . . . cannot renounce them'.[19] Heaney replies that he 'agree[s] partly', but insists on the necessity for dialogue with 'the obstinate voice of rationalist humanism'.[20] This insistence would, in fact, be the political gesture at the heart of *The Cure at Troy* fifteen years later. 'O'Brien did an utterly necessary job in rebuking all easy thoughts about the Protestant community in the North', Heaney maintained, because 'there should be some kind of clarity in southerners' thinking about' unionism. Therefore, O'Brien's 'obstinate insistence on facing up to . . . [the] reality' of their recalcitrance is 'his contribution'.[21] In this validating account of O'Brien's contribution, Heaney links clarity and obstinacy in a way that makes the colonial Hercules change places – for a moment, at least – with the dispossessed Antaeus. This is, in and of itself, a unionist trope and is consistent with his later merging, in *Cure*, of Revd Ian Paisley with Shakespeare's Caliban in the character of Philoctetes.

Although the terms of the conversation in 'Unhappy and at home' are aesthetic and political, they apply just as readily to the Aristotelian categories of rhetoric and ethics. In the opening quotation from Adorno, for instance, Deane invokes the idea of conciliation: the balanced work of art is conciliatory in relation to the coercive realities from which it arises. In order for Heaney's poetry of the 1970s to have a reconciling function in Northern Ireland, then, he decides that it had to address the psychology of the conflict in all of its mythic density and recalcitrance. Heaney's defence of O'Brien's obstinacy, moreover, continues the rhetorical and ethical tenor of this conversation by stressing the importance of audience. It is necessary, Heaney agrees with O'Brien, for citizens of the Republic to understand the unionist mindset. According to this argument, Southerners are too eager to assume that Ulster Protestants will easily identify with a united sense of Irishness, and this ignores the 'obstinate' reality of unionist recalcitrance. This recognition of psychological obstinacy and recalcitrance is central to the ethical and rhetorical point of Heaney's 'mythical' approach to the Troubles in *North* and in his much-criticised essay 'Feeling into words'. It is, therefore, ironic that O'Brien criticised these works for having a partisan or pessimistic endorsement of recalcitrance rather than an ethical recognition of it. In the 1980s, however, part of the Field Day ethos, as demonstrated by the theatrical output, would be to explore these mythical, recalcitrant positions in their historical specificity, and, by locating and exploring cracks and discontinuities in them, suggest ways forward on the cultural level.

Field Day's two most visionary movements in this direction were in the two plays of reconciliation: Stewart Parker's *Pentecost* and Heaney's *The Cure at Troy*. Both of these plays were about Protestant recalcitrance.

The first dealt with Protestant working-class culture during the Ulster Workers' Council strike of 1974, and the other strongly referenced Paisley's 'Ulster Says No' rhetoric against the Anglo-Irish Agreement. What distinguished these plays' treatment of the Protestant mindset from O'Brien's own *Antigone* allegory, however, was the fact that Parker's and Heaney's plays actually presented a vision whereby Protestant trust might actually on some level be engaged in a process of ethical reconciliation. These plays held fast to the principle that a good-faith conversation was possible despite considerable evidence to the contrary.

In *Cure*, Heaney continues the discussion of these themes in a different kind of Hellenic register. For instance, the version of Hercules who appears at the climax of *Cure* takes on a kind of Antaean quality. Further, Philoctetes is defined by his wounds, and represents those atavistic resentments and bigotries that Heaney and Deane identified with Antaeus back in 1975. Odysseus is the figure who speaks for the daylight gods of reason and the state, and so, like the Hercules of *North*, he recognises Philoctetes merely as an obstacle to victory. When Hercules speaks in *Cure*, however, he represents a version of the sky-born who actually can recognise and address the chthonic atavistic hero in the depths of his pain and recalcitrance.[22] Through the 'Hope and History' chorus, moreover, Heaney also presents a version of poetry that achieves freedom not through the easy evasions offered by the ideology of the aesthetic but, rather, by a visionary and emancipatory working-through of history.

During the period in which he was composing *The Cure at Troy*, Heaney was more heavily occupied with Yeats – and in a lighter mode – than he had been at any previous point in his career.[23] First of all, in 1988 he spent six weeks researching Yeats, largely at the National Library of Ireland, in preparation for his section on Yeats for *The Field Day Anthology*. This critical and creative engagement is manifest in his 1991 collection *Seeing Things*. In his introduction to Yeats, Heaney defends the poet against the long-established critical 'opposition' to Yeats' 'ultimate embrace of the high aesthetic mode as the basis not only of a poetic but of an ethic as well'.[24] Rather than trying to argue for aesthetic autonomy in any kind of depoliticising way, however, Heaney presents Yeats' poetic 'incitements to generous self-transcendence' as a reconciling ethos, a force of good in the political sphere.[25] He closes the introduction in a kind of reverie, where the 'limb-sweetening fullness' of Yeats' late poetry, while particularly absent from the worlds of 'consumer capitalism and clamant Marxism' alike, nevertheless 'marvellously promotes the savour of states of being where our social intelligence is animated, our emotional nature is replenished and our best-dreamt possibilities are corroborated'.[26] The 'states of being' Heaney says Yeats promotes are the same ones we find Philoctetes moving through in the conclusion to *Cure*.

Part of Heaney's ethical retrieval of Yeats was his attempt to associate the earlier poet with the discourse of reconciliation. He points, for instance, to Yeats' 'extreme exploration of the possibilities of reconciling the human impulse to transcendence and subversion with the antithetical project of continuity and consolidation' as being 'universally and inexhaustibly relevant'.[27] He repeats this emphasis on Yeats' antithetical reconciliation on the next page, when he writes that there 'is surely a political meaning, at once realistic and visionary, in his sense of life as an abounding conflict of energies; in his recognition of the necessity as well as the impossibility of the attempt "to hold in a single thought reality and justice"'.[28] Heaney will repeat the reality–justice–balance idea in the first chorus of *Cure*, and it will also resonate with the 'Hope and History' chorus. Just as his argument tried to retrieve Yeats from O'Brien for an ethical as well as poetic discourse of reconciliation, there are also hints of the 'daylight gods' language Tom Paulin had referenced in 'The making of a loyalist'. Heaney argues that Yeats' poetic consciousness, through its daemonic antitheses and search for 'unity of being', balances the 'chthonic, national, Celtic' impulses of the Irish nationalists with a surface 'artful expression of daylight opinion'.[29] Yeats reconciles this daylight opinion and the chthonic instincts by way of what Heaney calls 'True poetry . . . [which] had to be the speech of the whole man'. Heaney and Paulin did not always use the Hegelian terms to the same ends, but his echoes of them here demonstrate the degree to which Paulin's Hegelian–Sophoclean terms correspond to the notions of 'Hercules' and 'Antaeus' he had discussed with Seamus Deane in 1975.

In late summer 1990 Heaney became worried about how *Cure* might be attacked in the press by Field Day's critics.[30] As if to pre-empt hostile reviews, therefore, the poet gave copious interviews to local papers all over Ireland (in which Yeats' name came up very frequently).[31] Speaking to Jane Coyle in September 1990 for the theatre journal *Stet*, for instance, Heaney was asked if, having just returned from the Yeats Summer School, he had been influenced by Yeats' Sophocles. He answered that Yeats' 'verse medium was firmly in my mind', but that his *Oedipus* translations, being mainly done out in prose, were not: 'I very much wanted . . . to capture the clear, hard story-telling qualities of

Purgatory', he continued, 'and the melody and rhythms of the musicians' speeches [from] *At the Hawk's Well*'.[32] In writing *Cure*, therefore, Heaney draws on Yeats' 'original' plays, which he considers in some ways to be even more Greek than Yeats' translations of Sophocles.

In publicising his apologia, Heaney used similar terms to those Yeats had used to defend *Purgatory* in the press in 1938. For instance, Heaney told Barry White of the *Belfast Telegraph* that he 'had a special affection for Yeats' plays' such as *Purgatory* and *At the Hawk's Well* because he 'like[ed] symbolic drama'.[33] Heaney is likely to have known (or been reminded of) the controversy over *Purgatory* when he was consulting the Abbey Theatre collection in the Manuscripts Reading Room at the National Library of Ireland. If he did look at that collection while researching Yeats for *The Field Day Anthology*, he would have come across a folder containing newspaper clippings from *The Irish Times* detailing the controversy. During the Abbey Theatre Festival, one Fr Connolly of Boston College had prompted a debate over whether or not the poet owed his audience an explanation of what the occult philosophy behind the difficult play actually meant. *The Irish Times* followed the argument closely, and in August 1938 included an interview with Yeats about the play in which the poet asserted that 'There is no allegory in *Purgatory*, but . . . Symbolism is another matter . . . A work of art moves us because it expresses something in ourselves or in the general life of men.'[34] As if following Yeats, Heaney also told White that *Cure* was 'not a political allegory about solutions to the problems of Ireland'.[35] Not only does Heaney repeat the Yeatsian argument that his play is symbolic and universal, rather than allegorical and particular, but he also said that the play's meaning was on its surface rather than somewhere under or between the lines.[36]

Taking a cue from de Man, it is possible to call *Purgatory* (and, by extension, *Cure*) an emblematic drama as well as a symbolist one. Yeats practically identified the two himself in 1904 when he wrote in *Samhain* that the dramatist must 'take what is most creative out of himself, not from observation, but experience, yet he must master . . . a definite symbolism of incident and scene'.[37] According to this scheme, the symbol or emblem reconciles the experience of the individual and that of the community. What the individual invents or discovers through experience, moreover, becomes communicable through inherited tradition and language. If Yeats was figuring drama in terms of the emblem at the beginning of the century, then, at the end of his life the connection would be all the stronger. According to this scheme, by the time Yeats wrote his last play he had given himself entirely over to the poetics of the emblem.

Heaney was very interested in retrieving the visionary aspect of Yeats, but, of course, he had to reconfigure the politics behind the poetics. It was, therefore, his substitution of therapeutic psychology and human rights principles for Yeats' occult study and fascist sympathy that made the difference between Yeats' politically confusing vacillations between culture and emblem, on one hand, and Heaney's clearer and more positive contribution to the language of the peace process during the 1990s on the other. Heaney also explained to the *Galway Advertiser* that his symbolic drama 'enacts a profoundly true psychological scenario'.[38] As had been the case with Yeats, Heaney's insistence upon symbolism rather than allegory went against the de Manian assumption that the latter is more ethical than the former. For Heaney, however, symbolism was preferable to allegory because under the conditions of polarising conflict, the latter lends itself too easily to appropriation and propaganda. While *Cure* does actually work as an allegory for a poetics of human rights and reconciliation, this is very much in contrast to any kind of allegory that would suggest any specific political settlement between communities.

As Yeats had done before him, Heaney thinks about Sophocles largely in relation to Shakespeare. Parallels with *The Tempest* were obvious to *Cure*'s audiences from the start. In the *Daily Telegraph*, Charles Osborne called the *Philoctetes*, 'Sophocles' most Shakespearean play', and Des McAleer's Philoctetes was called 'Caliban-like' by two reviewers.[39] This is clearest when the character first emerges from his cave to meet Neoptolemus and the chorus. His entrance, then, is very similar to Caliban's own in Shakespeare's play.[40] The chorus expresses pity for his isolation. He is 'Out in the open always', it remarks, 'behaving like a savage', and with 'nothing left but his instincts'.[41] In the Sophoclean original, the chorus does not primarily regard Philoctetes as animalistic, although his isolation from human relationships does not allow him to be entirely human, in the Aristotelian sense of being a political animal, either. When Heaney's Philoctetes first appears, then, he resembles Caliban or the mad King Sweeney, both of whom belong to a tradition of medieval and early modern 'wild men' with no direct parallel in the classical Greek imagination. The character is more Greek than barbarian, however; insofar as he is Calibanic, he is clearly made, rather than born, that way. 'I know I look like a wild animal', Philoctetes exclaims, 'but . . . Don't treat me / Like an untouchable. / What I am / Is what I was made into by the traitors.'[42] The stage sets reinforce this point. Philoctetes' cave is made from the fragmented, knocked-over head of an Apollo Belvedere statue. What was balanced and classical has been broken down, but, as the staging will demonstrate by play's end, this can be reconciled.

When he recounts his story of having been wronged by Odysseus, moreover, Philoctetes descends into a kind of Calibanic rage against the sons of Atreus, his former lords. 'Ten years' misery and starvation', he laments: 'That's all my service ever got for me . . . / Gods curse them all!'[43] Philoctetes' speech parallels much of the unionist rhetoric against the Anglo-Irish Agreement whereby Protestants in the North described being unceremoniously abandoned after centuries of loyalty to London. Another notable aspect of the performance was the way McAleer growled and hollered his lines so that they sounded like Paisley. Based on the Paisley impression, some in Field Day started to call the play 'Ulcer Says No', referencing the unionist political-icon's catchphrase, 'Ulster Says No', against the Anglo-Irish Agreement. Moreover, Deane's pun 'Oranges and Lemnos' plays with the same connection. Furthermore, this parallel surfaces even more clearly later in the play when Neoptolemus returns the stolen bow to Philoctetes, and when he tries to persuade the hero to join the Greeks freely. 'I listened to you once and I believed you', Philoctetes tells Neoptolemus, 'but never again.'[44] Neoptolemus asks if he will be 'saying no forever', and he replies, 'I'll never join', calling any such reconciliation a 'surrender'.

Heaney has said that the problem of the ending gave him the most trouble while writing his version of the *Philoctetes*.[45] In a September 1990 interview with the *Sunday Tribune*, he explained that he had been 'thinking about adapting this play for the last few years', but that 'My hesitancy was due to the fact that a god appears at the end of it. That obviously created dramatic difficulties but I succeeded in dealing with it.'[46] Heaney also spoke about this problem with John Keyes for *Fortnight* in October 1990. Keyes reports that:

> The main theatrical problem for Heaney was the appearance of the deified Hercules. Here, he knew, the chorus had to appear in place of the *deus ex machina* . . . to demonstrate . . . a solution . . . neither arbitrary nor fortuitous . . . and realized by the psychological and spiritual crises that the play had shown. Vitally, Philoctetes had been brought, painfully, to a possible trust. Here the play enters into the realms of classical comedy where things are restored and the world is engulfed in golden possibility. There is inherent a masque of redemption.[47]

Agreeing in principle with Aristotle, Heaney considered the *deus ex machina* conclusion dramatically unsatisfying; it offers too easy an ethical and psychological resolution, and, indeed, lacks catharsis.[48] Heaney altered the conclusion, however, by making it more ethical, more visionary and more cathartic psychologically. First, he extended the two-part chorus. Whereas Sophocles has Hercules come onstage to convince Philoctetes with thirty-five lines of instructions, Heaney lets the chorus speak for the god. It does not speak for Hercules alone, however; the chorus also channels the voice of Poetry for thirty-three lines.[49] In the Field Day production, the chorus stands centre-stage during this section, flanked by Neoptolemus on the left and Philoctetes on the right, both in shadow against a brilliant-white background.

Although it did not work exactly that way in the Field Day production, the 'Hope and History' chorus is followed by what the stage directions call a 'ritual thunder-clap' and by Philoctetes' announcement that he has seen and heard Hercules. After this, the second part of the chorus begins, this time channelling the god himself for twenty-eight lines. The actors also shift positions. Now Philoctetes kneels centre stage in the brilliant light, his previous position taken by Odysseus. The chorus goes to the upper level, positioning itself above him so that all six characters make a pyramid with Philoctetes in the centre. This is where Hercules 'speaks' through the chorus, and Philoctetes looks out into the audience, 'seeing' the god. The chorus talks about opening 'the closed road / between the living and the dead' so that Hercules can 'make the right road clear to you'.[50] This comment corresponds with the staging and lighting:

> Lives that suffer and come right
> Are backlit by eternal light.
>
> So let my mind light up your mind.
> You must see straight and turn around.[51]

Although he does not actually appear onstage, these lines reproduce Hercules' original message faithfully. Heaney makes the metaphor of the voyage more explicit when he writes 'take just spoils and sail at last / Out of the bad dream of your past.'[52] Not only must the gods be shown respect in this version, moreover, but the warriors must also restrain their bloodlust when they sack Troy. 'Win by fair combat', the Herculean chorus says, 'But know to shun / Reprisal killings when it's done.'[53] Hercules' words convince Philoctetes to 'turn around' figuratively. They also convince Neoptolemus and Odysseus to turn around literally, bringing a robe to Philoctetes, who rises as a now clothed and reconciled member of the Greek community. At this point, Heaney's Philoctetes is no longer Calibanic (or Paisleyite); rather, he becomes a Caliban-turned-Prospero, a Caliban whose forgiveness makes him into a Prospero.

In the Field Day production, it was from this position of clothed, reconciled balance that Philoctetes delivered his final speech. It must be noted, however, that the Crowley–Rea staging is a departure from Heaney's own stage directions. Rather than calling for this super-symmetrical placement of actors, Heaney describes Philoctetes in an attitude of overwhelmed, subjective individuality, 'In a sort of a daze, on all fours perhaps, or clasping an upright support: knocked out, flattened.'[54] Perhaps the directors met him halfway by having him supported communally, as it were, by Neoptolemus and Odysseus rather than by some kind of post or stone. The staging has a Masonic look, however, and this may reflect set designer and co-director Bob Crowley's critically acclaimed set design for *The Magic Flute* at the English National Opera in 1988. Philoctetes says that his 'head's light at the thought of a different ground and a different sky'.[55] Working from the poetry alone, however, Philoctetes' farewell to Lemnos recalls Heaney's departure from 'Station Island' where the individualised poet is 'like a convalescent', 'fasted now, light-headed' and 'dangerous'.[56] In the larger context of that 1984 collection, one could argue Heaney's independent 'daze' is also a version of reconciliation, albeit not a communal one.

Whether delivered from a standing position or on all fours, Philoctetes' final speech in *Cure* transforms the Sophoclean original in such a way that it chimes with Heaney's other poetry of that era. In the original play, Sophocles gives a glimpse into the protagonist's interior world by having Philoctetes personify Lemnos as a kind of companion host, albeit a cold and often antagonistic one. 'Often the mountain of Hermes', he recalls in Hugh Lloyd-Jones' translation, 'brought back to me a groan answering my voice as the storm assailed me' when 'my head was drenched inside my cave by the battering of the wind'.[57] This actually sounds like something the protagonist would say in Heaney's 1983 translation of the medieval Irish poem *Sweeney Astray*. Indeed, in September 1990 Heaney told the *Irish News* that when he first read *Philoctetes* around 1985 he 'was struck by the relation to the Sweeney thing in my own work, the sense of his life on the Island'.[58] This connection would certainly justify Heaney's decision to leave us with a mad-seeming Philoctetes at the end of *The Cure*, although this is a significant addition to the Sophoclean original.

Where Sophocles offers personification, however, Heaney goes a step further and has Philoctetes actually identify himself psychologically with Lemnos. 'I'll never get over Lemnos', the character announces:

> this island's going to be the keel under me and the ballast inside me. I'm like a fossil that's being carried away, I'm nothing but cave stones and damp walls and an old mush of dead leaves. The sound of waves in draughty passages. A cliff that's wet with spray on a winter's morning.[59]

In addition to cementing the connection between Philoctetes and mad Sweeney, this is Philoctetes' way of saying that Lemnos, or the experience of having been stranded on Lemnos, has shaped him forever. This will not change even after he has moved beyond his self-regarding desire for retribution against his fellow Greeks. The process of forgiveness and reconciliation is ethically necessary but psychologically overwhelming, and will take a long time. As both 'ballast' and 'keel', Lemnos will be a burden that steadies Philoctetes, a connection to history that enables sea travel, progress and visionary experience.

It is worth remembering, therefore, that Heaney did not end *Cure* on an ecstatic note. When we look to the video of the original tour, we can see that the Field Day production did not close with this sense of other-worldly intensity either. For the final lines of the play, the chorus speaks clear-headedly; accordingly, in the Field Day production the lights went up and the characters all stood squarely on their own feet, facing the audience.

At this point, the chorus advises the audience to 'Suspect too much sweet talk / But never close your mind', even in a historical moment of visionary optimism. 'Now it's high watermark', it continues, 'And flood-tide in the heart / And time to go.'[60] Looking back at this poem from the present day, this chorus has sometimes been criticised for sounding like a catchphrase, and one, moreover, demanding the survivors of the Troubles to get over their losses and move on quickly without complaining. Taken in the context of the play itself, however, it is clear that Heaney did not intend 'Hope and History' to be read as any facile solution that outsiders might impose on the victims of violence, or on their survivors. 'The difficulty of a play with an optimistic ending', he told White, is that it can be mistaken for 'applying a poultice too quickly and not acknowledging the wound'.[61] This would make the play seem historically short-sighted and even insensitive. On the contrary, the chorus balances visionary hopes with sober insight, and reminds us that it may be only once in a lifetime that hope and history rhyme. When we contextualise 'hope and history' in Heaney's poetics of reconciliation, *Cure* appears to be even more prophetic now than it did in the 1990s.

At this point I want to return to the Deane–Heaney conversation with which this chapter began, and ask the question: does Heaney's play of reconciliation reproduce the aesthetic ideology that Deane said blunted the critical edge of Field Day's analysis of politics and culture in modern Ireland? Was it a 'colonial hangover', the hegemony of Arnoldian cultural Hellenism that rhymed hope and history for the Northern Ireland peace process? Considering some of Deane's writings regarding reconciliation, the aesthetic ideology, and the Field Day break-up in the early 1990s, however, one might, nevertheless, have expected from Deane a cool reception to *Cure*. On the contrary, his review 'Oranges and Lemnos' was positive and contained no hint of the 'ricochet effect' between critical theory and the ideology of the aesthetic to which he referred in *The Field Day Anthology*, his *Social Text* interview with Dympna Callaghan, or the unpublished interview with 'Jonathan'.

Deane was not just being evasive; in 'Oranges and Lemnos' he continued to address the key issues he took up with Heaney in 1975, and seemed to endorse Heaney's treatment of them in *Cure*. First, he gave an Adornian affirmation of Heaney's poetic response to the violence of the Troubles, even going so far as to identify this with a larger Field Day ethos. 'Heaney and Eagleton, Brian Friel and Thomas Kilroy, Tom Paulin and Derek Mahon', Deane wrote, 'and all the Field Day dramatists have had in common this preoccupation with freedom, won by coming through, not by skirting round, historical experience.'[62] This means Deane understood the chorus to be rhyming hope 'through' rather than 'round' history. In his reading of hope and history, moreover, Deane continued to address the ongoing dialectical relationship between Hercules and Antaeus. The way he did this furthermore reflected Paulin's recasting of Sophocles as an ethical dramatist of postcolonial subjectivity for Field Day, because here Neoptolemus is the subject split between the categories of Destiny (Philoctetes) and History (Odysseus), much the way Paulin's Ismene is split between Creon (daylight gods) and Antigone (instinctive powers). Deane described the problem:

> Neoptolemus is the anxious mediator who tries to make them [history and destiny] coincide. To stay in history is to remain in bitterness; to betray and be betrayed. To attain destiny is to become whole, to be healed. It is not just a matter of staying faithful to one's community; that is sectarian. Staying faithful to oneself is, paradoxically, truly communal.[63]

Here Deane is reading the ethical drama in terms that were natural to Heaney's poem 'Casualty'. Heaney, therefore, brings Neoptolemus into parallel with Paulin's Ismene.

As predicted by their conversation in 'Unhappy and at home', however, Deane sees Heaney working through these categories in a more nuanced way than O'Brien had argued Heaney had done in *North*. In 'Oranges and Lemnos', therefore, Deane describes Heaney's shift towards the visionary poetics of *Seeing Things*. History is 'ground-hugging' and 'provincial', Deane writes, and 'destiny presides over it'.[64] There are different versions of destiny, however, one of which has been particularly appealing in Ireland 'because of the devastations of colonial rule'.[65] The other makes one whole. The destiny Philoctetes chooses, however, is not the 'pre-ordained' one 'into which the past, history, snugly fits. It is a future the past could not imagine when it was embedded in its apparently inescapable stereotypes.'[66] Deane reads the 'hope and history rhyme' idea, therefore, as an ethical conception of Hercules in relation to Antaeus in the Northern Irish psyche. It is also meant to be therapeutic, and, as such, transcends the category of the 'colonial hangover'.[67]

Whether Deane had unpublished thoughts or an alternate reading of this play that he did not print, or whether Heaney actually intended anything of the sort that Deane read, would be a measure of the frictions within the Field Day board. In 'Oranges and Lemnos', however, Deane endorses the 'Hope and History' chorus as a poetic summation of Field Day's ethos of reconciliation. The terms Deane used to describe and affirm *Cure* were organic to the icon of reconciliation's history; he even reproduces the Aristotelian notion of 'ethical music' when he observes that Heaney's poetry of that time had an 'ethical tonality' which 'gives decency a good name by making it imperial'.[68] By way of that play, and the political figures who quoted it to endorse the peace process of the 1990s, that ethos was in fact widely adopted.

With this in mind, therefore, I want to return to an idea that Deane expressed in his email correspondence to 'Jonathan' about Field Day and why the board of directors broke up. 'Our failure', he wrote, 'was that we only attracted audiences; we did not create one.'[69] In this turn of phrase, Deane is referencing an argument he had recently made about Yeats and the Abbey Theatre, which he saw as an also-failed attempt to create an Irish audience.[70]As he noted in that essay, Yeats had attempted to create an audience through the force of style itself, and the problem of audience creation became a kind of defining subtext of that style. Heaney, by contrast, did not try to shape an audience; instead, he seemed perfectly content to attract one and model for them a poetic ethos of reconciliation for the peace process. Considering the role played by the 'Hope and History' chorus in the 1990s, moreover, we might say that Field Day actually did in a sense create an audience at the precise moment the group, as a theatrical enterprise, started to break up.

In this chapter I have looked to Field Day as a kind of case study for the viability of a modern Aristotelian project of civic art, one that might avoid the pitfalls of the statist ideology David Lloyd has attributed to the identarian projects of Arnoldian culture and national *Bildung*. I have also posed the question of whether the poetics of reconciliation can be something more substantial than a colonial ideology of the aesthetic, and suggested that, indeed, it can do so through an alternative to the exemplary subject of Arnoldian culture – namely, the icon of reconciliation. What makes Heaney an icon rather than an exemplary subject of culture is the fact that he has (following Paulin) delinked Hellenism from the state. This has allowed his visionary poetics (learned from Yeats) to figure forth emblems or 'symbol[s] of the resolved contradiction' rather than allegories or blueprints.[71] *The Cure at Troy* is the ideal drama in this regard, moreover, because it aims to teach through cathartic experience in the audience while at the same time raising questions about the ethics and psychology of conflict resolution. Compared to Yeats' *Oedipus at Colonus*, which sounds all too much like a Free State allegory, Heaney's *Cure* does not prescribe any specific political settlement, even though his exasperation with unionism is clear.

Although using a different approach, Deane has also attempted to retrieve civic art from statist ideology. Like Heaney, moreover, he has also undertaken this task somewhat in the shadow of Yeats. Given the terms of the Yeatsian antitheses I described in the first chapter of this book, it is ironic that Deane, whose scepticism about the rhetoric and aesthetics of reconciliation has been at the core of his critical output, has also shown a somewhat Yeatsian commitment to the foundation and maintenance of cultural and educational institutions. These commitments have led him in the direction of the 'cultural' Yeats, in that it has called him to endorse liberal pluralism in ways that he may have Adornian grounds for criticising. As a postcolonial critic, Deane has rigorously historicised and denaturalised historical discourses of 'national character'. Yet he has also measured Field Day's success by the criterion of whether or not it created an audience who would think about culture and politics from a critical perspective.

In their attempts to retrieve civic art from the statist ideology of culture, therefore, Deane and Heaney each followed a separate Yeatsian antithesis, but reversed their polarities. That is, Heaney has taken that which was most radically anti-foundationalist in the high-modernist Yeats, namely, the poetics of the emblem, and attached it to a much more accessible poetics and liberal politics of human rights. Deane, on the other hand, has followed Yeats down the more Arnoldian path of liberal democracy, pluralism and education. Nevertheless, he has tried at every turn to radicalise those liberal institutions by promoting a critique not just of state violence but also of the ideology of a culture that would authorise it.

Conclusion

Anthologising Reconciliation

> I think the Field Day collection is a symbol of the resolved contradiction.
>
> Seamus Heaney[1]

> [Edna Longley is] right about the difficulty of reconciling [canonisation and deconstruction] . . . But I think she's wrong in saying that, by trying to inhabit two unreconcilable positions, one is therefore caught in a state of paralyzing contradiction.
>
> Seamus Deane[2]

> Our job was easier when we were dealing with armed conflict. It was easy to get people to sign up to say stop the killing, but since the ceasefire it has been more difficult to get people to talk of reconciliation.
>
> Eileen Bell[3]

One might easily come away from this book with the impression that modern Irish Hellenism has been an entirely Sophoclean affair, given almost exclusively to new translations of *Antigone* as meditations on reconciliation in Northern Ireland. This is far from the case, however; Euripides has been almost as popular as Sophocles. Indeed, *Medea*, *Elektra*, *Hippolytus* and *The Bacchae* have all been translated and adapted by such distinguished modern playwrights as Brian Friel, Brendan Kennelly, Marina Carr, Frank McGuinness, Derek Mahon and Colin Teevan.[4] For instance, eight years after the election of President Mary Robinson and the Abbey performances of *The Cure at Troy*, and in the same year as the Good Friday Agreement, the Abbey Theatre staged Marina Carr's Medea-inspired 'Midlands tragedy' *By the Bog of Cats . . .* (1998).[5] The timing and success of this production (among others) attests not just to the pervasiveness of Greek tragedy in modern Irish drama, but also to a multiplicity of Irish Hellenisms, directed towards a variety of issues, transcending the Arnoldian tradition's narrower concern with reconciliation as a key term for addressing Irish culture and politics.[6]

As I have argued above, the Field Day productions of Sophocles' *Antigone* and *Philoctetes* reflect the board's general thinking about questions of identity and reconciliation. As we shall see in my concluding remarks here, reconciliation remains a major theme in the first three volumes of *The Field Day Anthology of Irish Writing* – but is largely displaced in the final two volumes, published in 2002. In terms of Field Day's intervention in Irish public debate, we might think of volumes one to three as a monument to the 'fifth province' idea, which had emerged from the *Crane Bag* (1977–84), edited by Richard Kearney and Mark Patrick Hederman.[7] Another goal of Deane's project was to boost the developing academic field of Irish studies in the direction of postcolonial theory.[8] This last achievement was qualified by the fact, however, that volumes one to three largely presented a gender-exclusive canon despite the editor's stated intentions both to be inclusive and to eschew canon formation as such.[9]

In terms of the Northern cultural intervention, we can say that the first three volumes, published in 1991, largely reflect the narrative of reconciliation John Hume used to promote the Northern Irish peace process.[10] However, the fourth and fifth volumes, published in 2002, are less defined by John Hume's approach to the peace process than by the desire to retrieve forgotten women's voices, and to speak in the distinctly modern voice of Mary Robinson's Ireland.[11] The first three volumes of the *Anthology* also deal with the language of reconciliation in a way that recalls the demolition of the Arnoldian critical tradition that took place in English departments during the canon wars of the 1980s. At the same time, Hume was using that very language to a political effect that Deane and his fellow editors could not fail to support. Therefore, despite the role of critical theory in the conception of the whole, *The Field Day Anthology* was not as radical in its critique of reconciliation as one might otherwise have expected. Although he had long criticised 'pluralism as a political question in relation to Joyce, to Roy Foster, and various others . . . [saying] in effect, for Christ's sake, save us from liberal pluralism', Deane admitted to Dympna Callaghan in 1993 that 'liberal pluralism permeates' his general introduction nonetheless.[12]

In the 1980s and 1990s, Hume spent a great deal of his energies trying to work past Conor Cruise O'Brien's bleak assessments of the North on a political level, while Field Day was trying to work past them on the level of art and cultural criticism. Seamus Heaney later wrote that Hume had not been able to find 'the political equivalent of a golden bough that would guarantee him a safe return from the underground of secret talks into the daylight of the old banal repetitions'.[13] Heaney returns to this analogy in his 1991 book *Seeing Things*, which he begins with a translation of Virgil's *Aeneid*, Book VI, about the golden bough. Like *The Cure at Troy*, *Seeing Things* begins with a visionary plan for constructing, through poetry (the golden bough), an imaginative space in which the irreconcilable differences between polarised communities in Northern Ireland might be reconciled ethically as well as poetically. The autonomous work of art was supposed to be a kind of golden bough, which meant that it allowed political movement that would otherwise not have been possible. The rhetorical situation was impossible. One was not allowed to speak to anyone without being attacked from at least one side, if not both. Heaney was therefore not so much presenting an impossible vision of social and political reconciliation through art as addressing a seemingly impossible rhetorical task through art.

As an organisation receiving funding from both the British and Irish states, and as one that toured the entire island with one of its intentions being to inspire constructive dialogue about partition, Field Day in many ways answered Hume's call for cross-border institutions as essential tools for conflict resolution. In this respect, among others, Field Day thought of itself, and was often considered to be, Ireland's true national theatre (contesting the Abbey's claim to that title) during the 1980s. Additionally, although Field Day was widely criticised as being too nationalist, a number of relatively liberal unionists were more or less sympathetic to it. This made Field Day a cross-border institution that was roughly acceptable to a unionist community that roundly rejected the establishment of other such institutions established by the Hillsborough Agreement. Field Day crossed the border in the manner of the SDLP (Social Democratic and Labour Party) rather than the IRA, and as a group of artists rather than an overtly political organisation, it was able to cross lines more fluidly than the SDLP was.

Hume's was, however, not the only liberal-nationalist perspective on reconciliation for Northern Ireland during the dark years leading to the IRA ceasefire of 1994. The future Irish President Mary Robinson also made important steps towards peace by winning favour with Northern unionism – precisely because she rejected the Hillsborough Agreement Hume had helped engineer. In fact, she resigned her membership of the Labour Party because the agreement had gone over the heads of the unionists; therefore, in 1990, when Robinson won the presidential election in the Republic, unionists applauded this victory as a break with the past in Irish politics. Her tenure in office signalled the kind of transformation of Irish-nationalist symbolism that Hume and others were calling for in 1985. According to many observers, the political discourse in the Republic about the North had become stultified and antiquated. This problem, along with objections to the Catholic Church's hegemony over social and political life in the South, were long-term features of unionist argument. Hume looked for new ways to think about all-Ireland solutions to the Northern crisis, while Robinson looked for ways to modernise social consciousness in the South. She was the feminist head of a state in which divorce was illegal and a ban on abortion was inscribed in the Constitution; her expertise in the Irish Constitution, her feminism and her advocacy of human rights all informed her rhetoric of reconciliation.

In her acceptance speech on 9 November, she framed her political success as a departure from the old narratives of Fine Gael versus Fianna Fáil, the two parties who had emerged from the opposing sides of the Irish civil war of 1922–23. 'I was elected by men and women of all parties and none', she told her audience at Dublin Castle,

> by many with great moral courage who stepped out from the faded flags of the Civil War and voted for a new Ireland, and above all by the women of Ireland, *mná na hÉireann*, who instead of rocking the cradle, rocked the system, and who came out massively to make their mark on the ballot paper and on a new Ireland. I will be a President for all the people, a symbol of reconciliation as well as renewal, not least in my commitment to pluralism and peace on this island.[14]

In this speech, Robinson suggested that one had to 'renew' social and political progress in the Republic before one could reconcile Ireland. These were welcome signs to Northern unionist politicians, whose statements to *The Irish Times* right after the election suggest they recognised Robinson as someone who at least represented the possibility of transformation in Irish politics and society.[15] In the years after the agreement, however, as the political movement towards full power sharing in the North lurched forward with stops, starts and significant reversals, the hope-and-history-style language of reconciliation became less popular.

Given the larger historical context of Ireland between 1998 and 2002, the relative lack of concern with reconciliation in volumes four and five makes sense.[16] Moreover, the 2002 volumes reflected more than simply the feminism of its editorial board, or even the changes in Irish society that took place during the 1990s. Readers familiar with the controversy in 1992 expected to find there a literary reflection of the shifts in public consciousness about gender and sexuality that prevailed in the 1990s. As expected, the gender politics of the later volumes were more progressive. However, the editorial methodology, which was more rigorously anti-aesthetic and anti-canonical than Deane's, was off-putting to readers who expected a more traditional approach.[17]

Here, also, the language of reconciliation was more substantially to be invoked in relation to the debate over divorce in the Republic than it was in relation to the nationalist–unionist conflict in the North. When the language was used in relation to the Northern Troubles, it was primarily invoked as a term to be critiqued in relation to the pervasive sexism of the peace process in the 1990s. As Bronagh Hinds asked about the *New Framework for Agreement* (1995) between London and Dublin, 'even though, to use the words of that document itself, the two governments may want to reconcile "the rights of both traditions in the fullest and most equitable manner", what "new beginning" can women expect?'[18] As several of the writers in Mary O'Dowd's section on 'Women and politics in Northern Ireland, 1993–2000' attest, there was considerable irony attached to the fact that women, who had been for so long invested with the symbolic function of peacemakers during the years of armed conflict, were nevertheless largely excluded from the political representation during the peace process itself. Kate Fearon, for instance, in her history of the Northern Ireland Women's Coalition, describes the experience of its two representatives in the Northern Ireland Forum for Political Understanding and Dialogue, which 'The NIWC soon came to refer to . . . as the "Forum for Political Misunderstanding and Monologue."'[19] This was not simply due to the unionist majority in the chamber but due also to the pervasive sexism of the male representatives in that body.

I want to end this discussion of reconciliation in the *Field Day Anthology* by considering a speech recorded therein by Bernadette McAliskey, the political activist from Derry, about whom O'Brien wrote his original *Antigone* analogy in 1968. Her speech illustrated the limitations of this concept from a feminist perspective, and even the limitations of popular perception of the struggle for peace and justice in Northern Ireland. 'Now violence is a big word', she told the Clár na mBan conference in 1994, and

> When the government [in the Downing Street Declaration] says they are talking about guaranteeing an end to violence, they are talking

> about the IRA handing over their weapons. They are not talking about an end to the Prevention of Terrorism Act. They are not talking about an end to the Payment of Debt Act. They are not talking about making it a criminal offence for a man to beat his wife or any other woman for whom he owns a valid certificate, a licence, a piece of paper that says he owns a property and, therefore, as long as he doesn't beat her on a public street it is nobody else's business. They are not talking about ending the violence of sexist or sexual abuse of women who are owned by men. We are not talking about the violence of people who think they own their children and therefore, in their own interests ought to beat them into submission.[20]

Her detractors might say that McAliskey is muddying the water when she brings up spousal or child abuse in her critique of the Downing Street Declaration, but what she is talking about is no less important to a 'tragic' understanding of the Troubles than O'Brien's Sophoclean intervention had been in 1968. Indeed, McAliskey's insights about the forms of domestic violence experienced during the Troubles, not substantially addressed in the course of the peace process, have become significant topics in journalistic accounts of conflict around the globe today. In terms of this book, her protest raises the question: can there be, and *should* there be, an ethical rhetoric of 'reconciliation' to counter the narratives that enable domestic violence and child abuse? Perhaps the icon of reconciliation will have to be wholly reconfigured yet again (perhaps to include Sinéad O'Connor), or perhaps a new term will have to be found for picturing a world where one can be what Adorno called 'different without fear'.[21]

One last example of the 'Hope and History' chorus' quotation in Irish politics deserves mention in this book. Over the decade that followed the signing of the Belfast Agreement, political progress in Northern Ireland moved forward at an agonisingly slow rate – and at some points it actually moved in reverse. Although the IRA has declared its campaign over, paramilitary violence never completely disappeared on either side. Held up by disagreements over the decommissioning of IRA weapons, moreover, the Northern Ireland Assembly was suspended from 2002 to 2007. It was hard to see the way forward after the general election of 2005, when Revd Ian Paisley's Democratic Unionist Party (which opposed the Belfast Agreement) decisively beat the Ulster Unionist Party – just as Sinn Féin displaced John Hume's SDLP. In May 2007, however, the Assembly reconvened with Paisley as first minister and Sinn Féin's Martin McGuinness as deputy first minister. The two got along surprisingly well in front of the cameras, however, and over the following year they developed something like a political friendship. When Paisley retired from Stormont in 2008, McGuinness gave him two framed gifts: the first was a poem of his own composition, and the second was a copy of the 'Hope and History' chorus, written out by Heaney himself. The gift was especially appropriate considering the fact that the only concrete political prediction to be found in *The Cure at Troy* was that Paisley would ultimately participate in the peace process. The Sinn Féin deputy first minister's gesture towards the real-life Philoctetes makes Heaney's version of Sophocles seem even more prescient than it did in 1998. But what did this mean to Philoctetes? *The Times* correspondent, David Sharrock, reported that 'Mr Paisley's response to the gift remains a secret.'[22]

Bibliography

Archives

Irish Film Institute Irish Film Archive: Field Day Archive

Three transcripts of interviews with Seamus Heaney for BBC *Arena* documentary, 'History Boys on the Rampage', VII.i.2, F/5

Transcript of interview with Tom Paulin for BBC *Arena* documentary, 'History Boys on the Rampage', VII.i.2, F/6

Recording of production of *The Cure of Troy* at Belltable Arts Centre, Limerick, 7 December 1990, VII.ii, VHS/5

National Library of Ireland Field Day Archive

Directors' correspondence, Stephen Rea, III.v.7, G/D/Rea/1a-4

Letter (undated) from Seamus Deane to Jonathan [Williams?], IX.i.9, D/4

Press cuttings for *High Time/The Riot Act*, V. PC/1984/1-3

Press cuttings for *The Cure at Troy*, V. PC/1990/1-6

Short essays by Seamus Deane on Field Day, circa 1985, III.x.1, G/Misc/8

National Library of Ireland W.B. Yeats Collection

The Study of Celtic Literature (London, 1891); Yeats' copy

Film

Arena, 'History Boys on the Rampage' (dir. Andrew Eaton), BBC, 1988

The Story of Field Day (dir. Johnny Muir), BBC Northern Ireland, 2006

Anne Devlin (dir. Pat Murphy), Bord Scannán na hÉireann, 1984

Periodicals

Atlantic Monthly

Belfast Telegraph

Daily Telegraph

Financial Times

Fortnight

Galway Advertiser

Guardian

Independent

Independent on Sunday
Irish News
Irish Press
The Irish Times
National Review
New Statesman & Society
New Yorker
New York Times
Northern Constitution
Sunday Independent
Sunday Tribune
The Listener
The Times
Times Literary Supplement

Personal Interviews

Mary Lawlor, June 2009
Stephen Rea, June 2009
Bill Shipsey, June 2009
Kevin Whelan, June 2009

Books, Articles, Web References

Adams, Gerry, *Hope and History: Making Peace in Ireland* (Dingle, 2003)
Address by Prime Minister of the United Kingdom, Dáil Éireann, vol. 497, 26 November 1998
Adorno, Theodor and Max Horkheimer, *Dialectic of Enlightenment*, trans. John Cumming (London, 1994)
—, *Minima Moralia: Reflections from Damaged Life*, trans. E.F.N. Jephcott (London, 1978)
—, *Negative Dialectics*, trans. E.B. Ashton (London, 1973)
—, *Notes to Literature*, 2 vols, ed. Rolf Tiedman, trans. Shierry Weber Nicholsen (New York, 1974)
Akenson, Donald H., *Conor: A Biography of Conor Cruise O'Brien* (Ithaca, NY, 1994)
Allison, Jonathan, 'Seamus Heaney's Yeats', *Yeats: An Annual of Critical and Textual Studies*, no. 14 (1996)
Althusser, Louis, *Lenin and Philosophy and Other Essays*, trans. Ben Brewster (London, 1971)
Alt, Peter and Russell Allspach (eds), *The Variorum Edition of the Poems of W.B. Yeats* (London, 1957)
Anonymous, 'Memorable Molière – but subverted Sophocles', *Northern Constitution*, 3 November 1984
—, 'Broad unionist welcome to election outcome', *The Irish Times*, 9 November 1990
Aristotle, *Nichomachean Ethics*, trans. C.J. Rowe and Sarah Broadie (Oxford, 2002)
—, *On Rhetoric: A Theory of Civic Discourse*, trans. with commentary George Alexander Kennedy (Oxford, 1991)
—, *The Art of Rhetoric*, trans. John Henry Freese (Cambridge, MA, 1975)
—, *The Poetics of Aristotle*, trans. with commentary Stephen Halliwell (Chapel Hill, NC, 1987)

——, *The Politics and the Constitution of Athens*, trans. Stephen Everson (Cambridge, 1988)
Arkins, Brian, 'Yeats's version of Colonus' Praise', *Classical and Modern Literature: A Quarterly*, no. 7 (1986)
——, *Builders of My Soul: Greek and Roman Themes in Yeats* (Gerards Cross, Bucks, 1990)
——, *Irish Appropriation of Greek Tragedy* (Dublin, 2010)
——, 'The duality of Oedipus in Yeats', *International Journal of the Classical Tradition*, vol. 18, no. 3 (September 2011)
——, 'Three Medeas from modern Ireland', in Heike Bartel and Anne Simon (eds), *Unbinding Medea: Interdisciplinary Approaches to a Classical Myth from Antiquity to the 21st Century* (London, 2010)
Arnold, Matthew, *The Complete Prose Works of Matthew Arnold: Volume I: On the Classical Tradition*, ed. R.H. Super (Ann Arbor, MI, 1960)
——, *The Complete Prose Works of Matthew Arnold: Volume III: Lectures and Essays in Criticism*, ed. R.H. Super (Ann Arbor, MI, 1962)
——, *The Complete Prose Works of Matthew Arnold: Volume IV: Culture and Anarchy*, ed. R.H. Super (Ann Arbor, MI, 1965)
——, *The Complete Prose Works of Matthew Arnold: Volume IX: English Literature and Irish Politics*, ed. R.H. Super (Ann Arbor, MI, 1977)
——, *The Complete Prose Works of Matthew Arnold: Volume XI: The Last Word*, ed. R.H. Super (Ann Arbor, MI, 1977)
——, *The Study of Celtic Literature* (London, 1891)
Art for Amnesty, 'Ambassador of Conscience Award', http://www.artforamnesty.org/view_event.php?id=5 (accessed 9 February 2009)
Barnard, Toby, 'An abrasive Palesman: Conor Cruise O'Brien and modern Ireland', *Times Literary Supplement*, 16 December 1994
Battersby, Eileen, 'Stalked by an agenda', *The Irish Times*, 5 October 2002
Benjamin, Walter, *The Arcades Project*, trans. Rolf Tiedemann (Cambridge, MA, 1999)
Berenson, Peter, 'The forgotten prisoners', *Observer*, 28 May 1961
Biggar, Nigel (ed.), *Burying the Past: Making Peace and Doing Justice after Civil Conflict* (Washington, DC, 2001)
Boland, Eavan, 'Daughters of colony: a personal interpretation of the place of gender issues in the postcolonial interpretation of Irish literature', *Éire-Ireland: A Journal of Irish Studies*, vol. 32, nos. 2–3 (summer/fall 1997)
Böss, Michael, 'The postmodern nation: a critical history of "fifth province" discourse', *Études Irlandaises*, vol. 27, no. 1 (spring 2002)
Bourke, Angela, Siobhán Kilfeather, Maria Lundy, Margaret MacCurtain, Gerardine Meaney, Máirín Ní Dhonnchadha, Mary O'Dowd and Clair Wills (eds), *The Field Day Anthology of Irish Writing: Vols 4–5: Irish Women's Writing and Traditions* (New York, 2002)
Bourke, Richard, 'Antigone and after: "ethnic" conflict in historical perspective', *Field Day Review*, no. 2 (2006)
——, *Peace in Ireland: The Battle of Ideas* (London, 2003)
Bracken, Claire, 'Becoming mother-machine: the event of Field Day vols iv and v', in Patricia Coughlan and Tina O'Toole (eds), *Irish Literature: Feminist Perspectives* (Dublin, 2008)
Bradley, A.C., *Oxford Lectures on Poetry* (London, 1909)
Brady, Ciaran (ed.), *Interpreting Irish History: The Debate on Historical Revisionism, 1938–1994* (Dublin, 1994)

Bromwich, David, 'The geneology of disinterestedness', *Raritan: A Quarterly Review*, no. 1 (1982)

Brown, John (ed.), *In the Chair: Interviews with Poets from the North of Ireland* (Cliffs of Moher, Co. Clare, 2002)

Buckler, William E., '*Literature and Dogma* and literature: new textual perspective on Matthew Arnold's critical organicism', *Victorian Newsletter*, no. 59 (1981)

Burke, Edmund, *Reflections on the Revolution in France: A Critical Edition*, ed. J.C.D. Clark (Stanford, CA, 2001)

Burris, Sidney, 'Reviewing contemporary poetry: Helen Vendler and the aesthetic method', *Contemporary Literature*, vol. 31, no. 2 (1990)

Cairns, Ed and Micheal D. Roe (eds), *The Role of Memory in Ethnic Conflict* (London, 2003)

Callaghan, Dympna, 'An interview with Seamus Deane, University College, Dublin, June 1993', *Social Text*, no. 38 (1994)

Campbell, Lewis, *Tragic Drama in Aeschylus, Sophocles, and Shakespeare* (New York, 1965)

Carr, Marina, *By the Bog of Cats* (New York, 2002)

Carroll, Joseph, *The Cultural Theory of Matthew Arnold* (Berkeley, CA, 1982)

Carson, Ciaran, 'Escaped from the massacre?', *Honest Ulsterman*, no. 50 (winter 1975)

Cavanagh, Michael, 'Tower and boat: Yeats and Seamus Heaney', *New Hibernia Review/Iris Éireannach Nua*, vol. 4, no. 3 (autumn/fómhar, 2000)

Chamberlain, Charles, 'From "haunts" to "character": the meaning of êthos and its relation to ethics', *Helios*, vol. 11, no. 2 (winter 1984)

Cicero, Marcus Tullius, *De Oratore I: Books I, II*, ed. E.W. Sutton (Cambridge, MA, 1942)

Cixous, Hélène, 'The laugh of the Medusa', in Elaine Marks and Isabelle de Courtivron (eds), *New French Feminisms* (New York, 1980)

Clark, David R. and James B. McGuire, 'The writing of Sophocles' *King Oedipus*', *Yeats: An Annual of Critical and Textual Studies*, no. 2 (1984)

Cleary, Joe, 'Domestic troubles: tragedy and the Northern Ireland conflict', *South Atlantic Quarterly*, no. 98 (1999)

Clinton, Bill, *Between Hope and History* (New York, 1996)

——, 'Presidential radio address – 11 April 1998', http://en.wikisource.org/wiki/Presidential_Radio_Address_-_11_April_1998 (accessed 29 January 2008)

Cole, Elizabeth (ed.), *Teaching the Violent Past: History Education and Reconciliation* (Plymouth, Devon, 2007)

Cohen, Michael A., 'Politics vs. drama in O'Brien's *Murderous Angels*', *Contemporary Literature*, no. 16 (1975)

Connolly, Claire, 'Ugly criticism: union and division in Irish literature', *Field Day Review*, no. 4 (2008)

Corr, Chris, 'Matthew Arnold and the younger Yeats: the manoeuvrings of cultural aesthetics', *Irish University Review: A Journal of Irish Studies*, no. 28 (1998)

Coughlan, Patricia, '"Bog queens": the representation of women in the poetry of John Montague and Seamus Heaney', in Toni O'Brien Johnson and David Cairns (eds), *Gender in Irish Writing* (Philadelphia, PA, 1991)

Crowley, Sharon and Debra Hawhee, *Ancient Rhetorics for Contemporary Students*, 3rd edn. (London, 2003)

Cullingford, Elizabeth, *Gender and History in Yeats's Love Poetry* (Cambridge, 1993)

——, *Yeats, Ireland and Fascism* (Oxford, 1981)

Curtis, L.P., *Coercion and Conciliation in Ireland, 1880–1892: A Study in Conservative Unionism* (Princeton, NJ, 1963)

Dawson, Graham, *Making Peace with the Past? Memory, Trauma and the Irish Troubles* (Manchester, 2011)

Deane, Seamus, 'Civilians and barbarians', in Thomas Flanagan (ed.), *Ireland's Field Day* (Notre Dame, IN, 1986)

——, and Barre Fitzpatrick, 'Interview with John Hume', *Crane Bag*, vol. 4, no. 2 (1980)

——, (ed.), *The Field Day Anthology of Irish Writing*, 3 vols (Derry, 1991)

——, 'Field Day's Greeks (and Russians)', in Marianne McDonald and J. Michael Walton (eds), *Amid Our Troubles: Irish Versions of Greek Tragedy* (London, 2002)

——, 'Heroic styles: the tradition of an idea', in Thomas Flanagan (ed.), *Ireland's Field Day* (Notre Dame, IN, 1986)

——, 'Irish theatre: a secular space?', *Irish University Review*, vol. 28, no. 1 (1998)

——, 'Oranges and Lemnos', *New Statesman & Society*, no. 120 (5 April 1991)

——, 'The poet's dream of an audience', *Times Literary Supplement*, 7 March 1986

——, 'Unhappy and at home: interview with Seamus Heaney', *Crane Bag*, vol. 1, no. 1 (1977)

——, 'Wherever green is read', Máirín Ní Dhonnchadha and Theo Dorgan (eds), *Revising the Rising* (Derry, 1991)

——, 'Yeats: the creation of an audience', in Nicholas Grene (ed.), *Tradition and Influence in Anglo-Irish Poetry* (Totowa, NJ, 1989)

de Bréadún, Deaglán, '"The Cruiser": still stirring things up after all these years', *The Irish Times*, 28 October 1998

de Man, Paul, *The Rhetoric of Romanticism* (New York, 1984)

De Selincourt, Aubrey, *Six Great Playwrights: Sophocles, Shakespeare, Molière, Sheridan, Ibsen, Shaw* (London, 1960)

DeLaura, David J., *Hebrew and Hellene in Victorian England: Newman, Arnold, and Pater* (Austin, TX, 1969)

Denard, Hugh, 'Seamus Heaney, colonialism, and the cure: Sophoclean re-visions', *PAJ: A Journal of Performance and Art*, no. 22 (2000)

Doyle, Maria-Elena, 'A gesture to indicate a presence: translation, dialect and Field Day Theatre Company's quest for an Irish identity', in Sherry Simon and Paul St-Pierre (eds), *Changing the Terms: Translating the Postcolonial Era* (Ottawa, 2000)

Elliott, Marianne (ed.), *The Long Road to Peace in Northern Ireland* (Liverpool, 2002)

Engelberg, Edward, 'Yeats and Sophocles', *English Literature in Transition, 1880–1920*, no. 33 (1990)

Fantham, Elaine, 'Ciceronian conciliare and Aristotelian ethos', *Phoenix*, vol. 27, no. 3 (1973)

Faverty, Frederic E., *Matthew Arnold the Ethnologist* (Evanston, IL, 1951)

Flannery, Eóin, 'Morning yet on Field Day? Ireland, Field Day and postcolonialism', in Helen Thompson (ed.), *The Current Debate about the Irish Literary Canon: Essays Reassessing the Field Day Anthology of Irish Writing* (Lewiston, NY, 2006)

Fleiss, Peter J., *Thucydides and the Politics of Bipolarity* (Baton Rouge, LA, 1966)

Forché, Carolyn (ed.), *Against Forgetting: Twentieth-century Poetry of Witness* (New York, 1993)

Fortenbaugh, William W., '*Benevolentiam Conciliare* and *Animos Permovere*: some remarks on Cicero's *De Oratore* 2.178–216', *Rhetorica*, no. 6 (1988)

Foster, Aisling, 'Too much, but still not enough', *Guardian*, 4 January 2003

Foster, Roy, 'Adams' original sin', *Financial Times*, 23 October 2004
——, 'Nations, yet again', *Times Literary Supplement*, 27 March 1992
——, *W.B. Yeats: A Life I: The Apprentice Mage, 1865–1914* (Oxford, 1997)
——, *W.B. Yeats: A Life II: The Arch-poet, 1915–1939* (Oxford, 2003)
——, 'Yeats at war: poetic strategies and political reconstruction from the Easter Rising to the Free State', *Transactions of the Royal Historical Society*, no. 11 (2001)
Frame, Frances, 'Arnold and the Irish question: anticipating communitarianism', *Nineteenth-century Prose*, no. 34 (2007)
Fugard, Athol, John Kani and Winston Ntshona, *Statements* (New York, 1986)
Gallagher, Susan V., *Truth and Reconciliation: The Confessional Mode in South African Literature* (Portsmouth, NH, 2002)
Garver, Eugene, *Aristotle's Rhetoric: An Art of Character* (Chicago, IL, 1994)
Gibbons, Luke, 'Dialogue without the other? A reply to Francis Mulhern', *Radical Philosophy*, no. 67 (1994)
Gibbons, Luke and Kevin Whelan, 'In conversation with Stephen Rea', *Yale Journal of Criticism: Interpretation in the Humanities*, no. 15 (2002)
Gibbs, David N., 'Dag Hammarskjöld, the United Nations, and the Congo Crisis of 1960–1: a reinterpretation', *Journal of Modern African Studies*, no. 31 (1993)
Goethe, Johann Wolfgang, *Essays on Art and Literature*, ed. John Gearey, trans. Ellen von Nardroff and Ernest Nardroff (Princeton, NJ, 1994)
Gossman, Lionel, 'Philhellenism and antisemitism: Matthew Arnold and his German models', *Comparative Literature*, no. 46 (1994)
Gould, Thomas, *The Ancient Quarrel Between Poetry and Philosophy* (Princeton, NJ, 1990)
Grab, Frederic D., 'Yeats' *King Oedipus*', *Journal of English and Germanic Philology*, no. 71 (1972)
Graham, Spencer (ed.), *Forgiving and Remembering in Northern Ireland: Approaches to Conflict Resolution* (London, 2011)
Gramsci, Antonio, *Prison Notebooks*, 3 vols, ed. and trans. Joseph A. Buttigieg (New York, 1992–2007)
Greene, John C., Patricia L. Haberstroh and Adrian Frazier, 'Wealth, gender, politics: three views of *The Field Day Anthology of Irish Writing*', *Éire-Ireland: A Journal of Irish Studies*, vol. 27, no. 2 (summer 1992)
Grene, David, *Reality and the Heroic Pattern: Last Plays of Ibsen, Shakespeare, and Sophocles* (Chicago, IL, 1967)
Griffiths, Martin, *Realism, Idealism, and International Politics: A Reinterpretation* (New York, 1992)
Halloran, S. Michael, 'Aristotle's concept of ethos, or if not his somebody else's', *Rhetoric Review*, vol. 1, no. 1 (September 1982)
Hammarskjöld, Dag, *Markings. Vägmärken*, trans. Leif Sjöberg and W.H. Auden (New York, 1964)
Hanks, Robert, 'The week in radio', *Independent*, 6 October 2004
Hardwick, Lorna, 'Classical texts in post-colonial literatures: consolation, redress and new beginnings in the work of Derek Walcott and Seamus Heaney', *International Journal of the Classical Tradition*, vol. 9, no. 2 (fall 2002)
——, 'Greek drama and anti-colonialism: decolonizing classics', in Edith Hall, Fiona Macintosh and Amanda Wrigley (eds), *Dionysus Since 69: Greek Tragedy at the Dawn of the Third Millennium* (Oxford, 2004)
Hardwick, Lorna and Carol Gillespie (eds), *Classics in post-colonial worlds* (Oxford, 2007)
Hardy, Molly O'Hagan, 'Symbolic power: Mary Robinson's presidency and Eavan

Boland's poetry', *New Hibernia Review/Iris Éireannach Nua*, vol. 12, no. 3 (fómhar/autumn 2008)

Harkin, Hugh, 'Irish Antigones: towards tragedy without borders?', *Irish University Review: A Journal of Irish Studies*, no. 38 (2008)

Heaney, Seamus, *Finders Keepers: Selected Prose, 1971–2001* (New York, 2002)

—, 'Human rights, poetic redress', *The Irish Times*, 15 March 2008

—, Interview, *Irish News*, 22 September 1990

—, Interview, *Sunday Tribune*, 30 September 1990

—, Interview with Barry White, *Belfast Telegraph*, 29 September 1990

—, Interview with John Keyes, *Fortnight*, 15 October 1990

—, Interview with 'J.O'C.', *Galway Advertiser*, 18 October 1990

—, *North* (London, 1975)

—, 'Old Derry's walls', *The Listener*, 24 October 1968

—, *Preoccupations: Selected Prose* (London, 1980)

—, 'Sophoclean', *New Yorker*, 3 March 2003

—, *Station Island* (London, 1984)

—, *Sweeney Astray* (Derry, 1983)

—, *The Burial at Thebes: A Version of Sophocles'* Antigone (New York, 2004)

—, *The Cure at Troy: A Version of Sophocles'* Philoctetes (New York, 1991)

—, '*The Cure at Troy*: production notes in no particular order', in Marianne McDonald and J. Michael Walton (eds), *Amid Our Troubles: Irish Versions of Greek Tragedy* (London, 2002)

—, *The Government of the Tongue: Selected Prose, 1978–1987* (New York, 1989)

—, *The Haw Lantern* (London, 1987)

—, 'The Trojan warrior', interview with Jane Coyle, *Stet* (September 1990)

—, *The Redress of Poetry* (New York, 1995)

—, 'Title deeds: translating a classic', *Proceedings of the American Philosophical Society*, vol. 148 (2004)

—, 'William Butler Yeats (1865–1939)', in Seamus Deane (ed.), *The Field Day Anthology of Irish Writing*, vol. 2 (Derry, 1991)

—, *Wintering Out* (London, 1972)

Hearfield, Colin, *Adorno and the Modern Ethos of Freedom* (Aldershot, 2004)

Hegel, Georg Wilhelm Friedrich, *Aesthetics: Lectures on Fine Art*, trans. T.M. Knox, 2 vols (Oxford, 1975)

—, *Philosophy of Fine Art*, trans. F.P.B. Osmaston, 4 vols (London, 1920)

—, *The Phenomenology of Spirit*, trans. J.N. Findlay (Oxford, 1977)

Higgins, Michael D., 'Culture, democracy and public service broadcasting', in Mary P. Corcoran and Mark O'Brien (eds), *Political Censorship and the Democratic State: The Irish Broadcasting Ban* (Dublin, 2005)

Higgins, Róisín, '"A drift of chosen females?": *The Field Day Anthology of Irish Writing*, vols. 4 and 5', *Irish University Review*, vol. 33, no. 2 (2003)

Hohenleitner, Kathleen, 'The book at the center of the stage: Friel's *Making History* and the *Field Day Anthology of Irish Writing*', in Stephen Watt, Eileen Morgan and Shakir Mustafa (eds), *A Century of Irish Drama: Widening the Stage* (Bloomington, IN, 2000)

Holland, Jack, *Hope Against History: The Course of Conflict in Northern Ireland* (New York, 1999)

Honig, Bonnie, 'Antigone's two laws: Greek tragedy and the politics of humanism', *New Literary History*, no. 41 (2010)

Horgan, John, *Irish Media: A Critical History Since 1922* (New York, 2001)

Hornblower, Simon and Antony Spawforth (eds), *The Oxford Classical Dictionary* (Oxford, 2009)

Horton-Smith, Lionel, *Ars Tragica Sophoclea cum Shaksperiana Comparata* (Cambridge, 1896)

Howe, Stephen, *Ireland and Empire: Colonial Legacies in Irish History and Culture* (Oxford, 2000)

Hughes, Eamonn, '"Could anyone write it?": place in Tom Paulin's poetry', in Colin Graham and Richard Kirkland (eds), *Ireland and Cultural Theory: The Mechanics of Authenticity* (London, 1999)

Huizinga, Johan, *Homo Ludens: A Study of the Play-element in Culture* (New York, 1950)

Hume, John, *A New Ireland: Politics, Peace, and Reconciliation* (Boulder, CO, 1996)

—, 'Reconciling the irreconcilable', in Seamus Deane (ed.), *The Field Day Anthology of Irish Writing*, vol. 1 (Derry, 1991)

Jameson, Fredric and Ronald Taylor (eds), *Aesthetics and Politics: Key Texts in the Debate Within German Marxism* (London, 1980)

Jepsen, Laura, *Ethical Aspects of Tragedy: A Comparison of Certain Tragedies by Aeschylus, Sophocles, Euripides, Seneca and Shakespeare* (Gainesville, FL, 1953)

Johnston, Dillon, 'Cross-currencies in the culture market: Arnold, Yeats, Joyce', *South Atlantic Quarterly*, vol. 95, no. 1 (1996)

Jones III, Richard C., '"Talking amongst ourselves": language, politics, and Sophocles on the Field Day stage', *International Journal of the Classical Tradition*, vol. 4, no. 2 (fall 1997)

Jordan, Eamonn, 'Unmasking the myths? Marina Carr's *By the Bog of Cats* and *On Raftery's Hill*', in Marianne McDonald and J. Michael Walton (eds), *Amid Our Troubles: Irish Versions of Greek Tragedy* (London, 2002)

Joseph, Gerhard, 'The *Antigone* as cultural touchstone: Matthew Arnold, Hegel, George Eliot, Virginia Woolf, and Margaret Drabble', *PMLA: Publications of the Modern Language Association of America*, vol. 96, no. 1 (1981)

Kaufman, Robert, 'Aura, still', in Andrew E. Benjamin (ed.), *Walter Benjamin and Art* (New York, 2005)

Keane, Elizabeth, *An Irish Statesman and Revolutionary: The Nationalist and Internationalist Politics of Seán MacBride* (New York, 2006)

Keane, Patrick J., 'Faithful in his fashion: Yeats and the Eros chorus from Sophocles' *Antigone*', *Yeats Eliot Review: A Journal of Criticism and Scholarship*, no. 8 (1986)

—, 'Revolutions French and Russian: Burke, Wordsworth, and the genesis of Yeats's "The Second Coming"', *Bulletin of Research in the Humanities*, no. 82 (1979)

Kearney, Richard, 'Ulysses returns to Ithaca: the odysseys and ambiguities of Conor Cruise O'Brien', *Times Literary Supplement*, 15 January 1999

Kelleher, Margaret, 'The cabinet of Irish literature: a historical perspective on Irish anthologies', *Éire-Ireland: A Journal of Irish Studies*, vol. 38, nos. 3–4 (fall/winter 2003)

—, '*The Field Day Anthology* and Irish women's literary studies', *Irish Review*, no. 30 (2003)

Kelly, John, *A W.B. Yeats Chronology* (New York, 2003)

Kennedy, Michael and Art Magennis, *Ireland: The United Nations and the Congo* (Dublin, 2014)

Keogh, Dermot and Michael Haltzel (eds), *Northern Ireland and the Politics of Reconciliation* (Cambridge, 1993)

Kermode, Frank, *The Romantic Image* (London, 1957)

Kiberd, Declan, *Inventing Ireland* (Cambridge, MA, 1997)

Kirkland, Richard, *Literature and Culture in Northern Ireland Since 1965: Moments of Danger* (London, 1996)

Knox, Colin and Pádraic Quirk (eds), *Peace Building in Northern Ireland, Israel and South Africa: Transition, Transformation and Reconciliation* (New York, 2000)

Laertius, Diogenes, *Lives of Eminent Philosophers*, ed. Tiziano Dorandi (Cambridge, MA, 2013)

Lambropoulos, Vassilis, 'Violence and the liberal imagination: the representation of Hellenism in Matthew Arnold', in Nancy Armstrong and Leonard Tennenhouse (eds), *The Violence of Representation: Literature and the History of Violence* (London, 1989)

Lane, Christopher, 'The Arnoldian ideal, or culture studies and the problem of nothingness', in Amanda Anderson and Joseph Valente (eds), *Disciplinarity at the Fin de Siècle* (Princeton, NJ, 2002)

Lebow, Richard, *The Tragic Vision of Politics: Ethics, Interests and Orders* (Cambridge, 2003)

Lecossois, Hélène, 'From Medea to Hester Swane: Marina Carr's rewriting of Ethos in *By the Bog of Cats*', in Thierry Dubost (ed.), *Drama Reinvented: Theatre Adaptation in Ireland 1970–2007* (Brussels, 2012)

Levinas, Emmanuel, *Totality and Infinity: An Essay on Exteriority*. trans. Alfonso Lingis (Pittsburg, PA, 1969)

Lloyd, David and Paul Thomas, *Culture and the State* (New York, 1998)

Lloyd, David, *Anomalous States: Irish Writing and the Post-colonial Moment* (Durham, NC, 1993)

——, 'Arnold, Ferguson and Schiller: aesthetic culture and the politics of aesthetics', *Cultural Critique*, no. 2 (1985)

Logan, Peter Melville, 'Fetishism and freedom in Matthew Arnold's cultural theory', *Victorian Literature and Culture*, no. 31 (2003)

Long, Christopher P., 'Totalizing identities: the ambiguous legacy of Aristotle and Hegel after Auschwitz', *Philosophy and Social Criticism*, vol. 29, no. 2 (2003)

——, 'The ethical culmination of Aristotle's metaphysics', *Epoché*, vol. 8, no. 1 (fall 2003)

Long, Joseph, 'The Sophoclean killing fields: an interview with Frank McGuinness', in Marianne McDonald and J. Michael Walton (eds), *Amid Our Troubles: Irish Versions of Greek Tragedy* (London, 2002)

Longley, Edna, 'Hospitable meta-narrative or hegemonic bid?', *Canadian Journal of Irish Studies*, vol. 18, no. 2 (1992)

——, '"Inner emigré" or "artful voyeur": Seamus Heaney's *North*', in Michael Allen (ed.), *New Casebooks: Seamus Heaney* (New York, 1997)

——, *The Living Stream: Literature and Revisionism in Ireland* (Newcastle upon Tyne, 1994)

Longley, Michael, *Collected Poems* (London, 2006)

Love, Mervyn, *Peace Building Through Reconciliation in Northern Ireland* (Aldershot, 1995)

Luddy, Maria, '*The Field Day Anthology of Irish Writing: Volumes Four and Five: Irish Women's Writing and Traditions*', *Women's Studies International Forum*, vol. 26, no. 4 (2003)

Lyons, F.S.L., *Culture and Anarchy in Ireland, 1890–1939* (Oxford, 1979)

——, *Ireland Since the Famine* (London, 1972)

McAliskey, Bernadette Devlin, *The Price of My Soul* (New York, 1969)

McCarthy, Conor, *Modernisation: Crisis and Culture in Ireland 1969–1992* (Dublin, 2000)

McCarthy, Gerry, 'Skirting the issue', *Sunday Times*, 24 November 2002

McDiarmid, Lucy, 'Isn't it a great pity?', *Times Literary Supplement*, 27 December 2002

McDonagh, John, '"Is Medea's crime Medea's glory?" Euripides in Dublin', in Marianne McDonald and J. Michael Walton (eds), *Amid Our Troubles: Irish Versions of Greek Tragedy* (London, 2002)

McDonald, Marianne, 'When despair and history rhyme: colonialism and Greek Tragedy', *New Hibernia Review/Iris Éireannach Nua*, vol. 1, no. 2 (samhradh/summer 1997)

——, 'The Irish and Greek tragedy', in Marianne McDonald and J. Michael Walton (eds), *Amid Our Troubles: Irish Versions of Greek Tragedy* (London, 2002)

McGuinness, Frank, 'Writing in Greek: *By the Bog of Cats* . . . programme note: Abbey Theatre 1998', in Cathy Leeny and Anna McMullan (eds), *The Theatre of Marina Carr: 'Before Rules Was Made'* (Dublin, 2003)

Macintosh, Fiona,'An Oedipus for our times? Yeats's version of Sophocles' *Oedipus Tyrranos*', in Martin Reverman and Peter Wilson (eds), *Performance, Reception, Iconography: Studies in Honour of Oliver Taplin* (Oxford, 2008)

——, *Dying Acts: Death in Ancient Greek and Modern Irish Tragic Drama* (Cork, 1994)

MacIntyre, Alasdair, 'Poetry as political philosophy: notes on Burke and Yeats', in Vereen Bell and Laurence Lerner (eds), *On Modern Poetry: Essays Presented to Donald Davie* (Nashville, TN, 1988)

McKenna, Colleen, 'Seeing "last things": reading Yeats through the eyes of Seamus Heaney', *Yeats Annual*, no. 13 (1998)

McNally, James, 'Cast a cold eye on Yeats and Arnold', *Victorian Poetry*, no. 25 (1987)

McNally, Mark, 'Conor Cruise O'Brien's conservative anti-nationalism: retrieving the postwar European connection', *European Journal of Political Theory*, vol. 7, no. 3 (2008)

Mahon, Derek, *Collected Poems* (Loughcrew, Co. Meath, 1999)

——, *High Time: A Comedy in One Act Based on Molière's* The School for Husbands (Dublin, 1985)

Maley, Patrick, 'Aeneas in Baile Beag: Friel's *Translations*, *The Aeneid*, and the humanism of the Field Day Theatre Company', *New Hibernia Review/Iris Éireannach Nua*, vol. 15, no. 4 (geimhreadh/winter 2011)

Martinich, Robert Anthony and Mary J. Harper (eds), *Yeats's Vision Papers: Volume III: Sleep and Dream Notebooks, Vision Notebooks 1 and 2, Card File* (Iowa City, IA, 1992)

Matthews, Stephen, *Irish Poetry: Politics, History, Negotiation: The Evolving Debate, 1969 to the Present* (New York, 1997)

Meaney, Gerardine, 'Engendering the postmodern canon? *The Field Day Anthology of Irish Writing, vols. IV & V: Women's Writing and Traditions*', in Patricia Boyle Haberstroh and Christine St Peter (eds), *Opening the Field: Irish Women: Texts and Contexts* (Cork, 2007)

——, 'Field Day's long-awaited list of women writers challenges existing notions of Irish writing', *The Irish Times*, 25 April 2002

Melnick, Daniel, 'Yeats's image of culture', *Studies in the Literary Imagination*, vol. 14, no. 1 (1981)

Miles, Edward T., 'The radical crusade of Conor Cruise O'Brien', *Modern Age*, no. 30 (1986)

Miller, Arthur B., 'Aristotle on habit (*ethos*) and character (*êthos*): implications for the *Rhetoric*', *Speech Monographs*, no. 41 (November 1974)
Mills, Patricia Jagentowicz, 'Hegel's Antigone', in Jon Stewart (ed.), *The Phenomenology of Spirit Reader* (Albany, NY, 1998)
Moloney, Ed, *A Secret History of the IRA* (New York, 2002)
—, 'Censorship and "The Troubles"', in Mary P. Corcoran and Mark O'Brien (eds), *Political Censorship and the Democratic State: The Irish Broadcasting Ban* (Dublin, 2005)
Morgenthau, Hans Joachim, *Politics Among Nations: The Struggle for Power and Peace* (New York, 1948)
Mulhern, Francis, 'A nation, yet again: *The Field Day Anthology*', *Radical Philosophy*, no. 65 (autumn 1993)
—, 'Postcolonial melancholy: a reply to Luke Gibbons', *Radical Philosophy*, no. 72 (1995)
Murray, Christopher, 'Three Irish Antigones', in Jacqueline Genet and Richard Alan Cave (eds), *Perspectives of Irish Drama and Theatre* (Gerrard's Cross, Bucks, 1991)
Nadler, Arie, Thomas B. Malloy and Jeffrey D. Fisher (eds), *The Social Psychology of Intergroup Reconciliation* (Oxford, 2008)
Ní Dhomhnaill, Nuala, 'The hidden island: women's inheritance', in Theo Dorgan (ed.), *Irish Poetry Since Kavanagh* (Dublin, 1996)
Nietzsche, Friedrich, *The Gay Science*, ed. Bernard Williams, trans. Josefine Nauckhoff and Adrian Del Caro (Cambridge, 2001)
O'Brien, Conor Cruise, *Ancestral Voices: Religion and Nationalism in Ireland* (Chicago, IL, 1994)
—, and William Dean Vanech (eds), *Power & Consciousness* (London, 1969)
—, 'A slow, north-east wind', in Elmer Andrews (ed.), *The Poetry of Seamus Heaney* (New York, 1998)
—, 'A "peace process" deadly as war', *New York Times*, 12 January 1997
—, 'Broadcasting and violence: the case for media restriction', in Mary P. Corcoran and Mark O'Brien (eds), *Political Censorship and the Democratic State: The Irish Broadcasting Ban* (Dublin, 2005)
—, 'Imagination and politics', in Conor Cruise O'Brien and William Dean Vanech (eds), *Power and Consciousness* (London, 1969)
—, *Memoir: My Life and Themes* (Dublin, 1998)
—, *Murderous Angels: A Political Tragedy and Comedy in Black and White* (London, 1969)
—, *Neighbours: Four Lectures Delivered in Memory of Christopher Ewart-Biggs* (London, 1980)
—, *Parnell and His Party, 1880–90* (Oxford, 1957)
—, *Passion & Cunning: Essays on Nationalism, Terrorism and Revolution* (New York, 1988)
—, 'Peace comes dropping hard', *National Review*, 12 September 1994
—, 'Police powers: how the IRA leverages the peace process', *Atlantic Monthly*, December 2001
—, *States of Ireland* (New York, 1972)
—, *The Suspecting Glance* (London, 1972)
—, *The United Nations: Sacred Drama*, with illustrations by Feliks Topolski (New York, 1968)
—, 'This peace means war: I will not applaud a Nobel Prize given to appeasers of the IRA', *Guardian*, 17 October 1998

——, *To Katanga and Back: A UN Case History* (New York, 1963)
——, 'Views', *The Listener*, 24 October 1968
——, *Writers and Politics* (New York, 1965)
O'Brien, Karen, 'Re-envisioning "woman": Medea as heroine in versions by Brendan Kennelly and Marina Carr', *Études Irlandaises*, vol. 37, no. 1 (2012)
O'Brien, Mark, 'Disavowing democracy: the silencing project in the South', in Mary P. Corcoran and Mark O'Brien (eds), *Political Censorship and the Democratic State: The Irish Broadcasting Ban* (Dublin, 2005)
O'Dowd, Mary (ed.), 'Women and politics in Northern Ireland', in Angela Bourke, Siobhán Kilfeather, Maria Lundy, Margaret MacCurtain, Gerardine Meaney, Máirín Ní Dhonnchadha, Mary O'Dowd and Clair Wills (eds), *The Field Day Anthology of Irish Writing: Vols 4–5: Irish Women's Writing and Traditions* (New York, 2002)
O'Driscoll, Dennis, *Stepping Stones: Interviews with Seamus Heaney* (New York, 2008)
Ó Duibhne, Cormac, '"Talk about the play!": an interview with Stephen Rea', *Princeton University Library Chronicle*, vol. 58, nos. 1–2 (2006)
——, (ed.), *The Field Day Archive* (Dublin, 2007)
O'Malley, Aidan, *Field Day and the Translation of Irish Identities: Performing Contradictions* (London, 2011)
Osborne, Charles, 'Greek drama with a Belfast rasp', *Daily Telegraph*, 20 September 1990
O'Toole, Fintan, 'Cruise O'Brien proud to be a Paisleyite', *The Irish Times*, 8 May 1998
——, 'Cruiser's new voyage', *The Irish Times*, 11 May 1996
——, 'Field Day: on the double', *Sunday Tribune*, 23 September 1984
Ostwald, Martin, *Ananke in Thucydides* (Atlanta, GA, 1988)
Paulin, Tom, 'A new look at the language question', in Field Day Theatre Company (ed.), *Ireland's Field Day* (London, 1986)
——, 'Antigone', in Marianne McDonald and J. Michael Walton (eds), *Amid Our Troubles: Irish Versions of Greek Tragedy* (London, 2002)
——, (ed.), 'Northern Protestant oratory and writing: 1791–1985', in Seamus Deane (ed.), *The Field Day Anthology of Irish Writing*, vol. 3 (Derry, 1991)
——, *Fivemiletown* (London, 1987)
——, *Ireland & the English Crisis* (Newcastle upon Tyne, 1984)
——, *Liberty Tree* (London, 1983)
——, *The Riot Act: A Version of Sophocles'* Antigone (London, 1985)
——, 'Whose side are you on?', *Independent on Sunday*, 28 September 2003, http://findarticles.com/p/articles/mi_qn4159/is_20030928/ai_n12745756/print (accessed 20 May 2008)
Plato, *The Republic*, trans. Tom Griffith (Cambridge, 2000)
Quayson, Ato, *Calibrations: Reading for the Social* (Minneapolis, MN, 2003)
Quilligan, Patrick, 'Field Day's new double-bill', *The Irish Times*, 18 September 1984
Randolph, Jody Allen, 'The shadow side of modern Ireland: Marina Carr's Midlands tragedies', *World Literature Today*, vol. 86, no. 4 (July–August 2012)
Richards, Sean, 'In the border country: Greek tragedy and contemporary Irish drama', in C.C. Barfoot and W.Z. Van Den Doel (eds), *Ritual Remembering: History, Myth and Politics in Anglo-Irish Drama* (Atlanta, GA, 1995)
Richards, Shaun, 'Field Day's fifth province: avenue or impasse?', in Eamonn Hughes (ed.), *Culture and Politics in Northern Ireland, 1960–1990* (Philadelphia, PA, 1991)

Richtarik, Marilynn J., *Acting Between the Lines: The Field Day Theatre Company and Irish Cultural Politics, 1980–1984* (Oxford, 1994)

Robinson, Daniel N., 'Rhetoric and character in Aristotle', *Review of Metaphysics*, no. 60 (2006)

Robinson, Mary, inaugural speech, Dublin Castle, 3 December 1990, https:// prelectur.stanford.edu/lecturers/robinson/inaugural.html (accessed 10 December 2010).

——, presidential-election acceptance speech, Dublin Castle, 9 November 1990, *The Irish Times*, 10 December 1990.

——, *Everybody Matters: My Life Giving Voice* (New York, 2013)

——, 'Speech at PEN World Voices Festival, 2008', http://www.wildriverreview.com/wrratlarge/2008/05/news-from-the-hug-watching-the.html (accessed 1 July 2008)

Roche, Anthony, 'Ireland's Antigones: tragedy North and South', in Michael Kenneally (ed.), *Cultural Contexts and Literary Idioms in Contemporary Irish Literature* (Gerrard's Cross, Bucks, 1988)

Roulston, Carmen and Celia Davies (eds), *Gender, Democracy, and Inclusion in Northern Ireland* (Basingstoke, 2000)

Russell, Richard Rankin, *Poetry & Peace: Michael Longley, Seamus Heaney, and Northern Ireland* (Notre Dame, IN, 2010)

Saddlemyer, Ann, *Becoming George: The Life of Mrs. W.B. Yeats* (Oxford, 2002)

Salis, Loredana, '"The root of all evil": Frank McGuinness' translations of Greek Drama', *Studi irlandesi. A Journal of Irish Studies*, no. 4 (2014)

Sanders, Mark, *Ambiguities of Witnessing: Law and Literature in the Time of a Truth Commission* (Stanford, CA, 2007)

Sattler, William M., 'Conception of ethos in ancient rhetoric', *Speech Monographs*, no. 14 (1947)

Schiller, Friedrich von, 'On naive and sentimental poetry', in H.B. Nisbett (ed.), *German Aesthetic and Literary Criticism: Winckelmann, Lessing, Hamann, Herder, Schiller and Goethe* (Cambridge, 1985)

——, *On the Aesthetic Education of Man in a Series of Letters*, trans. Elizabeth M. Wilkinson and L.A. Willoughby (Oxford, 1967)

Schlegel, Friedrich von, *On the Study of Greek Poetry*, trans. Stuart Barnett (Albany, NY, 2001)

Schuchard, Ronald, 'Yeats, Arnold, and the morbidity of modernism', *Yeats: An Annual of Critical and Textual Studies*, no. 3 (1985)

Schwartz, Daniel R., 'A humanist ethics of reading', in Todd F. Davis and Kenneth Womack (eds), *Mapping the Ethical Turn: A Reader in Ethics, Culture, and Literary Theory* (Charlottesville, VA, 2001)

Sena, Vinod, 'W.B. Yeats, Matthew Arnold, and the critical imperative', *Victorian Newsletter*, no. 56 (1979)

Shackford, Martha Hale, *Shakespeare, Sophocles: Dramatic Themes and Modes* (New Haven, CT, 1960)

Sharrock, David, 'McGuinness fishes for the right words to give Paisley his parting gift of poetry', *The Times*, 6 June 2008

Skelly, Joseph Morrison, *Irish Diplomacy at the United Nations 1945–1965: National Interests and the International Order* (Dublin, 1997)

Smyth, Marie, *Truth, Recovery and Justice after Conflict: Managing Violent Pasts* (NY, 2007)

Sophocles, *Antigone*, trans. Brendan Kennelly (Newcastle upon Tyne, 1986)

——, *Antigone*, in David Grene (ed.), *Sophocles I*, trans. Elizabeth Wyckoff (Chicago, IL, 1954)

——, *Sophocles: Volume 2: Antigone, The Women of Trachis, Philoctetes, Oedipus at Colonus*, trans. Hugh Lloyd-Jones (Cambridge, MA, 1994)

——, *The Oedipus Cycle*, trans. Dudley Fitts and Robert Fitzgerald (New York, 2002)

——, *The Three Theban Plays:* Antigone, Oedipus the King, Oedipus at Colonus, trans. Robert Fagles (New York, 1987)

——, *The Tragedies of Sophocles*, trans. Sir Richard C. Jebb (Cambridge, 1912)

Soyinka, Wole, *The Burden of Memory, the Muse of Forgiveness* (Oxford, 1999)

Stallworthy, Jon, 'The poet as archaeologist: W.B. Yeats and Seamus Heaney', *Review of English Studies: A Quarterly Journal of English Literature and the English Language*, no. 33 (1982)

Stanton, Domna C., 'Presidential address 2005: on rooted cosmopolitanism', *PMLA: Publications of the Modern Language Association of America*, vol. 121, no. 3 (2006)

Steiner, George, *Antigones* (Oxford, 1984)

Stoll, Elmer Edgar, *Shakespeare and other Masters* (Cambridge, MA, 1940)

Taplin, Oliver, 'Sophocles' *Philoctetes*, Seamus Heaney's, and some other recent half-rhymes', in Edith Hall, Fiona Macintosh and Amanda Wrigley (eds), *Dionysus Since 69: Greek Tragedy at the Dawn of the Third Millennium* (Oxford, 2004)

Taylor, Paul, 'A hit and myth', *Independent*, 8 April 1991

Teevan, Colin, 'Northern Ireland: our Troy? Recent versions of Greek tragedies by Irish writers', *Modern Drama*, no. 41 (1998)

Thatcher, Margaret, House of Commons speech on the Anglo-Irish Agreement, 26 November 1985, Margaret Thatcher Foundation, http://www.margaret-thatcher.org/document/106182 (accessed 19 August 2010)

——, speech in Belfast, 5 March 1981, Margaret Thatcher Foundation, http://www.margaretthatcher.org/document/104589 (accessed 19 August 2010)

Thompson, Peter, 'The contrast is only astonishing', *Irish Press*, 25 September 1984

Thucydides, *The Peloponnesian War*, trans. Thomas Hobbes (Chicago, IL, 1989)

Torchiana, Donald T., '"Among School Children" and the education of the Irish spirit', in Norman A. Jeffares (ed.), *In Excited Reverie: A Centenary Tribute to W.B. Yeats* (London, 1965)

——, 'Senator Yeats, Burke, and able men', *Newberry Library Bulletin*, no. 5 (1961)

Tracy, Robert, '"Intelligible on the Blasket Islands": Yeats's *King Oedipus*, 1926', *Éire-Ireland: A Journal of Irish Studies*, vol. 28, no. 2 (summer 1993)

——, 'When hope and history rhyme', *Irish Literary Supplement*, vol. 10, no. 2 (1 January 1991)

Turner, Paul, '*The Cure at Troy*: Sophocles or Heaney?', in Jason David Hall (ed.), *Seamus Heaney: Poet, Critic, Translator* (Basingstoke, 2007)

Twiddy, Iain, 'Visions of reconciliation: Longley, Heaney and the Greeks', *Irish Studies Review*, vol. 21, no. 4 (2013)

U2, *All That You Can't Leave Behind* (Island Records, 2000)

United Nations Universal Declaration of Human Rights, http://www.un.org/en/documents/udhr/ (accessed 28 February 2010)

Van de Kamp, Peter F.W., 'Field Day for women but it ain't an anthology', *Sunday Independent*, 10 August 2003

Vendler, Helen, *The Music of what Happens: Poems, Poets, Critics* (Cambridge, MA, 1988)

Vickers, Michael, 'A legend of wild beauty: Sophocles' *Antigone*', *Classics Ireland*, no. 14 (2007)

Wade, Allan (ed.), *The Letters of W.B. Yeats* (London, 1954)

Walker, Jeffrey, 'Pathos and katharsis in "Aristotelian" rhetoric: some implications', in Arthur E. Walzer (ed.), *Rereading Aristotle's Rhetoric* (Carbondale, IL, 2000)

Wallace, Nathan, 'Matthew Arnold, Edmund Burke, and Irish reconciliation', *Prose Studies*, vol. 34, no. 3 (December 2012)

Walton, J. Michael, 'Hit or myth: the Greeks and Irish drama', in Marianne McDonald and J. Michael Walton (eds), *Amid Our Troubles: Irish Versions of Greek Tragedy* (London, 2002)

Whelan, Diarmuid, 'Conor Cruise O'Brien and the legitimation of violence', *Irish Political Studies*, vol. 21, no. 2 (2006)

Whelan, Kevin, 'Rights of memory', http://www.epilogues.net/perspectives/KW%20Rights%20of%20memory.pdf (accessed 10 July 2012).

Williams, Julia McHatten, 'This is (not) a canon: staking out the tradition in recent anthologies of Irish writing', *Journal of Women's History*, vol. 7, no. 1 (1995–96)

Wills, Clair, *Improprieties: Politics and Sexuality in Northern Irish Poetry* (Oxford, 1993)

Wilmer, Steve, 'Women in Greek tragedy today: a reappraisal', *Theatre Research International*, vol. 32, no. 2 (July 2007)

Wilson, Edmund, *The Wound and the Bow: Seven Studies in Literature* (Oxford, 1947)

Woolford, John, 'Arnold on Empedocles', *Review of English Studies: A Quarterly Journal of English Literature and the English Language*, vol. 50, no. 197 (1999)

Worthen, W.B., 'Homeless words: Field Day and the politics of translation', *Modern Drama*, no. 38 (1995)

Wright, Julia, '"The order of time": nationalism and literary anthologies, 1774–1831', *Papers on Language and Literature*, vol. 33, no. 4 (fall 1997)

Yeats, W.B., *A Vision* (New York, 1966; first published 1937)

——, *Memoirs*, ed. Denis Donoghue (London, 1972)

——, 'Plain Man's Oedipus', *New York Times*, 15 January 1933

——, *Senate Speeches*, ed. Donald R. Pearce (Bloomington, IN, 1960)

——, *Sophocles'* Oedipus at Colonus: *Manuscript Materials*, ed. Jared Curtis (Ithaca, NY, 2008)

——, *The Collected Works of W.B. Yeats: Volume II: The Plays*, eds. David R. Clark and Rosalind E. Clark (New York, 2011)

——, *The Collected Works of W.B. Yeats: Volume III: Autobiographies*, eds. William H. O'Donnell and Douglas N. Archibald (New York, 1999)

——, *The Collected Works of W.B. Yeats: Volume IV: Early Essays*, eds. Richard J. Finneran and George Bornstein (New York, 2007)

——, *The Collected Works of W.B. Yeats: Volume V: Later Essays*, ed. William H. O'Donnell (New York, 1994)

——, *The Collected Works of W.B. Yeats: Volume VIII: The Irish Dramatic Movement*, eds. Mary FitzGerald and Richard J. Finneran (London, 2003)

——, The Tower *Manuscript Materials*, eds. Richard J. Finneran, Jared Curtis and Ann Saddlemyer (Ithaca, NY, 2007)

——, *Uncollected Prose*, vol. 1, ed. John P. Frayne (New York, 1970)

——, *Uncollected Prose*, vol. 2, eds John P. Frayne and Colton Johnson (NY, 1975)

——, 'W.B. Yeats explains his new play', *The Irish Times*, 13 August 1938

——, 'W.B. Yeats's unpublished talk on his version of *King Oedipus* broadcast from the BBC Belfast studio on 8 September 1931', ed. Karen Dorn, *Yeats Annual*, no. 5 (1987)

Yoos, George E, 'A revision of the concept of ethical appeal', *Philosophy & Rhetoric*, no. 12 (1979)

Young, Robert, *Colonial Desire: Hybridity in Theory, Culture, and Race* (New York, 1995)

Younger, Kelly, 'Antigone and terrorism: Seamus Heaney sends a letter to George W. Bush', in Stratos E. Constantinidis (ed.), *Text & Presentation: The Comparative Drama Conference Series* (New York, 2007)

——, 'Irish Antigones: burying the colonial symptom', *Colloquy: Text Theory Critique*, no. 11 (2006)

Zimmerman, Sarah M., *Romanticism, Lyricism and History* (Albany, NY, 1999)

Notes and References

Introduction

1. The theme of political and psychological reconciliation has been a popular topic of conferences, essay collections and book-length studies over the past two decades; this proliferation has been largely inspired by the Truth and Reconciliation Commission in South Africa, chaired by Archbishop Desmond Mpilo Tutu. Since that time, the scholarly world has found theologians, social psychologists, political scientists, sociologists and peace workers discussing this concept on many levels – usually with an eye towards healing communities in conflict not simply in South Africa but also around the world. The past fifteen years has seen a number of important studies of reconciliation from a literary perspective in Africa. Along with the Nigerian Nobel laureate Wole Soyinka's *The Burden of Memory, the Muse of Forgiveness* (Oxford, 1999), we have seen such literary critical histories as Susan V. Gallagher, *Truth and Reconciliation: The Confessional Mode in South African Literature* (Portsmouth, NH, 2002); Ato Quayson, *Calibrations: Reading for the Social* (Minneapolis, MN, 2003); and Mark Sanders, *Ambiguities of Witnessing: Law and Literature in the Time of a Truth Commission* (Stanford, CA, 2007).
2. Richard Bourke, *Peace in Ireland: The Battle of Ideas* (London, 2003), p. 9.
3. Although reconciliation had been an important concept in Irish political discourse for centuries, this new, interdisciplinary 'peace studies' approach to reconciliation has been prominent since the start of the peace process in 1993–94. The most widely read Irish book on this topic to be published in more than two decades since the IRA ceasefire of 1994 has been Nobel Prize-winner John Hume's *A New Ireland: Politics, Peace, and Reconciliation* (Boulder, CO, 1996). There are also many edited collections, moreover, devoted specifically to Northern Irish reconciliation. These include Dermot Keogh and Michael Haltzel (eds), *Northern Ireland and the Politics of Reconciliation* (Cambridge, 1993); Marianne Elliot (ed.), *The Long Road to Peace in Northern Ireland* (Liverpool, 2002); Carmen Rouston and Celia Davies (eds), *Gender, Democracy and inclusion in Northern Ireland* (Basingstoke, 2000); and Spencer Graham's *Forgiving and Remembering in Northern Ireland: Approaches to Conflict Resolution* (London, 2011). Book-length studies on Northern Irish reconciliation include Mervyn Love, *Peace Building Through Reconciliation in Northern Ireland* (Aldershot, 1995); Marie Smyth, *Truth, Recovery and Justice after Conflict: Managing Violent Pasts* (New York, 2007); and Graham Dawson, *Making Peace with the Past? Memory, Trauma and the Irish Troubles* (Manchester, 2011). In the field of literary criticism, Richard Rankin Russell's *Poetry and Peace: Michael Longley, Seamus Heaney,*

and Northern Ireland (Notre Dame, IN, 2010) concentrates on the subjects' 'reconciliationary aesthetic' as a positive influence on the peace process.

4. Margaret Thatcher, speech in Belfast, 5 March 1981, Margaret Thatcher Foundation, http://www.margaretthatcher.org/document/104589 (accessed 19 August 2010).
5. Tom Paulin parodied this in his 1984 Field Day play *The Riot Act: A Version of Sophocles'* Antigone (London, 1985) when Creon delivers his similarly uncompromising (yet initially reasonable-sounding) opening speech to the Thebans. He begins by talking about how he will rule by 'listen[ing] to the best advice', but ends with a demand that 'if ever any man here should find himself faced with a choice between betraying his country and betraying his friend, then he must swiftly place that friend in the hands of the authorities' (*The Riot Act*, p. 16). When Stephen Rea read the speech in the original Field Day production, he partly channelled Thatcher's secretary of state for Northern Ireland, Douglas Hurd. For a judgement that the opening satire of Creon ruins the tragic impact of the whole, see Fintan O'Toole, 'Field Day: on the double', *Sunday Tribune*, 23 September 1984. For a contrary argument, that Paulin's Creon is the central and most complex figure in *The Riot Act*, see Richard C. Jones III, '"Talking amongst ourselves": language, politics, and Sophocles on the Field Day stage', *International Journal of the Classical Tradition*, vol. 4, no. 2 (fall 1997), pp. 237–8.
6. Margaret Thatcher, House of Commons speech on the Anglo-Irish Agreement, 26 November 1985, Margaret Thatcher Foundation, http://www.margaretthatcher.org/document/106182 (accessed 19 August 2010).
7. John Hume, 'Reconciliation of the irreconcilable', in Seamus Deane (ed.), *The Field Day Anthology of Irish Writing*, vol. 3 (Derry, 1991), p. 788.
8. Conor Cruise O'Brien, *Passion and Cunning: Essays on Nationalism, Terrorism, and Revolution* (New York, 1988), p. 211.
9. Seamus Deane (ed.), *The Field Day Anthology of Irish Writing*, vol. 1 (Derry, 1991), p. xxvi.
10. The entire forty-five-minute episode of *Night Waves* was dedicated to the theme of Adams the writer. This particular exchange from that episode is quoted by Robert Hanks, 'The week in radio', *Independent*, 6 October 2004. For a more extended commentary on the episode, including the exasperated suggestion that no politician ever again quote the 'Hope and History' chorus, see Roy Foster, 'Adams' original sin', *Financial Times*, 23 October 2004.
11. Seamus Heaney, *The Cure at Troy: A Version of Sophocles'* Philoctetes (New York, 1991), p. 77.
12. Mary Robinson, inaugural speech at Dublin Castle, 3 December 1990, http://prelectur.stanford.edu/lecturers/robinson/inaugural.html (accessed 10 December 2010).
13. Seamus Heaney, '*The Cure at Troy*: production notes in no particular order', in Marianne McDonald and J. Michael Walton (eds), *Amid Our Troubles: Irish Versions of Greek Tragedy* (London, 2002), pp. 177–8.
14. Bill Clinton, *Between Hope and History* (New York, 1996); Jack Holland, *Hope Against History: The Course of Conflict in Northern Ireland* (New York, 1996); and also U2's song 'Peace on Earth'.
15. Bill Clinton, presidential radio address, 11 April 1998, http://en.wikisource.org/wiki/Presidential_Radio_Address_-_11_April_1998 (accessed 29 January 2008).
16. Address by Prime Minister of the United Kingdom, Ḍáil Éireann, vol. 497, 26 November 1998.
17. Mary Robinson, speech at PEN World Voices Festival, 2008, http://www.

wildriverreview.com/wrratlarge/2008/05/news-from-the-hug-watchingthe.html (accessed 1 July 2008).

18. Interview with Kevin Whelan, June 2009. 'Maybe it was understandable', Whelan continued, 'after thirty years of horror that people needed [that] kind of feeling to . . . get them to commit to the hard slog, but I kind of feel, looking back that . . . we should have emphasised more a trajectory . . . [or a] process and not an event . . . [although] even maybe for Heaney that's a little too easy. Not so much what Heaney said but the way it was taken up, the uses that it was put to . . . with Clinton and everybody. It was such a memorable line, but it could be evacuated of the difficulty because . . . in the poetry itself [Heaney] is very cognisant of the long-term damage.'
19. 'A common response by historians', Whelan has written, 'is to hector us . . . to forget about the past, and, in the famous phrase, "move on". This is a common liberal or scholarly view: if these foolish little people, trapped in their narrow streets and narrow minds, with their subjective tribal versions of history, could only see it as we detached professionals do, then all would become sweetness and light.' In opposition to this Arnoldian insensitivity, Whelan has proposed a 'duty to go beyond anger and hatred towards achieving a new horizon of justice, a culture with a just memory, while keeping alive the memory of the trauma, the trace of event, while reconciling past and future.' Whelan, unpublished paper, 'Rights of memory', delivered at a one-day conference on storytelling, for the organisation Healing Through Remembrance, Dunadry Hotel, Antrim, 29 September 2005. Text provided to me by the author, and available online at http://www.epilogues.net/perspectives/KW%20Rights%20of%20memory.pdf.
20. Hanks, 'The week in radio'.
21. It is unlikely that an American journalist would have asked Bill Clinton, who had also named a book after Heaney's poem, to explain what he liked about it. On the other hand, it is just as unlikely that Clinton would have done an interview about himself as a literary author.
22. Deane (ed.), *Field Day Anthology of Irish Writing*, vol. 1, p. xxvi.
23. Ibid.
24. Aristotle, *The Art of Rhetoric*, trans. John Henry Freese (Cambridge, MA, 1975), pp. 16–17. See also Sharon Crowley and Debra Hawhee, *Ancient Rhetorics for Contemporary Students* (London, 2003), in which the authors distinguish between the 'situated' and the 'invented' ethos in Aristotle's notion of the ethical proof. The situated ethos refers to the speaker's pre-existing reputation as trustworthy, while the invented ethos refers to the speaker's trustworthiness, established within the course of the argument itself. 'According to Aristotle', they write, 'rhetors can invent a character suitable to an occasion – this is invented ethos. However, if rhetors are fortunate enough to enjoy a good reputation in the community, they can use it as an ethical proof – this is situated ethos': Crowley and Hawhee, *Ancient Rhetorics for Contemporary Students*, p. 167. What Crowley and Hawhee term the 'invented' and 'situated' ethos are what Aristotle calls 'entechnoi' and 'atechnoi', or 'inartificial' and 'artificial', respectively: Aristotle, *Art of Rhetoric*, pp. 14–15. This artfulness does not necessarily imply that the invented ethos is false, however, because Aristotle attributes all character to habituation and custom.
25. Aristotle, *Art of Rhetoric*, p. 17.
26. See Aristotle, *Art of Rhetoric*, pp. 16–17. In *De Oratore*, Marcus Tullius Cicero revisits this Aristotelian triad, explaining that rhetoric works on the audience through 'instruction or persuasion of appeal to the emotions' ('*aut docendo aut conciliando aut permovendo*'; pp. 434–5). For more extended comparisons between the Greek and

Roman rhetorical theorists' treatment of this theme, see Elaine Fantham, 'Ciceronian conciliare and Aristotelian ethos', *Phoenix*, vol. 27, no. 3 (1973), and William W. Fortenbaugh, '*Benevolentiam conciliare and animos permovere*: some remarks on Cicero's *De Oratore* 2. 178–216', *Rhetorica*, no. 6 (1988).

27. Aristotle, *Art of Rhetoric*, pp. 308–9.
28. Ibid.
29. For a fuller overview of Sophocles' good reputation in antiquity, see the chapter 'Sophocles or Socrates?', in Thomas Gould, *The Ancient Quarrel Between Poetry and Philosophy* (Princeton, NJ, 1990), pp. 155–70. The immediate quotations from Aristophanes' *The Frogs*, Phrynicus' fragment on Sophocles and Plato's *Republic*, are cited on pp. 164–5.
30. Ibid., p. 164.
31. Plato, *The Republic* (Cambridge, 2000), p. 3.
32. Aristotle, *The Poetics of Aristotle*, trans. Stephen Halliwell (Chapel Hill, NC, 1987), p. 37.
33. August Wilhelm and Friedrich Schlegel were the first to make the comparison between these 'reconciled' playwrights when they invented the Romantic cult of Shakespeare at the turn of the nineteenth century, and by 1900 it had become more or less of a critical commonplace; a number of books since then have been written on this very topic. See Lionel Horton-Smith, *Ars tragica Sophoclea cum Shaksperiana comparata* (Cambridge, 1896); Elmer Edgar Stoll *Shakespeare and other Masters* (Cambridge, MA, 1940), the second chapter of which is called '"Reconciliation" in tragedy: Shakespeare and Sophocles'; Laura Jepsen, *Ethical Aspects of Tragedy: A Comparison of Certain Tragedies by Aeschylus, Sophocles, Euripides, Seneca and Shakespeare* (Gainesville, FL, 1953); Aubrey De Selincourt, *Six Great Playwrights: Sophocles, Shakespeare, Molière, Sheridan, Ibsen, Shaw* (London, 1960); Martha Hale Shackford, *Shakespeare, Sophocles: Dramatic Themes and Modes* (New Haven, CT, 1960); Lewis Campbell, *Tragic Drama in Aeschylus, Sophocles, and Shakespeare* (New York, 1965); and David Grene's *Reality and the Heroic Pattern: Last Plays of Ibsen, Shakespeare, and Sophocles* (Chicago, IL, 1967). As the title of Grene's book suggests, one major topic for comparison has been in the respective playwrights' later careers. Each dramatist enacted qualitative shifts of emphasis, whereby tragic and comic elements came together in new ways, resulting in a tragic-comic form with optimistic rather than fatalistic conclusions.
34. Aristotle, *Art of Rhetoric*, pp. 155–7.
35. Ibid., pp. 220, 226. We can see the link between the *Rhetoric* and the *Poetics* when we note that Aristotle lists these emotions as primary in both works. In Book II of the *Rhetoric*, for instance, he analyses the 'emotions' as 'all those affections which cause men to change their opinion in regard to their judgments, and are accompanied by pleasure and pain; such are anger, pity, fear, and all similar emotions and their contraries': Aristotle, *Art of Rhetoric*, p. 173.
36. Ibid., pp. 238, 242.
37. Ibid., p. 243.
38. Ibid., p. 147.
39. In this regard, Heaney's *Cure* has frequently been compared with Michael Longley's sonnet 'Ceasefire', a loose translation from Book XXIV of the *Iliad*, published in *The Irish Times* shortly after the IRA ceasefire in 1994. See Michael Longley, *Collected Poems* (London, 2006), p. 225. In Longley's poem, the grieving Priam approaches Achilles for the return of his son Hektor's body. This sonnet, which has the two men 'stare at each other's beauty as lovers might', is significantly more intimate than what

we find at the closing of Homer's epic. As Richard Rankin Russell and Iain Twiddy have shown, however, this short statement reflects the profundity of Longley's poetic meditation on the ethics and psychology of reconciliation. In the Homeric episode, we find a pause in hostilities – but no intimation of a coming peace. Heaney's *Cure*, on the other hand, actually does recommend optimism because it stages a cathartic reconciliation. While the Neoptolemus of Sophocles and Aristotle considers his role in the conflict from the perspective of an ethicist, psychologist, actor and rhetorician, Twiddy reminds us that, at the end of the Trojan War, Neoptolemus will be Priam's killer; p. 427

40. The Greeks also took Homer as an authority on a wide range of topics, but the Hiberno-Hellenic parallel should not be taken too far. None of the medieval Irish cycles are attributed to particular poets in the way the *Iliad* and *Odyssey* are attributed to Homer, and conversely nothing we know of the Homeric bards suggests they performed all of the functions or undertook the same formalised educational requirements that various classes of Irish poets did up until the ultimate collapse of the Gaelic order.
41. Emmanuel Levinas, *Totality and Infinity: An Essay on Exteriority* (Pittsburg, PA, 1969), p. 196.
42. Ibid.
43. This treatise does not survive from antiquity, but Diogenes Laertius lists it (*Alexandros ê hyper apoíkôn*) as one of Aristotle's works in *Lives of Eminent Philosophers*, ed. Tiziano Dorandi (Cambridge, MA, 2013), p. 357.
44. See Christopher P. Long, 'The ethical culmination of Aristotle's metaphysics', *Epoché*, vol. 8, no. 1 (fall 2003), p. 122. Long also counters Levinas' claims even more specifically in 'Totalizing identities: the ambiguous legacy of Aristotle and Hegel after Auschwitz', *Philosophy and Social Criticism*, vol. 29, no. 2 (2003).
45. Several proponents of the ethical turn have in fact drawn on this very point to justify their positions. Daniel R. Schwartz writes that, in following Aristotle, he believes 'that the aesthetic, ethical, and political are inextricably linked': Schwartz, 'A humanist ethics of reading', in Todd F. Davis and Kenneth Womack (eds), *Mapping the Ethical Turn: A Reader in Ethics, Culture, and Literary Theory* (Charlottesville, VA, 2001), p. 9.
46. William Sattler argues that the ethos we find in Aristotle's *Rhetoric* is 'clearly divorced from the ethical' as we find it in his other philosophical works: Sattler, 'Conceptions of ethos in ancient rhetoric', *Speech Monographs*, no. 14 (1947), pp. 59–60.
47. S. Michael Halloran argues that because character in Aristotle is a matter of habituated custom, *The Art of Rhetoric* contains a 'theory of rhetorical pedagogy as a form of moral education and character development': Halloran, 'Aristotle's concept of ethos, or if not his somebody else's', *Rhetoric Review*, vol. 1, no. 1 (September 1982), p. 61. Moreover, Lois Self agues that the *Rhetoric* and the *Ethics* do in fact overlap where Aristotle uses the term *phronimos*, or 'man of practical wisdom', to describe the ideal figure in both works: Self, 'Rhetoric and phronesis: the Aristotelian ideal', *Philosophy & Rhetoric* (1979), p. 131. See also Arthur B. Miller, 'Aristotle on habit (*ethos*) and character (*êthos*): implications for the *Rhetoric*', *Speech Monographs*, no. 41 (November 1974). For more studies of this topic, see Charles Chamberlain, 'From "haunts" to "character": the meaning of éthos and its relation to ethics', *Helios*, vol. 11, no. 2 (winter 1984), and Daniel N. Robinson, 'Rhetoric and character in Aristotle', *Review of Metaphysics*, no. 60 (2006).
48. Eugene Garver, *Aristotle's Rhetoric: An Art of Character* (Chicago, IL, 1994), pp. 6–7.

49. See Aristotle, *The Politics and the Constitution of Athens*, trans. Stephen Everson (Cambridge, 1988), p. 195: 'Music should be studied . . . for the sake of . . . many benefits, that is to say, with a view to education, or purgation [*katharsis*] (the word 'purgation' we use at present without explanation, but when hereafter we speak of poetry . . . we will treat the subject with more precision).' If the *Poetics* ever did contain the more elaborate treatment of catharsis to which Aristotle refers here, however, that part of his lecture notes have of course been lost to posterity. For another reading of catharsis in relation to rhetorical theory, see Jeffrey Walker, 'Pathos and katharsis in "Aristotelian" rhetoric: some implications', in Arthur E. Walzer (ed.), *Rereading Aristotle's Rhetoric* (Carbondale, IL, 2000).
50. In *Art of Rhetoric*, Aristotle explains that the audience is most likely to believe ethical arguments that conform to the speaker's character. If the speaker's natural behaviour 'seems incredible', he writes, 'the reason must be added; of this Sophocles gives an example, where his Antigone says that she cared more for her brother than for her husband or children; for the latter can be replaced after they are gone, "But when father and mother are in the grave, no brother can ever be born." If you have no reason, you should at least say that you are aware that what you assert is incredible, but that it is your nature . . .' Aristotle, *Art of Rhetoric*, pp. 447, 449.
51. Aristotle, *Nicomachean Ethics* (Oxford, 2002), p. 202: 'There are also some who fail to stick to what has seemed right to them not because of lack of self-control, e.g. Neoptolemus in Sophocles' *Philoctetes*: true, it was because of pleasure that he departed from his judgment, but the pleasure was a fine one – telling the truth was, to him, a fine thing, but he had been persuaded by Odysseus to lie. Not everyone who does something because of pleasure is self-indulgent, or bad, or un-self-controlled; only one who does it because of a shameful pleasure.'
52. Edmund Burke, *Reflections on the Revolution in France* (Stanford, CA, 2001), p. 243.
53. See David Lloyd, 'The poetics of politics: Yeats and the founding of the state', in Lloyd, *Anomalous States: Irish Writing and the Post-colonial Moment* (Durham, NC, 1993), pp. 59–87; and Paul de Man, 'Image and emblem in Yeats', in de Man, *The Rhetoric of Romanticism* (New York, 1984), pp. 145–238.
54. See David Lloyd and Paul Thomas, *Culture and the State* (New York, 1988).
55. 'The making of a loyalist' was originally a review, for the 14 November 1980 edition of the *Times Literary Supplement*, of Conor Cruise O'Brien's *Neighbours: Four Lectures Delivered in Memory of Christopher Ewart-Biggs* (London, 1980). In that review, Paulin criticised an analogy O'Brien had earlier drawn between Sophocles' Antigone and Northern Ireland, in the latter's 1972 book *States of Ireland* (New York, 1972). Paulin's review later appeared in his essay collection *Ireland & the English Crisis* (Newcastle upon Tyne, 1984), pp. 23–38.
56. Theodor Adorno, *Minima Moralia: Reflections from Damaged Life* (London, 1978), p. 103.
57. Lloyd's 'Pap for the dispossessed' appears in Lloyd, *Anomalous States*, pp. 13–40.
58. Angela Bourke, Siobhán Kilfeather, Maria Lundy, Margaret MacCurtain, Gerardine Meaney, Máirín Ní Dhonnchadha, Mary O'Dowd and Clair Wills (eds), *The Field Day Anthology of Irish Writing: Vols 4–5: Irish Women's Writing and Traditions* (New York, 2002).

Chapter 1

1. De Man's last-published essay on the poet, 'Image and emblem in Yeats', was actually a chapter from his 1960 dissertation, and was published in *Rhetoric of Romanticism*,

his posthumous essay collection. This constituted de Man's most sustained account of Yeats' poetic career, and furthermore contained the seeds of some arguments that would appear in later writings.

2. De Man, *Rhetoric of Romanticism*, p. 172.
3. Ibid., pp. 187–8.
4. Ibid., p. 189.
5. For a very different view of Yeats' development as a political thinker and poet during this same period, see R.F. Foster, 'Yeats at war: poetic strategies and political reconstruction from the Easter Rising to the Free State', *Transactions of the Royal Historical Society*, no. 11 (2001).
6. The classic study of Arnoldian Hellenism can be found in David DeLaura's *Hebrew and Hellene in Victorian England: Newman, Arnold, and Pater* (Austin, TX, 1969). More recent analyses of Arnoldian Hellenism's underlying ideology include Vassilis Lambropoulos, 'Violence and the liberal imagination: the representation of Hellenism in Matthew Arnold', in Nancy Armstrong and Leonard Tennenhouse (eds), *The Violence of Representation: Literature and the History of Violence* (London, 1989), and Lionel Gossman, 'Philhellenism and antisemitism: Matthew Arnold and his German models', *Comparative Literature*, no. 46 (1994). For more on Yeats' reading of Arnold, see Chris Corr, 'Matthew Arnold and the younger Yeats: the manoeuvrings of cultural aesthetics', *Irish University Review: A Journal of Irish Studies*, vol. 28 (1998); Dillon Johnston, 'Cross-currencies in the culture market: Arnold, Yeats, Joyce', *South Atlantic Quarterly*, vol. 95, no. 1 (1996); James McNally, 'Cast a cold eye on Yeats and Arnold', *Victorian Poetry*, no. 25 (1987); Daniel Melnick, 'Yeats' image of culture', *Studies in the Literary Imagination*, vol. 14, no. 1 (1981); Ronald Schuchard, 'Yeats, Arnold, and the morbidity of modernism', *Yeats: An Annual of Critical and Textual* Studies, no. 3 (1985); and Vinod Sena, 'W.B. Yeats, Matthew Arnold, and the critical imperative', *Victorian Newsletter*, no. 56 (1979).
7. Matthew Arnold, *The Complete Prose Works of Matthew Arnold, Volume III: Lectures and Essays in Criticism*, ed. R.H. Super (Ann Arbor, MI, 1962), p. 345. The classic study of the racial theory underlying the Arnoldian Celticism is Frederic Faverty, *Matthew Arnold the Ethnologist* (Evanston, IL, 1951); this has been supplemented in postcolonial criticism by Robert Young in *Colonial Desire: Hybridity in Theory, Culture, and Race* (New York, 1995). Arnold first presented his Celticist arguments in a series of four lectures at Oxford between December 1865 and May 1866. These lectures were then printed as a four-part series in the *Cornhill Magazine*, between March and July 1866, under the title of 'On the study of Celtic literature'. Smith, Elder and Co. in 1867 published them as a book: *On the Study of Celtic Literature*. In 1891, moreover, the publisher issued a popular edition entitled *The Study of Celtic Literature*. Yeats owned and annotated a copy of this edition, and it is now part of the Yeats manuscript collection in the National Library of Ireland. Arnold's thinking about Ireland goes beyond his Celticism, however, as can be seen by such studies as Claire Connolly, 'Ugly criticism: union and division in Irish literature', *Field Day Review*, no. 4 (2008), and Frances Frame, 'Arnold and the Irish question: anticipating communitarianism', *Nineteenth-century Prose*, no. 34 (2007).
8. Arnold, *Complete Prose Works of Matthew Arnold*, vol. 3, pp. 296–7.
9. Ibid., p. 330.
10. Ibid., p. 345. The term 'architectonicé' comes initially from the conclusion of Aristotle's *Politics*, although Arnold seems to borrow it more directly from Goethe and Schiller's essay 'On dilettantism' in Johann Wolfgang Goethe, *Essays on Art and Literature* (Princeton, NJ, 1994), pp. 213–15.

11. Schlegel, *On the Study of Greek Poetry*, trans. Stuart Barnett (Albany, NY, 2001).
12. Ibid., p. 61.
13. Ibid.
14. Arnold, *Complete Prose Works of Matthew Arnold*, vol. 3, p. 345.
15. Schlegel, *On the Study of Greek Poetry*, p. 61.
16. See W.B. Yeats, *The Collected Works of W.B. Yeats: Volume IV: Early Essays*, eds. Richard J. Finneran and George Bornstein (New York, 2007). In this collection we find Yeats very critical of Arnold's aesthetics, often noting that the Victorian poet was a valuable critic, but hardly the organicist he had considered himself to be. In his 1913 essay 'Art and ideas', for instance, Yeats wrote that 'Arnold when he withdrew his *Empedocles on Etna*, though one had been sorry to lose so much lyrical beauty for ever, showed himself a great critic by his reasons, but his *Sohrab and Rustum* proves that the unity he imagined was a classical imitation and not an organic thing, not the flow of flesh under the impulse of passionate thought'; p. 255. For more readings of Arnold as an organicist critic, see Joseph Carroll, *The Cultural Theory of Matthew Arnold* (Berkeley, CA, 1982); William E. Buckler, '*Literature and Dogma* and literature: new textual perspective on Matthew Arnold's critical organicism', *Victorian Newsletter*, no. 59 (1981); and Peter Melville Logan, 'Fetishism and freedom in Matthew Arnold's cultural theory', *Victorian Literature and Culture*, no. 31 (2003). One especially powerful ideological critique of Arnold's cultural theory is Christopher Lane, 'The Arnoldian ideal, or culture studies and the problem of nothingness', in Amanda Anderson and Joseph Valente (eds), *Disciplinarity at the Fin de Siècle* (Princeton, NJ, 2002).
17. In his copy of *The Study of Celtic Literature*, Yeats underlines words from two passages about Titanism: first, about the 'chord of penetrating passion and melancholy . . . in Byron', and then 'the Titanism of the Celt, his passionate, turbulent, indomitable reaction against the despotism of fact'; pp. 127, 130. He also underlines a passage about the Celt's 'magically vivid and near interpretation of nature'; p. 135.
18. Yeats, *Collected Works of W.B. Yeats*, vol. 4, p. 130.
19. See W.B. Yeats, *The Collected Works of W.B. Yeats: Volume V: Later Essays*, ed. William H. O'Donnell (New York, 1994), p. 239. For Yeats' own account of these translations and their first performances, see 'W.B. Yeats' unpublished talk on his version of *King Oedipus* broadcast from the BBC Belfast studio on 8 September 1931', ed. Karen Dorn, *Yeats Annual*, no. 5 (1987). See also David R. Clark and James B. McGuire, 'The writing of Sophocles' *King Oedipus*', *Yeats: An Annual of Critical and Textual Studies*, no. 2 (1984); Frederic Grab, 'Yeats' *King Oedipus*', *Journal of English and Germanic Philology*, no. 71 (1972); and Robert Tracy, '"Intelligible on the Blasket Islands": Yeats's *King Oedipus*, 1926', *Éire-Ireland: A Journal of Irish Studies*, vol. 28, no. 2 (summer 1993). For a very illuminating account of the translation's influence on modern drama and criticism, see Fiona Mackintosh's 'An Oedipus for our times? Yeats' version of Sophocles' *Oedipus Tyrranos*', in Martin Reverman and Peter Wilson (eds), *Performance, Reception, Iconography: Studies in Honour of Oliver Taplin* (Oxford, 2008), in which the author describes what Sir Laurence Olivier and Tyrone Guthrie did with Yeats' translation in the 1940s and fifties, and how the former influenced Francis Fergusson's classic work, *The Idea of a Theatre* (Princeton, NJ, 1949).
20. See Yeats, *Collected Works of W.B. Yeats*, vol. 5, pp. 239–40.
21. Yeats' attention to the Sophoclean chorus gestures back to Arnold's preface to *Merope*. See Matthew Arnold, *The Complete Prose Works of Matthew Arnold: Volume I: On the Classical Tradition*, ed. R.H. Super (Ann Arbor, MI, 1977), pp. 61–2, in which the Victorian critic described 'the aim of tragedy' as '*profound moral impression*', and

identified the chorus as 'the ideal spectator' through whom the poetics of reconciliation operated because they 'collect[ed] and weigh[ed]' for the audience 'the impressions which the action would at that stage naturally make on a pious and thoughtful mind; and . . . when the issue of the action appeared to strike the final balance . . . [it] combine[d] . . . harmonise[d] . . . [and] deepen[ed] . . . the feelings naturally excited . . . by the sight of what was passing on the stage.' In Arnold's reading, the chorus brought the audience into emotional harmony with their own human nature, providing a glimpse of the idealised subject position offered by aesthetic education in the first place. For another explanation of Yeats' 'Sophoclean' reconciliation, see 'Preface to *Oedipus the King*', in W.B. Yeats, *The Collected Works of W.B. Yeats: Volume II: The Plays* (New York, 2011), eds. David E. Clark and Rosalind E. Clark, p. 885, where he described how, when the audience is properly moved by the chorus, 'past ages are called up before us, vast emotions are aroused, and our attention is no longer concentrated on a single spot, a single man'. In contrast with the Arnoldian tragic chorus, which would elevate us through a kind of Wordsworthian therapeutic music, the Yeatsian tragic chorus provided audiences connection with the *Anima Mundi*. For more on this chorus in particular, see Brian Arkins, 'Yeats' version of Colonus' Praise', *Classical and Modern Literature: A Quarterly*, no. 7 (1986).

22. Yeats, *Collected Works of W.B. Yeats*, vol. 4, p. 132.
23. Arnold, *Complete Prose Works of Matthew Arnold*, vol. 3, p. 30.
24. Ibid., p. 30.
25. W.B. Yeats, *Uncollected Prose*, vol. 2, eds. John P. Frayne and Colton Johnson (New York, 1975), pp. 141–2.
26. See Yeats, *Collected Works of W.B. Yeats*, vol. 4, p. 153. As Yeats put it in his 1901 essay 'Ireland and the arts': 'the end of art is peace'.
27. Ibid., p. 122.
28. Ibid., p. 123.
29. Ibid., pp. 124–5.
30. Ibid., p. 123.
31. W.B. Yeats, *Uncollected Prose*, vol. 1, ed. John P. Frayne (New York, 1975), p. 269.
32. W.B. Yeats, *The Collected Works of W.B. Yeats: Volume III: Autobiographies*, eds. William H. O'Donnell and Douglas N. Archibald (New York, 1999), p. 364.
33. A longer version of this journal would be included in his *Memoirs: Autobiography and First-draft Journal* (New York, 1972).
34. See Yeats, *Collected Works of W.B. Yeats*, vol. 3. In his 1909 journal entitled *Estrangement: Extracts from a Diary kept in 1909*, Yeats even suggests that he would close the Abbey or simply leave it in order not to make personal compromises with 'the vulgarity . . . [of] the Irish town mind' (p. 357). He also writes that 'A young man in Ireland meets only crude, impersonal things, things that make him like others. One cannot discuss his ideas or ideals, for he has none. He has not the beginning of aesthetic culture . . . I can only wish that a young Irishman of talent and culture may spend his life, from eighteen to twenty-five, outside Ireland. Can one prescribe duties to a developed soul?' (p. 352). In another section he refers to Thomas MacDonagh, who would later be executed as a leader of the Easter Rising in 1916, as 'a man with some literary faculty which will probably come to nothing through lack of culture and encouragement' (p. 360).
35. See Yeats, *Collected Works of W.B. Yeats*, vol. 3. 'Culture is the sanctity of the intellect', Yeats wrote in one entry from *Estrangement*, and added in another that 'Anarchic revolt is coming to an end . . . [as] the arts are about to reinstate the traditional

morality' (pp. 361–2). Lest he effectively abandon his earlier critique, however, Yeats attributed the degeneration of morality to an English poetic tradition 'passed from Milton to Wordsworth and to Arnold' (p. 362). Even when he borrowed from the earlier writer to critique Irish nationalism, therefore, Yeats was still inclined to subvert its imperial source.

36. Yeats, *Collected Works of W.B. Yeats*, vol. 3, p. 362.
37. Ibid., p. 364.
38. Ibid.
39. Ibid.
40. Ibid., p. 365.
41. See W.B. Yeats, *Memoirs*, ed. Denis Donoghue (London, 1972), p. 247, where he calls it their 'old argument about Sinn Féin and its attack on Synge, and the general circumstances that surrounded the first split in the Theatre. I notice that this old quarrel is the one difference about which she feels strongly. I for this very reason allow myself to get drawn into it again and again, thinking to convince her at last that apart from wrongs and rights impossible to settle so long after, it was fundamental. I could not have done otherwise. My whole movement, my integrity as a man of letters, were alike involved.'
42. Ibid., p. 248.
43. Matthew Arnold, *The Complete Prose Works of Matthew Arnold: Volume IX: English Literature and Irish Politics*, ed. R.H. Super (Ann Arbor, MI, 1977), p. 52.
44. Lloyd and Thomas borrow the term 'ethical state' from Antonio Gramsci, and the language of the 'ideological apparatus' from Louis Althusser. For an overview of how they use these two thinkers more generally, see their introduction to the text in Lloyd and Thomas, *Culture and the State*, pp. 1–30. See also Louis Althusser, 'Ideology and ideological state apparatuses', in Louis Althusser, *Lenin and Philosophy and Other Essays*, trans. Ben Brewster (London, 1971), pp. 123–73; and Antonio Gramsci, *Prison Notebooks*, ed. and trans. Joseph A. Buttigieg, 3 vols (New York, 1992–2007).
45. Yeats, *Collected Works of W.B. Yeats*, vol. 4, p. 246.
46. Lloyd and Thomas, *Culture and the State*, p. 27.
47. Yeats, *Collected Works of W.B. Yeats*, vol. 3, p. 365.
48. See Yeats' letter to John Quinn on 2 April 1916 in Allan Wade (ed.), *The Letters of W.B. Yeats* (London, 1954), p. 610.
49. See Robert Anthony Martinich and Mary J. Harper (eds), *Yeats' Vision Papers: Volume III: Sleep and Dream Notebooks, Vision Notebooks 1 and 2, Card File* (Iowa City, IA, 1992), p. 63.
50. Ibid.
51. Wade (ed.), *Letters of W.B. Yeats*, p. 665.
52. Ibid., p. 667. 'If I only express it', the letter to Russell continued, 'it will seem but a deduction from one man's unpopular system. They will say "O that is Yeats" and pass it by. You spoke it all long ago and I would like to hear you speak it again – not indirectly only as in a dialogue but directly so that men can act upon it, and not only as culture but as economics. We writers are not politicians, the present is not in our charge but some part of the future is.'
53. See W.B. Yeats, *The Senate Speeches*, ed. Donald R. Pearce (Bloomington, IN, 1960), pp. 75–6.
54. Ibid., p. 76.
55. For further analysis of Arnold's evolving 'Burkean' reading of Irish politics, see my 'Matthew Arnold, Edmund Burke, and Irish reconciliation', *Prose Studies*, vol. 34, no. 3 (December 2012). Just as Arnold did over the course of his career, Yeats also

turned from a model of Burkean conciliation to one of Burkean coercion. For an overview of these strategies in the British government's Irish policy during that period, see L.P. Curtis, *Coercion and Conciliation in Ireland: 1880–1892* (Princeton, NJ, 1963). We can see how Yeats' turn to a coercive Burke impacted on his mature poetry in Donald T. Torchiana, 'Senator Yeats, Burke, and Able Men', *Newberry Library Bulletin*, no. 5 (1961), and in Patrick J. Keane, 'Revolutions French and Russian: Burke, Wordsworth, and the genesis of Yeats' "The Second Coming"', *Bulletin of Research in the Humanities*, no. 82 (1979), and also in Alasdair MacIntyre, 'Poetry as political philosophy: notes on Burke and Yeats', in Vereen Bell and Laurence Lerner (eds), *On Modern Poetry: Essays Presented to Donald Davie* (Nashville, TN, 1988).

56. Arnold, *Complete Prose Works of Matthew Arnold*, vol. 3, p. 386.
57. See Martinich and Harper (eds), *Yeats' Vision Papers*, vol. 3.
58. Ibid., p. 121.
59. Ibid., p. 122.
60. Ibid.
61. Ibid., pp. 121–2.
62. See David Lloyd, 'Arnold, Ferguson and Schiller: aesthetic culture and the politics of aesthetics', *Cultural Critique*, no. 2 (1985).
63. Yeats, *Uncollected Prose*, vol. 2, p. 470.
64. Wade (ed.), *Letters of W.B. Yeats*, pp. 710–11.
65. See Donald T. Torchiana, 'Among school children and the education of the Irish spirit', in Norman A. Jeffares (ed.), *In Excited Reverie: A Centenary Tribute to W.B. Yeats* (London, 1965); Roy Foster, *W.B. Yeats: A Life II: The Arch-poet, 1915–1939* (Oxford, 2003); Ann Saddlemyer, *Becoming George: The Life of Mrs. W.B. Yeats* (Oxford, 2002); and John Kelly, *A W.B. Yeats Chronology* (New York, 2003). Torchiana placed the St Otteran's visit in February; in late March, however, the Yeatses wrote letters about the visit (not included in Wade, but included in Foster and Saddlemyer) that would suggest they actually toured the school on 21 and 22 March. Kelly's *Chronology* also places the visit in March. This means that Yeats' most substantial Senate speech on the topic of education, the one that mentions the school directly, would have been given only days after the actual visit.
66. See W.B. Yeats, The Tower *Manuscript Materials*, eds. Richard J. Finneran, Jared Curtis and Ann Saddlemyer (Ithaca, NY, 2007), p. 361.
67. He would not have wanted the poem to undermine his authority as a senator to speak about education; 'Leda and the Swan' had already been invoked by the *Catholic Bulletin* as reason not to let him near the education debate. Yeats was happy enough to scandalise the Church to some degree, but he was also interested in the political results of his efforts.
68. Peter Alt and Russell Allspach (eds), *The Variorum Edition of the Poems of W.B. Yeats* (London, 1957), p. 407.
69. Ibid., p. 408.
70. Ibid., p. 445.
71. Ibid.
72. Ibid.
73. See Elizabeth Butler Cullingford, *Gender and History in Yeats' Love Poetry* (Cambridge, 1993), p. 202. More specifically, she writes that the final stanza's 'evocation of unalienated labor and joyful learning can be read both as an impossible Utopia and as a plea for a humane and decent system of primary education' (p. 199).
74. Alt and Allspach (eds), *Variorum Edition of the Poems of W.B. Yeats*, p. 443.

75. In one key passage in their introduction to *Culture and the State*, Lloyd and Thomas use Gramscian and Althusserian terms to describe the ideological achievement of the British educational reformers David Stow (1793–1864) and Sir James Kay-Shuttleworth (1804–77) by the time of the 1870 Education Act: 'Stow in effect invents the modern classroom that Kay succeeds in generalizing and does so in the form of the "gallery" whose architecture we recognize as the contemporary lecture hall or "theater". It permits the simultaneous surveillance of multiple subjects and, more importantly, their simultaneous interpellation as individuals through their "training" on the same elevated object, the teacher. The elevation of the teacher, and his constitution as exemplary representative of ethical formation, places him *before* the class in both temporal and spatial senses of the word. He represents the ethical to them as the single, spatially isolated common object of their regard as much as by the superior development that his position in the pyramidal structure of the classroom instantiates . . . [and] prefigures the yet more abstract role of the state as ultimate representative of ethical subjectivity. The school, in other words, permits the transfer of the subject from the private domain of the family into the public world of the political, not by teaching civics but by representing representation' (p. 20). This idea of ethics in relation to the movement from the family to the public world is also essential to my later discussion of Sophocles' *Antigone*, in chapters two and three.
76. Lloyd and Thomas, *Culture and the State*, p. 5.
77. Alt and Allspach (eds), *Variorum Edition of the Poems of W.B. Yeats*, p. 443.
78. Foster, *W.B. Yeats*, vol. 2, p. 321. See also Torchiana, 'Among school children and the education of the Irish spirit', p. 123, which begins with a child's perspective on Yeats' visit: 'One Monday morning in February 1926, a present member of the Convent of Mercy, Waterford, at that time a thirteen-year-old student, watched from a window as Senator W.B. Yeats, in soft hat and with a magisterial presence, took his distinguished way up the driveway of St. Otteran's School. His famed turkey strut – a gait combining short, jerky steps with body erect, head thrown back and hands clasped behind his back – was unforgettable.'
79. His self-consciousness about appearances returns at the end of stanza four, by which point it is obvious that he has phased out of whatever presentation was being made, and decided it is 'Better to smile on all that smile, and show / There is a comfortable kind of old scarecrow.' Alt and Allspach (eds), *Variorum Edition of the Poems of W.B. Yeats*, p. 444.
80. Yeats, *Collected Works of W.B. Yeats*, vol. 5, p. 8.
81. See Arnold, *Complete Prose Works of Matthew Arnold*, vol. 1. Here we might recall Arnold's own explanation of why he left *Empedocles on Etna* out of the 1853 edition of his *Poems*: namely that it took place at the moment 'the disinterested objectivity' of the classical Greek era had 'disappeared' and 'the dialogue of the mind with itself [had] commenced' (p. 1). For a very fine reading of how Arnold fits into a longer history and larger context of thinkers in this vein, see David Bromwich, 'The genealogy of disinterestedness', *Raritan: A Quarterly Review*, no. 1 (1982). See also John Woolford, 'Arnold on Empedocles', *Review of English Studies: A Quarterly Journal of English Literature and the English* Language, vol. 50, no. 197 (1999). In *The Tower* (1928) and *The Winding Stair* (1933), however, Yeats eschews the Arnoldian notion of critical disinterest, and places his own inner quarrel at the centre of the creative process.
82. W.B. Yeats, *A Vision* (New York, 1966; first published 1937), p. 240. This final image of the dancer is related to one of the greatest images of reconciliation in his occult system: the 'Thirteenth Cone', which is as close to the image of God as anything else

we find in Yeats' philosophy. He concludes the last prose section of *A Vision*, for instance, with the idea that 'The particulars [of the system] are the work of the thirteenth sphere or cycle which is in every man and called by every man his freedom. Doubtless, for it can do all things and know all things, and it knows what it will do with its own freedom but has kept it a secret' (pp. 301–2).

83. Alt and Allspach (eds), *Variorum Edition of the Poems of W.B. Yeats*, p. 446.
84. W.B. Yeats, The Tower *Manuscript Materials*, p. 21.
85. See Yeats, *Collected Works of W.B. Yeats*, vol. 3. As far back as 1909, however, when he was re-conceiving his mission as an apostle of Arnoldian culture, Yeats recognised that the Greek sculptor would be an ineffective exemplar; 'Plutarch was right when he said the artist should not be too prominent in the State', the poet wrote, 'because no young man, born for war and love, desires to be like Phidias' (p. 351). Yeats thought the idea was relevant (or perhaps ironic) enough during his Senatorial period that he included the entry in his published diary from 1909: Yeats, *Estrangement* (pp. 339–65).
86. Alt and Allspach (eds), *Variorum Edition of the Poems of W.B. Yeats*, p. 446.
87. Ibid., pp. 407, 445.
88. Ibid., p. 447.
89. Ibid., p. 441.
90. Yeats, *A Vision*, p. 26.
91. Ibid., p. 27.
92. Ibid.
93. Ibid.
94. Ibid., pp. 27–8.
95. Ibid., p. 28.
96. Ibid.
97. Alt and Allspach (eds), *Variorum Edition of the Poems of W.B. Yeats*, p. 540. For another reading of this poem, see Patrick J. Keane, 'Faithful in his fashion: Yeats and the Eros chorus from Sophocles' *Antigone*', *Yeats Eliot Review: A Journal of Criticism and Scholarship*, no. 8 (1986).
98. See Arnold, *Complete Prose Works of Matthew Arnold*, vol. 1, p. 12: 'An action like the action of the *Antigone* of Sophocles, which turns upon the conflict between the heroine's duty to her brother's corpse and that to the laws of her country, is no longer one in which it is possible that we should feel a deep interest.' History has not borne Arnold's judgement on this matter out, but Gerhard Joseph nonetheless finds a great deal of significance in Arnold's reading in relation to other modern writers, in 'The *Antigone* as cultural touchstone: Matthew Arnold, Hegel, George Eliot, Virginia Woolf, and Margaret Drabble', *PMLA: Publications of the Modern Language Association of America*, vol. 96, no. 1 (1981).

Chapter 2

1. The standard (and generally sympathetic) biography is Donald Harman Akenson's *Conor: A Biography of Conor Cruise O'Brien* (Ithaca, NY, 1994). For a briefer and somewhat more critical overview, see Tom Garvin, 'Imaginary Cassandra: Conor Cruise O'Brien as public intellectual in Ireland', *Irish University Review* (2007).
2. See Akenson, *Conor*, p. 418: 'When it became clear that Conor did not intend to abolish Section 31 or even to withdraw the earlier orders under Section 31 made by Fianna Fail [sic], this confused many of his old friends and backers. They could not help but contrast his longtime opposition to censorship in general to his new

behavior, now that he was the censor. In 1974, Conor replaced the obscure banning order that Fianna Fail [sic] had formulated under Section 31, with a very precise order that was drafted by his son-in-law Nicholas Simms. The vague wording was gone: now the Provos, Officials, Provisional Sinn Fein [sic] (but not Official Sinn Fein [sic]) were unambiguously banned from the airwaves, as were their advocates.' See also Ed Moloney, 'Censorship and "The Troubles"', in Mary P. Corcoran and Mark O'Brien (eds), *Political Censorship and the Democratic State: The Irish Broadcasting Ban* (Dublin, 2005), pp. 99–110, which describes the stifling atmosphere of self-censorship in Irish journalism under O'Brien, and argues this delayed the peace process until the 1990s.

3. For an excerpt from O'Brien's own 1975 speech to the Oireachtas recommending the passage of the 1976 Broadcasting (Amendment) Act, see Conor Cruise O'Brien, 'Broadcasting and violence: the case for media restriction', in Corcoran and O'Brien (eds), *Political Censorship and the Democratic State*. Diarmuid Whelan, in 'Conor Cruise O'Brien and the legitimation of violence', *Irish Political Studies*, vol. 21, no. 2 (2006), analyses O'Brien's attitude to discussions of violence in the Republic. John Horgan, in *Irish Media: A Critical History Since 1922* (New York, 2001), notes the 1976 Act 'bore a passing – and in all probability not coincidental – resemblance to the British Broadcasting Act of 1973' (p. 121).
4. O'Brien's draft of section 3 read: 'Any person who expressly or by implication, directly or through another person or persons, or by advertisement, propaganda or any other means, incites or invites another person (or persons generally) to join an unlawful organisation or take part in, support, or assist its activities, shall be guilty of an offence and shall be liable on conviction on indictment to imprisonment for a term not exceeding ten years'; quoted in Horgan, *Irish Media*, p. 116.
5. The minister for justice, Patrick Cooney, denied the existence of a 'Heavy Gang', and accused the media of having been misled by the Provisional IRA. According to then-minister for foreign affairs Garrett Fitzgerald, however, he and the Taoiseach, Liam Cosgrave, had both been alerted to this practice shortly before *The Irish Times* story broke. In his *Memoirs: My Life and Themes* (Dublin, 1998), moreover, O'Brien divulged that he had learned of it back in 1975 – and kept the information to himself (p. 355). For an overview of these events, see Mark O'Brien, 'Disavowing democracy: the silencing project in the South', in Corcoran and O'Brien (eds), *Political Censorship and the Democratic State*, pp. 48–58.
6. Michael D. Higgins was minister for the arts, culture and Gaelteacht at that time, and was thus responsible for recommending renewal. For his account of how he decided not to, see his 'Culture, democracy and public service broadcasting', in Corcoran and O'Brien (eds), *Political Censorship and the Democratic State*, pp. 136–46.
7. Less than two weeks after the IRA's announcement of a cessation of military operations on 31 August 1994, O'Brien published 'Peace comes dropping hard' (*National Review*, 12 September 1994), concluding that 'the now-discredited "peace process" has been a political bonanza for Sinn Féin-IRA' (p. 26). His *Ancestral Voices: Religion and Nationalism in Ireland* (Chicago, IL, 1994) had recently been published, and in each of its new editions during the 1990s he would append a new postscript predicting ever-increasing catastrophic outcomes for this 'discredited' peace process. Irish historians Toby Barnard and Brendan Bradshaw wrote reviews of *Ancestral Voices*, noting in each case that the author was brilliant but out of touch with the spirit of the time. Barnard wrote that 'far from being swept along in the orchestrated euphoria of the recent cease-fires', the author 'returns to his apocalyptic mode, warning that truces and compacts belong to a ruthless nationalist

strategy'; Toby Barnard, 'An abrasive Palesman: Conor Cruise O'Brien and modern Ireland', *Times Literary Supplement*, 16 December 1994, p. 3. In 'Republican rebellion to Catholic fury', *Review of Politics*, vol. 60, no. 1 (winter 1998), Bradshaw dismissed the historical argument as politically tendentious, and concluded that 'The elderly Conor Cruise O'Brien of this polemic . . . [expends] so much intelligence and energy . . . in the heroically futile endeavor, Canute-like to stem the tide of history' (p. 216). For other op-eds from O'Brien denouncing the peace process, see 'A "peace process" deadly as war', *New York Times*, 12 January 1997; 'This peace means war: I will not applaud a Nobel Prize given to appeasers of the IRA', *Guardian*, 17 October 1998; and 'Police powers: how the IRA leverages the peace process', *Atlantic Monthly*, vol. 288, no. 5 (December 2001). This last article called for the imposition of martial law and suspension of ordinary courts in Northern Ireland, reasoning that even the US would be sympathetic to these measures, in the wake of the 11 September attacks.

8. Bourke et al. (eds), *Field Day Anthology of Irish Writing*, vol. 5, p. 1521.
9. O'Brien, *States of Ireland*, p. 293.
10. See Seamus Deane and Barre Fitzpatrick, 'Interview with John Hume', *Crane Bag*, vol. 4, no. 2 (1980), p. 679.
11. See O'Brien's *The Irish Times* interview with Fintan O'Toole, 'Cruiser's new voyage' (11 May 1996): 'I have no qualms or heart searching, though I would have had six years ago certainly. But I am a bit sorry for decent people who have been defending me for years among their friends and saying that I'm not a unionist, as I hadn't formally said I was.'
12. See Fintan O'Toole, 'Cruise O'Brien proud to be a Paisleyite', *The Irish Times*, 8 May 1998: 'One of the saddest sentences I have read in a long time is this: "I am glad to be an ally of Paisley's in the defence of the Union" . . . how poignant that a man who should be honoured for breaking the intellectual ground in which the possibilities of lasting peace have taken root asks instead that we should remember him marching arm-in-arm with a foolish old reactionary into a swamp of decaying obscurities.' For a similarly bittersweet image, see Richard Kearney's review of O'Brien's *Memoirs* in the *Times Literary Supplement*: 'It is probably in this last role that most contemporary observers will remember him. Sitting tight-lipped and resolute between Bob McCartney and Ian Paisley, walking stick in hand, staunchly denouncing the evils of the Good Friday Agreement – to the bitter end, a defender of the most misunderstood and maligned cause (as he sees it)', even though 'If things had really turned out as they should have, and his initial hopes for the national question been heeded, he might have received the Nobel Peace Prize rather than his enemies MacBride and Hume. O'Brien is Ireland's *prophète maudit* and *manqué*'; Richard Kearney, 'Ulysses returns to Ithaca: the odysseys and ambiguities of Conor Cruise O'Brien', *Times Literary Supplement*, 15 January 1999. As it turns out, O'Brien's eulogies and critical reassessments have tactfully overlooked the controversialist's final period, and spent more time engaging with the more challenging and influential ideas of the 1960s and Seventies.
13. O'Brien explained himself to Deaglán de Bréadún, in '"The Cruiser": still stirring things up after all these years', *The Irish Times*, 28 October 1998.
14. Paulin, *Ireland & the English Crisis*, pp. 25, 30, 33.
15. Mark McNally describes the 'two key arguments on the nature of Irish nationalism' O'Brien formulated in *States of Ireland*, and to which he returned consistently throughout his career, namely that Irish republicanism, while pretending to be secular, was 'based on the collective emotional bonds of the descendants of a

colonised Gaelic and Catholic people', and that 'the religious dimension of this identity was primary', and this led him to 'condemn the hypocrisy of the Irish State's claims over Northern Ireland'; Mark McNally, 'Conor Cruise O'Brien's conservative anti-nationalism: retrieving the postwar European connection', *European Journal of Political Theory*, vol. 7, no. 3 (2008), pp. 308–9.

16. He was not the only Irish revisionist to combine Arnold with Yeats: in 1979 F.S.L. Lyons published a series of Oxford lectures that takes as its end points the Parnell split and the death of Yeats; F.S.L. Lyons, *Culture and Anarchy in Ireland, 1890–1939* (Oxford, 1979). Moreover, R.F. Foster inherited from Lyons the job of writing Yeats' official (and monumental) biography.
17. Conor Cruise O'Brien, 'Imagination and politics', in Conor Cruise O'Brien and William Dean Vanech (eds), *Power and Consciousness* (London, 1969), p. 213.
18. Ibid., p. 214.
19. Ibid.
20. Ibid., p. 213.
21. See Joseph Morrison Skelly, *Irish Diplomacy at the United Nations 1945–1965: National Interests and the International Order* (Dublin, 1997), pp. 149–65.
22. Conor Cruise O'Brien, *To Katanga and Back: A UN Case History* (New York, 1963), p. 14.
23. Ibid., pp. 14–15.
24. Ibid., p. 15.
25. It was hard to argue with the general charge against the UN's Western bias in the case, but the Hammarskjöld cult was strong and O'Brien like many others at the time defended him from the charge of complicity. O'Brien would, however, later be convinced that Hammarskjöld had in fact played a conscious role in Lumumba's betrayal, and this would become the subject of his 1968 play *Murderous Angels*. For more on this work, see Michael Cohen, 'Politics vs. drama in O'Brien's *Murderous Angels*', *Contemporary Literature*, no. 16 (1975).
26. For an overview of these operations, see Akenson, *Conor*, pp. 149–83.
27. O'Brien had tried to convince the secretary general not to go at all, and was even denied permission to accompany him on the flight. The plane had a crew of six, and Hammarskjöld was also accompanied by a party of nine, including functionaries, security officers and Swedish soldiers.
28. O'Brien, *To Katanga and Back*, p. 41.
29. Akenson, *Conor*, p. 188.
30. Ibid.
31. He was also expected to observe a customary silence. Instead of falling quietly on his sword, however, O'Brien called a press conference and started granting interviews the next day. This was a radical departure from UN protocol, and O'Brien took it even further by publishing *To Katanga and Back*, in which he argued that Hammarskjöld, taking a broad view of the UN's ambiguous mandate to resolve the crisis, personally authorised the author to use a greater amount of force than some members of the Security Council believed they were authorising. For a critical revision of O'Brien's account, see Michel Kennedy and Art Magennis, *Ireland: The United Nations and the Congo* (Dublin, 2014).
32. Akenson, *Conor*, pp. 187–8.
33. Ibid., p. 188.
34. Conor Cruise O'Brien, *United Nations: Sacred Drama* (New York, 1968), pp. 89–90.
35. See Johan Huizinga, *Homo Ludens: A Study of the Play-element in Culture* (New York, 1950). O'Brien devotes chapter eighteen of *United Nations* to Huizinga, contrasting his 'play' of peace with the 'play' of war in Nietzsche and Yeats.

36. O'Brien, *United Nations*, p. 10.
37. Ibid., p. 11.
38. Ibid., pp. 11–12.
39. Morgenthau emigrated from Nazi Germany in the late 1930s, and became a colleague of Leo Strauss and David Grene (a friend of O'Brien's) at the University of Chicago. Morgenthau's *Politics Among Nations: The Struggle for Power and Peace* (New York, 1948) was a major textbook on political science in the US for the better part of the Cold War. For intellectual histories of political realism and Morgenthau's place in that history, see Richard Lebow, *The Tragic Vision of Politics: Ethics, Interests and Orders* (Cambridge, 2003); and Martin Griffiths, *Realism, Idealism, and International Politics: A Reinterpretation* (New York, 1992).
40. Thucydides, *The Peloponnesian War* (Chicago, IL, 1989), pp. 14–15.
41. See Henry George Liddell and Robert Scott, *A Greek-English Lexicon* (Oxford, 1985). Liddel and Scott also translate *anagkê* as 'kindred', likening it to the Latin *necessitudo*, which Lewis renders as 'inevitableness', or 'necessary connection'. The possible and probable meanings of this term have been the foci of many books and articles on Thucydides; see Peter J. Fleiss, *Thucydides and the Politics of Bipolarity* (Baton Rouge, LA, 1996); and Martin Ostwald, *Ananke in Thucydides* (Atlanta, GA, 1998).
42. O'Brien, *United Nations*, p. 133.
43. Ibid., p. 247.
44. See Conor Cruise O'Brien, *Writers and Politics* (New York, 1965), p. 204.
45. O'Brien, *United Nations*, pp. 131–2.
46. Ibid., p. 245.
47. Within the Council of Europe, moreover, Northern Ireland was considered an internal issue for the UK. The US was sympathetic to Irish nationalist claims for most of the twentieth century, but it also had a 'special relationship' with Britain.
48. O'Brien, *States of Ireland*, p. 142.
49. Ibid., p. 143.
50. For more on the controversy over historical revisionism in Ireland, see Ciaran Brady (ed.), *Interpreting Irish History: The Debate on Historical Revisionism* (Dublin, 1994).
51. F.S.L. Lyons, *Ireland Since the Famine* (London, 1972), p. 201.
52. Seamus Deane has commented on this paradox in his anti-revisionist essay 'Wherever green is read', in Máirín Ní Dhonnchadha and Theo Dorgan (eds), *Revising the Rising* (Derry, 1991), p. 234. On the same page he dismisses O'Brien as a revisionist and a unionist: 'The revisionists are now themselves more vulnerable to revision because their pseudo-scientific orthodoxy is so obviously tailored to match the prevailing political climate – especially in relation to the Northern crisis – that its claims to "objectivity", to being "value-free", have been abandoned as disguises no longer needed. Conor Cruise O'Brien has declared himself to be a unionist and, in that light, his writings can be understood as a polemic in favour of that position.'
53. Conor Cruise O'Brien, *Parnell and his Party* (Oxford, 1957), p. 356.
54. Yeats, *Collected Works of W.B. Yeats*, vol. 3, p. 410.
55. This essay would later appear in *Passion and Cunning*. When he introduced this bombshell argument, O'Brien astonished the editors who had commissioned it. It inflicted long-term damage on Yeats' reputation, and remains an important topic for scholarship nearly a half-century later. O'Brien's 'fascist charge' went largely unchallenged until Elizabeth Cullingford's response in *Yeats, Ireland and Fascism* (Oxford, 1981).
56. O'Brien, *Passion and Cunning*, p. 54.
57. Ibid.

58. Ibid., p. 50.
59. O'Brien, *Memoirs*, p. 297.
60. He stayed until his contract ran out, and in his parting meeting with Nkumra, the president thanked him 'for what you did for the University of Ghana . . . Whatever it was'; quoted in Akenson, *Conor*, pp. 270–1. This became one of O'Brien's favourite stories about himself.
61. O'Brien, *Memoirs*, p. 298.
62. O'Brien nevertheless revisited the charge of Yeats' hypothetical collaboration with a Nazi regime in the introduction to *Passion and Cunning*. Most importantly, he retracted any suggestion that Yeats would have approved of the hypothetical transportation of Jews from Britain or Ireland. 'I acknowledge now', he wrote in the book's introduction, 'as I think about the matter further, that the passage as it stands is unjust to Yeats. It is unjust because of where it stops. He might indeed have accepted participation in the kind of government I have hypothesised; he could well have been persuaded that it was his duty to do so. But I cannot imagine him remaining in such a government, or continuing to support it, while it complied with the actual demands of the new masters of Europe': O'Brien, *Passion and Cunning*, p. 2. Perhaps O'Brien had stopped the controversial passage too soon because when he wrote it, his analogous relation to the dictatorial regime of Kwame Nkrumah had itself not stopped *yet*. Even so, it remained a part of O'Brien's Enlightenment principles that one should support the universities even of non-democratic regimes. In the 1980s, for instance, O'Brien would enrage the Anti-Apartheid Movement in Ireland by breaking the international academic boycott against South Africa.
63. O'Brien, *United Nations*, p. 315.
64. Conor Cruise O'Brien, 'A slow, north-east wind', in Elmer Andrews (ed.), *The Poetry of Seamus Heaney* (New York, 1998), p. 82.
65. Ibid., p. 84.
66. Ibid.
67. Ibid., p. 82.
68. Ibid.
69. Ibid.
70. Ibid.
71. Seamus Heaney, *North* (London, 1975), p. 31. In making this omission, O'Brien also condensed lines into a quatrain that did not exist in the original.
72. O'Brien, *United Nations*, p. 120.
73. Conor Cruise O'Brien, *The Suspecting Glance* (London, 1972), p. 87.
74. Ibid., p. 88.
75. Seamus Heaney, 'Old Derry's walls', *The Listener*, 24 October 1968. Heaney observed that 'a cliché-mongering movement begins to be discerned in Unionist speeches associating civil rights with "communist and republican elements" and dropping the matter there – not that the rest of us are particularly reassured by the presence of Orangemen in the Cabinet. Since the administration is so unwilling to recognise shades of grey even while pleading for their existence in other spheres, they must not feign surprise if opinion hardens. *They* will have been responsible: not the local police, who must bear the brunt; nor the special reserve force, who are trained and ordered to do what they do' (p. 522).
76. Conor Cruise O'Brien, 'Views', *The Listener*, 24 October 1968.
77. Ibid.
78. Ibid.
79. Ibid.

80. O'Brien, *States of Ireland*, p. 153.

CHAPTER 3

1. Paulin, *The Riot Act*, p. 15.
2. Tom Paulin, *Fivemiletown* (London, 1987), pp. 42–3.
3. By the time O'Brien published *States of Ireland*, of course, the anti-colonial possibilities for reading and performing Greek drama were not as widely recognised as they are today. Largely thanks to dramatic re-appropriations from Africa to the Caribbean to Ireland and elsewhere, the study of this topic has undergone a further paradigm shift. Lorna Hardwick nicely sums up this transformation at the end of her essay 'Greek drama and anti-colonialism: decolonizing classics', in Edith Hall, Fiona Macintosh and Amanda Wrigley (eds), *Dionysus Since 69: Greek Tragedy at the Dawn of the Third Millennium* (Oxford, 2004), p. 242.
4. See Marianne McDonald, 'The Irish and Greek tragedy', in McDonald and Walton (eds), *Amid Our Troubles*, pp. 80–2. McDonald counts thirty-nine Irish translations or adaptations of Greek drama written or performed between 1899 and 2000. For some essays on Greek plays dealing with the Troubles in Northern Ireland, see Joe Cleary, 'Domestic troubles: tragedy and the Northern Ireland conflict', *South Atlantic Quarterly*, no. 98 (1999); Anthony Roche, 'Ireland's Antigones: tragedy North and South', in Michael Kenneally (ed.), *Cultural Contexts and Literary Idioms in Contemporary Irish Literature* (Gerrard's Cross, Bucks, 1988); Shaun Richards, 'In the border country: Greek Tragedy and contemporary Irish drama', in C.C. Barfoot and W.Z. Van Den Doel (eds), *Ritual Remembering: History, Myth and Politics in Anglo-Irish Drama* (Atlanta, GA, 1995); Kelly Younger: 'Irish Antigones: burying the colonial symptom', *Colloquy: Text Theory Critique*, no. 11 (2006); and Christopher Murray, 'Three Irish Antigones', in Jacqueline Genet and Richard Alan Cave (eds), *Perspectives of Irish Drama and Theatre* (Gerrard's Cross, Bucks, 1991).
5. Negative criticism of Field Day came primarily from critics in the 'revisionist' school of Irish history, the origins of which were discussed in the previous chapter. For the most extended argument that Field Day was smuggling IRA propaganda into the Anglo-American academy under the cover of fashionable French literary theory, see Edna Longley, *The Living Stream: Literature and Revisionism in Ireland* (Newcastle upon Tyne, 1994), pp. 22–44. For an extended analysis of Deane's debate with Longley (which largely sides with Deane against Longley's perceived Arnoldianism), see chapter five of Conor McCarthy's *Modernisation: Crisis and Culture in Ireland, 1969–1992* (Dublin, 2000), pp. 197–228. For a revisionist historian's critique of the entire postcolonial school of Irish studies that emerged alongside Field Day in the 1980s, see chapter 7 of Stephen Howe's *Ireland and Empire* (Oxford, 2000), pp. 107–45. Strangely enough, I have not been able to locate any substantial published response – either to Paulin or to Field Day – by Conor Cruise O'Brien himself.
6. Dympna Callaghan and Seamus Deane, 'An interview with Seamus Deane: University College, Dublin, June 1993', *Social Text* (1994), p. 45.
7. See 'Short essays by Seamus Deane on Field Day, circa 1985', National Library of Ireland Field Day archive, III.x.1, G/Misc/8. According to Cormac Ó Duibhne's description in *The Field Day Archive* (Dublin, 2007), 'this essay was intended for the May 1985 issue of *Ireland Today*, the bulletin of the Irish Department of Foreign Affairs' (p. 112).
8. For the definitive historical account of the company's genesis and dramatic productions from 1980 to 1984, see Marilyn Richtarik's *Acting Between the Lines: The*

Field Day Theatre Company and Irish Cultural Politics, 1980–1984 (Oxford, 1994).

9. See Cormac Ó Duibhne, '"Talk about the play!": an interview with Stephen Rea', *Princeton University Library Chronicle*, vol. 58, nos. 1–2 (2006), p. 579.
10. Scholars stressing Field Day's liberalism have emphasised Friel and the theme of translation. See Patrick Maley, 'Aeneas in Baile Beag: Friel's *Translations*, *The Aeneid*, and the humanism of the Field Day Theatre Company', *New Hibernia Review/Iris Éireannach Nua*, vol. 15, no. 4 (geimhreadh/winter 2011), and Maria-Elena Doyle, 'A gesture to indicate a presence: translation, dialect and Field Day Theatre Company's quest for an Irish identity', in Sherry Simon and Paul St-Pierre (eds), *Changing the Terms: Translating the Postcolonial Era* (Ottawa, 2000). See also W.B. Worthen, 'Homeless words: Field Day and the politics of translation', *Modern Drama*, no. 38 (1995), in which Worthen contrasts Friel's *Translations* with Paulin's *Riot Act*, and concludes that Friel's statement is more central to the group's ethos. For a Gramscian analysis of Field Day, placing greater emphasis on Paulin's Sophoclean quarrel with O'Brien, see Richard Kirkland, *Literature and Culture in Northern Ireland Since 1965: Moments of Danger* (London, 1996), pp. 136–40. More recently, in *Field Day and the Translation of Irish Identities* (London, 2011), Aidan O'Malley splits the difference by using translation theory to argue that Field Day was an anti-hegemonic enterprise (actually on the grounds of its emphasis on translation), and that *The Riot Act* was a key text because it 'foregrounds the inherent, ghostly, anachrony of translation' (p. 101).
11. In the BBC *Arena* documentary 'History Boys on the Rampage' (dir. Andrew Eaton), BBC, 1988, Rea described the importance, to him, of performing Friel's *Making History* to local communities such as Dungannon, which is where the protagonist of the play, Hugh O'Neill, had actually lived. 'One of the important things that I think we do', he told the interviewer, 'is that people aren't getting ideas second-hand; they're getting them from the horse's mouth; . . . We're delivering them to the people that should be hearing them, you know. They're not second-hand on television, it isn't an RSC tour, it's not being delivered from Headquarters. It's being delivered from within.' In this and other statements made over the years, Rea stresses that there is something vital, organic, authentic, and un-official about Field Day's critical and creative intervention.
12. *Arena*, 'History Boys on the Rampage'.
13. For a particularly illuminating discussion of Paulin's and Heaney's versions of Sophocles in relation both to the Athenian playwright's ancient context and to the deep history of his interpretation, see Michael Vickers, 'A legend of wild beauty: Sophocles' *Antigone*', *Classics Ireland*, no. 14 (2007).
14. Tom Paulin, 'Whose side are you on?', *Independent on Sunday*, 28 September 2003.
15. Paulin, *Ireland & the English Crisis*, pp. 27–8. There is an Arnoldian parallel to Paulin's 'Hellenic' counterargument: when he claims that O'Brien misreads Northern Ireland the same way he misreads Sophocles, this recalls Arnold's contention, in the 1886 essay 'The nadir of liberalism', that Gladstone misread Parnellism in the same way he mistranslated Homer; see Matthew Arnold, *The Complete Prose Works of Matthew Arnold: Volume XI: The Last Word*, ed. R.H. Super (Ann Arbor, MI, 1977), p. 64. In this passage from 'The making of a loyalist', Paulin splices F.P.B. Osmaston's 1920 translation of Hegel's *Philosophy of Fine Art*, vol. 2 ((London, 1920), p. 215) with T.M. Knox's 1975 rendering of the same passage in *Aesthetics: Lectures on Fine Art*, vol. 1 (Oxford, 1975), p. 465. He also makes an unattributed quotation from A.C. Bradley's essay, *Hegel's Theory of Tragedy* (London, 1904), p. 74. Hegel also describes Sophocles' play in similar terms in *The Phenomenology of the Spirit*, trans. J.N. Findlay (Oxford, 1977), pp. 267–8.

16. See Seamus Deane, 'Field Day's Greeks (and Russians)', in McDonald and Walton (eds), *Amid Our Troubles*, pp. 153–4, and Seamus Heaney, 'Title deeds: translating a classic', *Proceedings of the American Philosophical Society*, vol. 148 (2004), pp. 413–14. For a valuable cautionary note about invoking Hegel in Northern Ireland, see Clair Wills, *Improprieties: Politics and Sexuality in Northern Irish Poetry* (Oxford, 1993), p. 133: 'Hegel's theory has obvious attractions for anyone hoping for a solution to the situation in Northern Ireland, yet there is a danger both that the irreconcilability of political differences will be glossed over in the ideal of synthesis or resolution, and that such differences will be polarised into the by now familiar distinction between tradition and modernity, or, more problematically still, between Protestantism and Catholicism.' Deane had sounded a similarly cautionary note in his Field Day pamphlet, *Heroic Styles: The Tradition of an Idea*; see Seamus Deane, 'Heroic styles: the tradition of an idea', in Thomas Flanagan (ed.), *Ireland's Field Day* (Notre Dame, IN, 1986), p. 58: 'It is about time we put aside the idea of essence – that hungry Hegelian ghost looking for a stereotype to live in.' But considering Paulin's crucial presence in *The Field Day Anthology of Irish Writing*, alongside Deane's own positive comments on *The Riot Act*, it appears that he ultimately approved of at least some use of Hegel in Northern Ireland. For Wills' more critical view of how Paulin used the German philosopher, see Wills, *Improprieties*, pp. 135–6.
17. McDonald and Walton (eds), *Amid Our Troubles*, p. 152.
18. See Patricia Jagentowicz Mills, 'Hegel's Antigone', in Jon Stewart (ed.), *The Phenomenology of Spirit Reader* (Albany, NY, 1998), pp. 243–71. Mills' analysis concentrates on Hegel's *Phenomenology of Spirit*, whereas Paulin concentrates on the *Aesthetics*.
19. Ibid., p. 266.
20. Ibid., p. 285.
21. Ibid., pp. 287–8.
22. Ibid., p. 259.
23. Paulin, 'Whose side are you on?'
24. Tom Paulin, 'Antigone', in McDonald and Walton (eds), *Amid Our Troubles*, p. 169.
25. Ibid.
26. Ibid., p. 166.
27. Ibid., p. 170.
28. For an overview of these events, see David Beresford, *Ten Men Dead: The Story of the 1981 Hunger Strike* (London, 1987). For a behind-the-scenes account of what these events meant to the leadership of the Provisional IRA, see Ed Moloney, *A Secret History of the IRA* (New York, 2002), chapter six, 'A long, hot summer', pp. 196–217.
29. *The Story of Field Day* (dir. Johnny Muir), BBC Northern Ireland, 2006.
30. See John Brown (ed.), *In the Chair: Interviews with Poets from the North of Ireland* (Cliffs of Moher, Co. Clare, 2002), p. 155.
31. O'Toole, 'Field Day: on the double'.
32. Patrick Quilligan, 'Field Day's new double-bill', *The Irish Times*, 18 September 1984.
33. Ibid.
34. Ibid.
35. Peter Thompson, 'The contrast is only astonishing', *Irish Press*, 25 September 1984. The longer passage reads: 'Set (with aching obviousness) in Northern Ireland, [Paulin] introduces the villain, Creon (– the State, N.I. –) . . . the heroine, Antigone (– the Oppressed, the One who tries to bury her brother –) and the self-serving mob most of us are for most of our lives . . . This done, it spoon-feeds us into an understanding of their respective qualities as if we were imbeciles. Mercilessly

didactic, this piece belongs to that hopelessly outdated and ironically, peculiarly British genre, the Theatre of the Political Whinge.'

36. Anonymous, 'Memorable Molière – but subverted Sophocles', *Northern Constitution*, 3 November 1984.
37. Ibid.
38. Ibid.
39. Quilligan, 'Field Day's new double-bill'.
40. For another reading of Paulin's Antigone as a drama of identity, see Cleary, 'Domestic troubles', p. 530.
41. Tom Paulin, *Liberty Tree* (London, 1983), p. 13.
42. Ibid. 'Under Creon' begins in what seems to be a Romantic landscape, but by the end of the poem that relationship is transformed by Paulin's unresolved questions about identity and aesthetics. In '"Could anyone write it?": place in Tom Paulin's poetry', in Colin Graham and Richard Kirkland (eds), *Ireland and Cultural Theory: The Mechanics of Authenticity* (London, 1999), Eamonn Hughes contrasts Paulin's sense of place with Seamus Heaney's, because the former resists the ideological formulations of authenticity that have traditionally been associated with landscape in Irish poetry (p. 184). For a feminist critique of Irish landscape poetry, see Patricia Coughlan, '"Bog queens": the representation of women in the poetry of John Montague and Seamus Heaney', in Toni O'Brien Johnson and David Cairns (eds), *Gender in Irish Writing* (Philadelphia, PA, 1991).
43. Paulin, *Liberty Tree*, p. 13. The set designer for *The Riot Act* was Brian Vahey.
44. Ibid.
45. Ibid.
46. McDonald and Walton (eds), *Amid Our Troubles*, p. 167.
47. Ibid., p. 168 (my italics).
48. For a more sceptical reading of how Paulin negotiates the tension between Enlightenment and myth in *Liberty Tree*, see Wills, *Improprieties*, pp. 143–4.
49. *Sophocles: Volume 2: Antigone, The Women of Trachis, Philoctetes, Oedipus at Colonus*, trans. Hugh Lloyd-Jones (Cambridge, MA, 1994), pp. 36–7.
50. Paulin, *The Riot Act*, p. 27.
51. *Sophocles*, vol. 2, trans. Hugh Lloyd-Jones, pp. 44–5.
52. For two versions of this translation see Seamus Heaney, 'Sophoclean', *New Yorker*, 3 March 2003, and Seamus Heaney, *The Burial at Thebes: A Version of Sophocles'* Antigone (New York, 2004), pp. 24–5.
53. See Derek Mahon, *Collected Poems* (Loughcrew, Co. Meath, 1999), p. 14.
54. Paulin, *The Riot Act*, pp. 23–4.
55. *Sophocles*, vol. 2, trans. Hugh Lloyd-Jones, p. 37.
56. For further historical context to Heaney's translation of *Antigone*, see Kelly Younger, 'Antigone and terrorism: Seamus Heaney sends a letter to George W. Bush', in Stratos E. Constantinidis (ed.), *Text & Presentation: The Comparative Drama Conference Series* (New York, 2007).
57. *Sophocles*, vol. 2, trans. Hugh Lloyd-Jones, pp. 36–7. There are other options to consider for this antithesis as well. Richard C. Jebb, *The Tragedies of Sophocles* (Cambridge, 1912), p. 139: 'proudly stands his city' vs 'no city hath he'; Sophocles, *Antigone*, in David Grene (ed.), *Sophocles I*, trans. Elizabeth Wyckoff (Chicago, IL, 1954), p. 171: 'high indeed is his city' vs 'stateless the man'; Sophocles, *The Three Theban Plays:* Antigone, Oedipus the King, Oedipus at Colonus, trans. Robert Fagles (New York, 1987), p. 77: 'he and his city rise high' vs 'the city casts out'; Sophocles, *The Oedipus Cycle*, trans. Dudley Fitts and Robert

Fitzgerald (New York, 2002), p. 199: 'proudly his city stands' vs 'what of his city then?'. In the revised version of 'Sophoclean' that appears in Heaney's *Burial at Thebes*, Heaney renders the 'hypsopolis' idea with 'The city will reward him', and renders the 'apolis' idea with the phrase 'He'll have put himself beyond the pale' (p. 25).

58. For further explanation of Paulin's antagonism towards Heidegger in this poem, see Wills, *Improprieties*, pp. 153–5, and Hughes, 'Could anyone write it?', pp. 182–3.
59. Paulin, *Fivemiletown*, p. 59.
60. *Arena*, 'History Boys on the Rampage'.
61. See Tom Paulin's edited section on 'Northern Protestant oratory and writing: 1791–1985', in Deane (ed.), *Field Day Anthology of Irish Writing*, vol. 3, pp. 314–79.
62. Ibid., pp. 318–19.
63. Ibid., pp. 314–15.
64. Ibid.
65. Ibid., p. 315.
66. Ibid., p. 318. For the concept that inspired Paulin to theorise Protestant writing in this way, see Hélène Cixous' explanation of *écriture féminine* in 'The laugh of the Medusa', in Elaine Marks and Isabelle de Courtivron (eds), *New French Feminisms* (New York, 1980), pp. 245–64.
67. Ibid., p. 372.
68. Ibid., pp. 372–3 (my italics).
69. Transcript of interview with Tom Paulin for BBC *Arena* documentary, 'History Boys on the Rampage' [(dir. Andrew Eaton), BBC, 1988], Irish Film Institute Irish Film Archive: Field Day archive, VII.i.2, F/6.
70. Simultaneously with his presentation of these problems through the poetry of *Liberty Tree*, Paulin also addressed them in his 1983 Field Day pamphlet, *A New Look at the Language Question*; Tom Paulin, 'A new look at the language question', in Field Day Theatre Company (ed.), *Ireland's Field Day* (London, 1986).
71. Paulin, *Fivemiletown*, p. 42.
72. Paulin, *The Riot Act*, p. 14.
73. Paulin, *Fivemiletown*, p. 42.
74. Ibid., p. 54.
75. This critical gesture fitted nicely into Field Day's larger project, which Deane described to John Brown in *In the Chair: Interviews with Poets from Northern Ireland*, 'to redesign the linkage between authority and power and show that the possession of the latter was no prelude or condition for the possession of the former'; Brown (ed.), *In the Chair*, p. 105.
76. Heaney, 'Title deeds', p. 413.
77. Ibid., p. 412.
78. Ibid.
79. See Seamus Heaney, *The Redress of Poetry* (New York, 1995), p. 186.
80. Ibid., p. 187.

Chapter 4

1. Personal interview with Mary Lawlor, June 2009.
2. See Theodor Adorno, 'Reconciliation under duress', in Fredric Jameson and Ronald Taylor (eds), *Aesthetics and Politics* (London, 1980), p. 160.
3. United Nations Universal Declaration of Human Rights. Kevin Whelan, 'Rights of memory', http://www.epilogues.net/perspectives/KW%20Rights%20of%20memory.pdf (accessed 10 July 2012)

4. Seamus Heaney, 'Human rights, poetic redress', *The Irish Times*, 10 December 2008.
5. See Dennis O'Driscoll, *Stepping Stones: Interviews with Seamus Heaney* (New York, 2008), pp. 291–2. The main reference to Amnesty International occurs in the discussion of 'From the Republic of Conscience'.
6. Heaney's reference to the 'Wonders of Man' chorus is also a reference to his own *Burial at Thebes*, discussed in chapter three.
7. A winner of the Nobel Peace Prize (1974) and the Lenin Peace Prize (1977), MacBride is sometimes cited as a co-founder of Amnesty International, although the original spark came from Peter Berenson's editorial, 'The forgotten prisoners', *Observer*, 28 May 1961. See Elizabeth Keane, *An Irish Statesman and Revolutionary: The Nationalist and Internationalist Politics of Seán MacBride* (New York, 2006), pp. 180–98. Amnesty International's Irish section is located at Seán MacBride House in Dublin, although the organisation in the Dublin area is extensive enough that it has other addresses. Heaney's commission to write 'From the Republic of Conscience', for instance, came from the members of the Sandymount branch.
8. Ciaran Carson, 'Escaped from the massacre?', *Honest Ulsterman*, no. 50 (winter 1975), p. 186.
9. Seamus Heaney, 'The Tollund Man', in Heaney, *Wintering Out* (London, 1972), pp. 36–7. Also, 'Feeling into Words', in Heaney, *Preoccupations: Selected Prose* (London, 1980), pp. 41–60.
10. Heaney, *Preoccupations*, p. 36.
11. Ibid., p. 37.
12. Edna Longley, '"Inner Emigré" or "Artful Voyeur": Seamus Heaney's *North*', in Michael Allen (ed.), *New Casebooks: Seamus Heaney* (New York, 1997), p. 42.
13. Carson, 'Escaped from the massacre?', p. 184.
14. Lloyd, *Anomalous States*, p. 19.
15. Ibid.
16. Ibid., p. 27.
17. Heaney, *Preoccupations*, p. 57.
18. In *Preoccupations*, Heaney calls this metaphor only 'to some extent' applicable insofar as we wish to understand 'the bankrupt psychology and mythologies implicit in the terms Irish Catholic and Ulster Protestant' (p. 57). The choice of the word 'bankruptcy' suggests disgust with (not endorsement of) identity politics and its mythologies of violence. At the end of his list of names for Mother Ireland, he says 'whatever'. And finally, far from placing the conflict outside of history, he identifies the Troubles as 'the tail end' of a historical conflict (ibid.). Whether we can locate identity politics or mythologised violence in Heaney's bog poems or not, this passage does not reflect either one of those things.
19. The expression comes from Yeats' 'Meditations in Time of Civil War'; Alt and Allspach (eds), *Variorum Edition of the Poems of W.B. Yeats*, p. 420.
20. Heaney, *Preoccupations*, p. 56.
21. See Edmund Wilson, *The Wound and the Bow* (Oxford, 1947), pp. 272–95. A long quotation from this essay appears in the programme notes for *The Cure at Troy*. Like most of the other Field Day theatre programmes, this booklet featured an impressive collage of similarly interesting passages, each one hinting in its own way at the critical and cultural depth of what the audience was about to experience.
22. Seamus Heaney, *The Government of the Tongue: Selected Prose, 1978–1987* (New York, 1989), pp. xi–xxiii.
23. Seamus Heaney, 'Place and displacement: recent poetry from Northern Ireland', in Heaney, *Finders Keepers: Selected Prose, 1971–2001* (New York, 2002), pp. 122–45.

Some sections of the essay are also worked into 'The interesting case of Nero, Chekhov's cognac and a knocker'; see Heaney, *Government of the Tongue*, pp. xi–xxiii. 'Place' and 'Case' are closely interrelated essays, one being delivered as a lecture in 1984 and the other in 1986. During the year between, Heaney published 'From the Republic of Conscience', and so it is fair to say that his ideas in these essays are relevant to the development of his human rights poetic.

24. Heaney, *Government of the Tongue*, p. xvi.
25. Ibid., p. xix.
26. Ibid., pp. 191–6.
27. Seamus Heaney, *Station Island* (London, 1984), p. 93.
28. Ibid.
29. Heaney, *Finders Keepers*, p. 128.
30. See Robert Kaufman, 'Aura, still', in Andrew E. Benjamin (ed.), *Walter Benjamin and Art* (New York, 2005), p. 123: 'Following Benjamin, Adorno consistently argues for the "critical" nature of a modern aura whose point of departure he, like Benjamin, tends to locate in romantic lyric poetry. Adorno's rewritings of aura traces its criticality first from romanticism, and then from the later nineteenth century, on to modernism and after.'
31. Theodor Adorno, *Notes to Literature*, vol. 1, ed. Rolf Tiedman, trans. Shierry Weber Nicholsen (New York, 1991), p. 44.
32. Helen Vendler, *The Music of what Happens: Poems, Poets, Critics* (Cambridge, MA, 1988), pp. 149–65. For a review and critique of Vendler's 'aethetic criticism' in that volume, see Sidney Burris, 'Reviewing contemporary poetry: Helen Vendler and the aesthetic method', *Contemporary Literature*, vol. 31, no. 2 (1990).
33. Heaney, *Finders Keepers*, p. 129.
34. Adorno, *Notes to Literature*, vol. 1, p. 38.
35. Ibid. For a more extended discussion of this idea, see Sarah M. Zimmerman, *Romanticism, Lyricism and History* (Albany, NY, 1999), p. 8: 'Theodor Adorno . . . confirms that lyricism is the genre of the individual apart from society, but he claims this detachment as the site of political resistance.'
36. Adorno, *Minima Moralia*, p. 103: 'An emancipated society would not be a unitary state, but the realization of universality in the reconciliation of differences'; in other words, 'a better state' would be one in which 'people could be different without fear'. In the introduction to *Negative Dialectics* (trans. E.B. Ashton, London, 1973; moreover, Adorno expresses how this utopian vision might be approached through an ethos of non-coercive reconciliation that would 'release the nonidentical, would rid it of coercion . . . [and] would open the road to the multiplicity of different things and strip dialectics of its power over them' (p. 6).
37. Adorno, *Notes to Literature*, vol. 1, p. 41.
38. Adorno, 'Reconciliation under duress', p. 160. For another Adornian reading of Heaney's poetry of this period, see Stephen Matthews, *Irish Poetry: Politics, History, Negotiation: The Evolving Debate, 1969 to the Present* (New York, 1997), pp. 158–85. Matthews has also related the idea of 'negative knowledge' to Heaney's poetry, with particular reference to *The Cure at Troy*. He interprets the phrase 'reconciliation under duress' as meaning that reconciliation is itself being coerced, where I read it to mean the 'false universalism', in which reconciliation operates by coercively subsuming the object.
39. Personal interview with Mary Lawlor, June 2009. When Lawlor started at Amnesty International, it was run by international human rights icon Seán MacBride, but had, as former chair Mary Lawlor said, 'no office, no staff, nothing', when Amnesty in

Ireland was, as Lawlor puts it, 'work[ing] out of somebody's back bedroom, a tiny little bedroom, and everything was manual and all that'. From these early days, however, artists have played an important role in promoting the organisation in Ireland. Amnesty in Ireland was able to move from someone's back bedroom to its own building in Dublin – MacBride House on Shaw Street – due to the proceeds of an art auction, 'Artists for Amnesty', that included paintings by the Catalan painter Joan Miro, and the Irish painters Francis Bacon and Louis le Brocquy. Also, in a personal interview with Bill Shipsey in June 2009, Shipsey, who was Lawlor's successor as chair of Amnesty International's Irish section, adds that there was also a Heaney poetry manuscript and a Samuel Beckett fragment manuscript. Shipsey also recalls that U2 was at the opening of MacBride House – now called Amnesty House. Not long after this, inspired by Amnesty's 'Secret Policeman's Ball' concerts of the 1970s, U2 and other major acts, such as Peter Gabriel and Sting, carried out a 'Conspiracy of Hope' tour in the US; it ended with a massive sold-out concert in Giants Stadium, covered by MTV, which raised Amnesty's profile in the US tremendously. Shipsey and Lawlor were also both involved with this event.

40. It is interesting to consider how well this poem speaks to an economy like Ireland's; in the 1980s, tourism was the major industry.
41. Personal interview with Bill Shipsey, June 2009.
42. Ibid.
43. Personal interview with Mary Lawlor, June 2009.
44. Ibid.
45. Heaney, 'Human rights, poetic redress'. In this source, Heaney says that he was asked to contribute the poem to Amnesty International for United Nations Day (24 October), but in fact the pamphlet appeared on Human Rights Day (10 December).
46. Ibid.
47. O'Driscoll (ed.), *Stepping Stones*, p. 292.
48. Ibid.
49. The theme of travel in 'Republic' was relevant to Amnesty International's policy of impartiality, and this was particularly significant during the Cold War, when each section would take on three cases simultaneously: one in the West, one in the East, and one in the 'South'. It was also against Amnesty policy to address human rights concerns in one's own country; Amnesty in Ireland, for instance, was not allowed to address human rights violations in the North of Ireland, or Britain. It was therefore a breach of protocol for Seán MacBride, for instance, to write in support of Bobby Sands and the IRA hunger strikers in 1981.
50. O'Driscoll, *Stepping Stones*, p. 292.
51. Seamus Heaney, *The Haw Lantern* (London, 1987), p. 12.
52. Ibid., p. 13.
53. Ibid.
54. Ibid., p. 12.
55. Personal interview with Mary Lawlor, June 2009.
56. Heaney, *Haw Lantern*, p. 13.
57. Personal interview with Bill Shipsey, June 2009.
58. Heaney, *Haw Lantern*, p. 13.
59. Domna C. Stanton, 'Presidential address 2005: on rooted cosmopolitanism', *PMLA: Publications of the Modern Language Association of America*, vol. 121, no. 3 (2006), p. 638.
60. 'Ambassador of Conscience Award', Art for Amnesty.
61. Personal interview with Bill Shipsey, June 2009. Describing human rights work 'can be incredibly grim', says Shipsey; 'the successes are not always visible. You are

dealing with individual human misery and torture and disappearances and I thought that it was important that we also be able to celebrate the inspiring lives and I wanted to couple it with . . . the bards, as Seamus says, and the poets who were the ones who were involved with it.'

62. Personal interview with Mary Lawlor, June 2009.
63. The term 'relieved' also suggests being dismissed from a post, as Mary Robinson noted at the end of her term as United Nations commissioner for human rights from 1997 to 2002. Indeed, reading this poem at a function in the cathedral at Geneva was her final official act in that post. For her own account of the political events leading to her departure, see chapter sixteen of Mary Robinson, *Everybody Matters: My Life Giving Voice* (New York, 2013), pp. 249–60.
64. Colin Hearfield, *Adorno and the Modern Ethos of Freedom* (Aldershot, 2004), p. 155.
65. Carolyn Forché, *Against Forgetting* (New York, 1993), p. 46. In a similar vein, while Forché invokes *Negative Dialectics* as a philosophical basis for the poetry of witness, she does not accept Adorno's most famous comment about poetry being mere barbarism in the wake of Auschwitz. Her poetry of witness draws enough influence from Adorno's sense of immediate catastrophe, however, that her poetic of human rights can be easily distinguishable from Heaney's.
66. Theodor Adorno and Max Horkheimer, *Dialectic of Enlightenment* (London, 1994), p. 6.
67. Adorno, *Minima Moralia*, pp. 102–3.
68. *The Cure at Troy* has subsequently been recognised as an anti-colonial play – very much in keeping with modern criticism of other Irish versions of Greek tragedy. See Hugh Denard, 'Seamus Heaney, colonialism, and the cure: Sophoclean re-visions', *PAJ: A Journal of Performance and Art*, no. 22 (2000); Lorna Hardwick, 'Classical texts in post-colonial literatures: consolation, redress and new beginnings in the work of Derek Walcott and Seamus Heaney', *International Journal of the Classical Tradition*, vol. 9, no. 2 (fall 2002); and Oliver Taplin, 'Sophocles' *Philoctetes*, Seamus Heaney's, and some other recent half-rhymes', in Hall et al. (ed.), *Dionysus Since 69*.
69. Heaney, *The Cure at Troy*, p. 77.
70. Ibid., p. 1.
71. Ibid., p. 2.
72. Ibid.
73. Ibid.
74. Ibid.
75. Ibid. Despite the heady poetic theory on display in this section of the opening chorus, there is, nevertheless, something prosaic (and even didactic) about it. It slows down even so far as to explain the meaning of the volcano prop, even though the prop is not essential. 'If a volcano can be suggested in the background', Heaney notes in the opening stage directions to *Cure*, 'all the better; but it should not be overemphasized' (p. 1). We can explain this by recognising that Heaney is not trying to create that hypnotic moment that comes at the end of the play. Instead, he is giving the audience directions for how to interpret that final chorus.

CHAPTER 5

1. 'Letter (undated) from Seamus Deane to Jonathan [Williams?]', National Library of Ireland Field Day archive, IX.i.9, D/4, 'Deane letters'.
2. Transcript of interview with Tom Paulin for BBC *Arena* documentary, 'History Boys on the Rampage' [(dir. Andrew Eaton), BBC, 1988], Irish Film Institute Irish Film Archive: Field Day archive, VII.i.2, F/6.

3. Deane (ed.), *Field Day Anthology of Irish Writing*, vol. 1, p. xxvi. For further discussion of Coleridge's writings on Ireland, see also Deane, 'Civilians and barbarians', in Flanagan (ed.), *Ireland's Field Day*, p. 34.
4. Deane (ed.), *Field Day Anthology of Irish Writing*, vol. 1, p. xxv.
5. Deane's attitude towards the state, however, is anything but Platonic. That is, whereas Plato saw poetry as a dangerous threat to the properly functioning state, Deane sees the ideology of the aesthetic as an aid to the state's monopoly on violence.
6. Dympna Callaghan, 'An interview with Seamus Deane, University College, Dublin, June 1993', *Social Text*, no. 38 (1994), p. 47.
7. 'Letter (undated) from Seamus Deane to Jonathan [Williams?]', National Library of Ireland Field Day archive, IX.i.9, D/4, 'Deane letters'.
8. Ibid.
9. For an account of this growing conflict, see Richtarik, *Acting Between the Lines*, pp. 267–8.
10. 'Letter (undated) from Seamus Deane to Jonathan [Williams?]', National Library of Ireland Field Day archive, IX.i.9, D/4, 'Deane letters'.
11. Deane, 'Heroic styles', p. 50.
12. 'Letter (undated) from Seamus Deane to Jonathan [Williams?]', National Library of Ireland Field Day archive, IX.i.9, D/4, 'Deane letters'.
13. Seamus Deane, 'Unhappy and at home: interview with Seamus Heaney', *Crane Bag*, vol. 1, no. 1 (1977), p. 68.
14. Ibid.
15. Heaney, *North*, pp. 4, 47–8.
16. Deane, 'Unhappy and at home', p. 68.
17. Ibid.
18. Ibid., p. 67.
19. Ibid., p. 68.
20. Ibid.
21. Ibid., p. 69.
22. This is the term Heaney uses to describe Hercules in two different poems in *North*: 'Antaeus' (p. 12) and 'Hercules and Antaeus' (pp. 52–3).
23. Yeats was, of course, a major presence in Heaney's poetry, with the series 'Singing School', in Heaney, *North*, pp. 62–7, and 'Casualty', in Heaney, *Field Work* (London, 1979), pp. 21–2, being only the most celebrated examples. Yeats was no less important a figure in Heaney's critical essays, however. We find the 'early' Heaney's ambivalent reading of Yeats in two 1978 essays, 'The makings of a music' and 'Yeats as an exemplar?', in Heaney, *Preoccupations: Selected Prose, 1968–1978* (New York, 1980), pp. 61–78, 98–114, while a more enthusiastic connection shines through in the 1988 essay 'The place of writing: W.B. Yeats and Thoor Ballylee' and the 1990 essay 'Joy or night', in Heaney, *Finders Keepers: Selected Prose, 1971–2001* (New York, 2002), pp. 252–61, 343–60, and in his introduction to the Yeats section of the *Field Day Anthology* in Seamus Deane (ed.), *The Field Day Anthology of Irish Writing*, vol. 2 (Derry, 1991), pp. 783–90. There is, moreover, a considerable secondary literature on Heaney and Yeats, the foundational statements of which are Jon Stallworthy, 'The poet as archaeologist: W.B. Yeats and Seamus Heaney', *Review of English Studies: A Quarterly Journal of English Literature and the English Language*, no. 33 (1982), pp. 158–74, and Jonathan Allison, 'Seamus Heaney's Yeats', *Yeats: An Annual of Critical and Textual Studies*, no. 14 (1996), pp. 19–47. These essays concentrate on the early, somewhat anxious, phase of Heaney's engagement with the Yeatsian inheritance. Two later essays, Michael Cavanagh's 'Tower and boat: Yeats and Seamus Heaney', *New*

Hibernia Review/Iris Éireannach Nua, vol. 4, no. 3 (autumn/fómhar 2000), and Colleen McKenna's 'Seeing "last things": reading Yeats through the eyes of Seamus Heaney', *Yeats Annual*, no. 13 (1998), explore the more positive charge of Heaney's mature engagement with Yeats from the late 1980s onward.

24. Seamus Heaney, 'William Butler Yeats (1865–1939)', in Deane (ed.), *Field Day Anthology of Irish Writing*, vol. 2, p. 783.
25. Ibid., p. 790.
26. Ibid.
27. Ibid., p. 789.
28. Ibid., p. 790. Heaney repeats this Yeatsian formulation in the first chorus of *The Cure at Troy*, which defines 'Poetry' as 'the voice of reality and justice': Heaney, *The Cure at Troy*, p. 2.
29. Heaney, 'William Butler Yeats (1865–1939)', p. 785.
30. Heaney described this trepidation in an interview with Jane Coyle, 'Trojan warrior', *Stet* (September 1990), p. 17: 'Let's face it . . . I'm no little choirboy going up for my first communion in a clean white surplice. No doubt, it will become the subject for some kind of "cultural debate" and yes, that prospect is a little unnerving.'
31. National Library of Ireland Field Day archive, V., 'Press cuttings', contains more interviews from Heaney's publicity campaign for *The Cure at Troy* than can be found from all the other playwrights' publicity campaigns put together. This reflects Heaney's talent for giving interesting interviews; practically every one of them provides some new food for thought not contained in the others. It also suggests how earnestly Heaney wished to shape the popular understanding of his play's argument.
32. Coyle, 'Trojan warrior', p. 17.
33. Seamus Heaney, interview with Barry White, *Belfast Telegraph*, 29 September 1990.
34. W.B. Yeats, 'W.B. Yeats explains his new play', *The Irish Times*, 13 August 1938.
35. Seamus Heaney, interview with Barry White, *Belfast Telegraph*, 29 September 1990.
36. See Yeats, 'W.B. Yeats explains his new play': 'Father Connolly says my plot is perfectly clear . . . but that he does not understand my meaning. The plot is my meaning.'
37. W.B. Yeats, *The Collected Works of W.B. Yeats: Volume VIII: The Irish Dramatic Movement*, eds. Mary FitzGerald and Richard J. Finneran (London, 2003), p. 65.
38. Seamus Heaney, interview with 'J.O'C.', *Galway Advertiser*, 18 October 1990.
39. See Charles Osborne, 'Greek tragedy with a Belfast rasp', *Daily Telegraph*, 20 September 1990. He adds that Heaney's Philoctetes moves past 'pain' and 'rage' and 'puts one in mind of Shakespeare's Prospero'. See also Paul Taylor, 'A hit and myth', *Independent*, 8 April 1991: 'Des McAleer's transfixing Caliban-like hero sets up just the right conflicting responses.'
40. There are also compound parallels in the Sophoclean characters of Odysseus and Neoptolemus. As a master manipulator, Odysseus embodies a more unsavoury part of Prospero's character – but as the person who abandoned Philoctetes in the first place, he is like Duke Antonio, the brother who had usurped Prospero. Neoptolemus, for that matter, is a kind of Ferdinand and/or Miranda character insofar as he is a gallant but confused youth caught in the centre of a larger plot leading to reconciliation. He is also a kind of reluctant Ariel, in that he carries out the trick on Caliban/Philoctetes on behalf of a master manipulator hidden behind the scenes.
41. Heaney, *The Cure at Troy*, p. 13.
42. Ibid., p. 15.
43. Ibid., p. 19.
44. Ibid., p. 69.

45. As Deane wrote about the Field Day production in 'Oranges and Lemnos', Heaney's version was 'in blank verse and minus the *deus ex machina*'; Deane, 'Oranges and Lemnos', *New Statesman & Society*, no. 120 (5 April 1991).
46. Seamus Heaney, interview, *Sunday Tribune*, 30 September 1990.
47. Seamus Heaney, interview with John Keyes, *Fortnight*, 15 October 1990.
48. Aristotle, *Poetics*, p. 48: 'It is evident that the dénouements of plot-structures should arise from the plot itself, and not, as in Medea, from a *deus ex machina* . . .'.
49. Personal interview with Stephen Rea, June 2009. 'It was stunning to hear that around the country', Rea said, 'because of the even-handedness of it . . . you understand the suffering wherever it happens. That's what people find very hard in the North of Ireland.' Contrary to contemporary critics' accusations of ideological one-sidedness, in *The Cure at Troy* we can see that Field Day was calling everyone to rethink, with Neoptolemus, their own ethical positions with regard to the island's intractable conflict.
50. Heaney, *The Cure at Troy*, p. 78.
51. Ibid., pp. 78–9.
52. Ibid., p. 79.
53. Ibid.
54. Ibid., p. 80.
55. Ibid.
56. Heaney, *Station Island*, pp. 92–3.
57. *Sophocles*, vol. 2, trans. Lloyd-Jones, p. 407.
58. Seamus Heaney, interview, *Irish News*, 22 September 1990.
59. Heaney, *The Cure at Troy*, p. 80.
60. Ibid., p. 81.
61. Seamus Heaney, interview with Barry White, *Belfast Telegraph*, 29 September 1990.
62. Deane, 'Oranges and Lemnos'.
63. Ibid.
64. Ibid.
65. Ibid. For a longer description of the negative kind of destiny that *Cure* eschews, see Deane, 'Heroic styles', where he writes that in Northern Ireland the two 'communities have been stereotyped into their roles of oppressor and victim to such an extent that the notion of a Protestant or Catholic sensibility is now assumed to be a fact of nature rather than a product of these very special and ferocious conditions . . . In such a situation, nothing is more likely to perpetuate or even galvanise these stereotypes than the dream of a community's attaining, through a species of spiritual-military heroics, its longed-for destiny. Each begins to seek, in such a climate, a leadership which will definitely embody the univocal style which is the expression of its inner essence or nature' (pp. 54–5).
66. Ibid., p. 19.
67. 'Letter (undated) from Seamus Deane to Jonathan [Williams?]', National Library of Ireland Field Day archive, IX.i.9, D/4, 'Deane letters'.
68. Deane, 'Oranges and Lemnos', p. 19.
69. 'Letter (undated) from Seamus Deane to Jonathan [Williams?]', National Library of Ireland Field Day archive, IX.i.9, D/4, 'Deane letters'.
70. The argument first appeared as 'The poet's dream of an audience', which Deane later developed into 'Yeats: the creation of an audience'; Seamus Deane, 'The poet's dream of an audience', *Times Literary Supplement*, 7 March 1986; Deane, 'Yeats: the creation of an audience', in Nicholas Grene (ed.), *Tradition and Influence in Anglo-Irish Poetry* (Totowa, NJ, 1989), pp. 31–47.

71. Transcript of interview with Seamus Heaney for BBC *Arena* documentary, 'History Boys on the Rampage' [(dir. Andrew Eaton), BBC, 1988], Irish Film Institute Irish Film Archive: Field Day archive, VII.i.2, F/5.

CONCLUSION

1. Ibid.
2. Callaghan, 'An interview with Seamus Deane', p. 47.
3. Bourke et al. (eds), *Field Day Anthology of Irish Writing*, vol. 5, p. 415.
4. For comparative overviews of Euripides and Sophocles on the modern Irish stage, see McDonald, 'The Irish and Greek tragedy', and J. Michael Walton, 'Hit or myth: the Greeks and Irish drama', in McDonald and Walton (eds), *Amid Our Troubles*. For overviews of Euripides' *Medea* in Dublin, see John McDonagh, '"Is Medea's crime Medea's glory?" Euripides in Dublin', in McDonald and Walton (eds), *Amid Our Troubles*; Steve Wilmer, 'Women in Greek tragedy today: a reappraisal', *Theatre Research International*, vol. 32, no. 2 (July 2007); and Brian Arkins, 'Three Medeas from modern Ireland', in Heike Bartel and Anne Simon (eds), *Unbinding Medea: Interdisciplinary Approaches to a Classical Myth from Antiquity to the 21st Century* (London, 2010).
5. For analyses of Carr's Euripides, see Eamonn Jordan, 'Unmasking the myths? Marina Carr's *By the Bog of Cats* and *On Raftery's Hill*', in McDonald and Walton (eds), *Amid Our Troubles*; Hélène Lecossois, 'From Medea to Hester Swane: Marina Carr's rewriting of Ethos in *By the Bog of Cats*', in Thierry Dubost (ed.), *Drama Reinvented: Theatre Adaptation in Ireland 1970–2007* (Brussels, 2012); and Karen O'Brien, 'Re-envisioning "woman": Medea as heroine in versions by Brendan Kennelly and Marina Carr', *Études Irlandaises*, vol. 37, no. 1 (2012). The most famous comment on Carr's Hellenism is Frank McGuinness' 'Writing in Greek: *By the Bog of Cats* . . . programme note: Abbey Theatre 1998', in Cathy Leeny and Anna McMullan (eds), *The Theatre of Marina Carr: Before Rules Was Made* (Dublin, 2003).
6. One might just as easily have written a Euripides-centric account of Irish Hellenism, but reconciliation would no longer be the key term and the Troubles would no longer be the historical focus. J.M. Synge, Brendan Kennelly, Marina Carr and Frank McGuinness would probably be the central playwrights to such a study, rather than Yeats, Heaney and Paulin. Fiona Mackintosh's *Dying Acts: Death in Ancient Greek and Modern Irish Tragic Drama* (Cork, 1994) is crucial to understanding Revival-era foundations for the modern Irish Euripides.
7. For an account of this concept, see Michael Böss, 'The postmodern nation: a critical history of "fifth province" discourse', *Études Irlandaises*, vol. 27, no. 1 (spring 2002). Richard Kearney is responsible for writing Mary Robinson's inauguration speech in 1990, and it contains both the fifth-province idea, and the first instance of an Irish politician's quotation of the 'Hope and History' chorus. For a critique of Field Day's use of the concept, see Shaun Richards, 'Field Day's fifth province: avenue or impasse?', in Eamonn Hughes (ed.), *Culture and Politics in Northern Ireland, 1960–1990* (Philadelphia, PA, 1991).
8. As had been the case with many other Field Day efforts, Deane's postcolonial approach to editing the Anthology was criticised as a nationalist polemic. Roy Foster, in 'Nations, yet again', *Times Literary Supplement*, 27 March 1992, found Deane's postcolonial critique of liberal pluralism 'puzzlingly incompatible with the "Fifth Province" idealism of the original Field Day. I suspect it indicates something about the backwards route travelled since 1980, which has led in some quarters to a sort of glorification of cultural atavism.' For further negative reviews of the anthology's

perceived republican bias, see Edna Longley, 'Hospitable meta-narrative or hegemonic bid?', *Canadian Journal of Irish Studies*, vol. 18, no. 2 (1992), and Francis Mulhern's two essays: 'A nation, yet again: *The Field Day Anthology*', *Radical Philosophy*, no. 65 (autumn 1993), and 'Postcolonial melancholy: a reply to Luke Gibbons', *Radical Philosophy*, no. 72 (1995). See also Luke Gibbons' defence: 'Dialogue without the other? A reply to Francis Mulhern', *Radical Philosophy*, no. 67 (1994). Adrian Frazier celebrates Deane's overtly political approach (without endorsing what he saw as Deane's politics) in John C. Greene, Patricia L. Haberstroh and Adrian Frazier, 'Wealth, gender, politics: three views of *The Field Day Anthology of Irish Writing*', *Éire-Ireland: A Journal of Irish Studies*, vol. 27, no. 2 (summer 1992).

9. For reviews concentrating on gender in *The Field Day Anthology of Irish Writing*, vols. 1–3, see Patricia Haberstroh's contribution in Greene, Haberstroh and Frazier, 'Wealth, gender, politics', and Julia McHatten, 'This is (not) a canon: staking out the tradition in recent anthologies of Irish writing', *Journal of Women's History*, vol. 7, no. 1 (1995–96). For criticism by women poets who were included in the actual anthology, see Eileán Ní Chuilleanáin, 'Review of *The Field Day Anthology of Irish Writing*, vols. I–III', *Cyphers*, no. 35 (1992), p. 52; Eavan Boland, 'Daughters of colony: a personal interpretation of the place of gender issues in the postcolonial interpretation of Irish literature', *Éire-Ireland: A Journal of Irish Studies*, vol. 32, nos. 2–3 (summer/fall 1997); and Nuala Ní Dhomhnaill, 'The hidden island: women's inheritance', in Theo Dorgan (ed.), *Irish Poetry Since Kavanagh* (Dublin, 1996).
10. Volumes 1–3 were initially published in 1991, and then reprinted in 1992. Most of the reviews appeared in 1992, and the public debates over the anthology took place then as well.
11. For one reflection of Robinson's impact on Irish women's writing of the 1990s, see Molly O'Hagan Hardy, 'Symbolic power: Mary Robinson's presidency and Eavan Boland's poetry', *New Hibernia Review/Iris Éireannach Nua*, vol. 12, no. 3 (fómhar/autumn 2008). Hardy reminds us that Robinson officiated at the launch of *The Field Day Anthology of Irish Writing*, volumes 4–5, in 2002, whereas then-Taoiseach Charles Haughey had thrown the launch party for *The Field Day Anthology of Irish Writing*, volumes 1–3, in 1991. See Deane (ed.), *Field Day Anthology of Irish Writing*, vol. 3, p. 68, for Deane's comments on Haughey, which became a source of ridicule in the review literature because the Taoiseach resigned over a wire-tapping scandal shortly after publication.
12. Callaghan, 'An interview with Seamus Deane', p. 46.
13. Heaney, *Redress of Poetry*, p. 188.
14. Mary Robinson, inaugural speech at Dublin Castle, 3 December 1990, http://prelectur.stanford.edu/lecturers/robinson/inaugural.html (accessed 10 December 2010).
15. In an article entitled 'Broad unionist welcome to election outcome' (9 November 1990), *The Irish Times* reporter describes how unionists respected Robinson because of her record of 'regular visits to the North to address and meet various organisations, and particularly her resignation from the Labour party' after Hillsborough. The reporter interviewed the unionist MP John Taylor, who 'expressed his "absolute delight" at the outcome and said Ms Robinson was "a break with the past and a breath of fresh air . . . [who] appealed to me as a unionist even though she is a republican, as somebody who understood unionist feelings and someone we could do business with"'. Another unionist politician, Peter Robinson, said, 'If it is friendship she is seeking, that is attainable.'
16. In subsequent years, the history of anthology production has received significant

attention from feminist scholars. For examples of this in the field of Irish studies specifically, see Julia Wright, '"The order of time": nationalism and literary anthologies, 1774–1831', *Papers on Language and Literature*, vol. 33, no. 4 (fall 1997), and Margaret Kelleher, 'The cabinet of Irish literature: a historical perspective on Irish anthologies', *Éire-Ireland: A Journal of Irish Studies*, vol. 38, nos. 3–4 (fall/winter 2003).

17. The editorial board for *The Field Day Anthology of Irish Writing*, volumes 4–5, explained its methods and aims in many places. Of course, its general introduction offers the most official explanation, and its closing paragraph reads: 'In ranging so broadly across forms of writing, historical records and oral traditions, where the words of poets jostle with those of paupers and politicians, these volumes seek to do more than propose a new or extended canon of Irish writing, or a subaltern history for academics. Irish women are entitled to know about their history, culture and traditions. We offer this anthology to all our readers as a sampler of texts which are historically interesting, aesthetically accomplished and politically indispensable'; Bourke et al. (eds), *Field Day Anthology of Irish Writing*, vol. 4, p. xxxvi. In addition to this collectively authored introduction, three of the editors published reviews and articles giving their own individual perspectives. See Margaret Kelleher, '*The Field Day Anthology* and Irish women's literary studies', *The Irish Review*, no. 30 (2003); Gerardine Meaney, 'Engendering the postmodern canon?: *The Field Day Anthology of Irish Writing, vols. IV & V: Women's Writing and Traditions*', in Patricia Boyle Haberstroh and Christine St Peter (eds), *Opening the Field: Irish Women: Texts and Contexts* (Cork, 2007); and Maria Luddy, '*The Field Day Anthology of Irish Writing: Volumes Four and Five: Irish Women's Writing and Traditions*', *Women's Studies International Forum*, vol. 26, no. 4 (2003). For reviews disapproving of the new approach, see Eileen Battersby, 'Stalked by an agenda', *The Irish Times*, 5 October 2002; Peter Van de Kamp, 'Field Day for women but it ain't an anthology', *Sunday Independent*, 10 August 2003; Aisling Foster, 'Too much, but still not enough', *Guardian*, 4 January 2003; and Gerry McCarthy's unfortunately-titled 'Skirting the issue', *Sunday Times*, 24 November 2002. For more positive readings of this approach, however, see Helen Meany, 'Field Day's long-awaited list of women writers challenges existing notions of Irish writing'; Róisín Higgins, '"A drift of chosen females?": *The Field Day Anthology of Irish Writing*, vols. 4 and 5', *Irish University Review*, vol. 33, no. 2 (2003); Lucy McDiarmid, 'Isn't it a great pity?', *Times Literary Supplement*, 27 December 2002; and Claire Bracken's 'Becoming mother-machine: the event of Field Day vols iv and v', in Patricia Coughlan and Tina O'Toole (eds), *Irish Literature: Feminist Perspectives* (Dublin, 2008).
18. Bourke et al. (eds), *Field Day Anthology of Irish Writing*, vol. 5, p. 424.
19. Ibid., p. 427.
20. Ibid., p. 422.
21. Adorno, *Minima Moralia*, p. 103.
22. David Sharrock, 'McGuinness fishes for the right words to give Paisley his parting gift of poetry', *The Times*, 6 June 2008.

Index